GETTING THROUGH TO JEHOVAH'S WITNESSES

Approaching Bible Discussions in Unexpected Ways

David A. Englund

Visit the author's website at:
www.DAEnglund.com

GRACE & JOY PUBLISHING
Belvidere, Illinois

TABLE OF CONTENTS

SECTION 1: ENCOUNTERING JEHOVAH'S WITNESSES

Chapter 1:
Here They Come—Now What?

When I was a young boy, my family followed a popular strategy in dealing with Jehovah's Witnesses.

We hid from them.

Our house was located in the middle of the block, so we usually spotted them as they were coming up the street doing their door-to-door witnessing. My parents would close all the curtains and pull down the shades. We would stay out of sight and pretend we weren't at home. The Witnesses would ring the doorbell, wait a few minutes, and then leave.

That was fun for me, sort of like a game of hide-and-seek initiated by adults. I have to confess, though, that I wondered what was so bad about those people that we had to hide from them. My parents explained that Jehovah's Witnesses weren't bad people but that they were annoying, always trying to push their religion on everyone else. Many of them wouldn't take no for an answer, so in order to avoid unpleasantness the best thing to do was to avoid encountering them at all.

Of course, total avoidance wasn't always possible. If we didn't spot them coming, we would answer the doorbell and find ourselves face-to-face with them. What then? We would politely say, "Thank you, but I'm not interested. I have my own religion." Some of the time, that was the end of it; they would thank us for our time and leave.

More often, they would try to get past that initial rebuff and get a dialogue going. "I'm glad to hear that you have an interest in spiritual things," they would say. "Do you read your Bible on a regular basis? We have come to your door to offer you a free home Bible study." At that point, my parents would tell them firmly, "No, thank you," and close the door.

Coming to Christ

Fast forward several years. I was now age 17 and my college roommate shared the gospel with me. He led me through an inductive chapter-by-chapter, verse-by-verse study of the New Testament book of Romans. Wanting to make sure I was right with God, I repented of my sins. I asked Christ to forgive me and save me based on his sacrifice on the cross.

Like many—perhaps most—Christians, I got busy with my life. Although I continued to read the Bible, I didn't begin any systematic study of doctrine. I didn't see the need for it, and even if I had wanted to I wouldn't have known where to start. Truth be told, there were vast portions of the Bible I had never read, not even superficially.

I knew that as a Christian I was supposed to be a witness for Christ, but I wasn't very good at it. My main problem was with getting conversations about religion started. Many people seemed to want to avoid discussing the topic altogether. The few such conversations I did start often led to fruitless arguments and bad feelings. Because of those negative experiences, I had pretty much given up trying. Deep down, though, I felt guilty about my lack of effort. I promised God that if he would open the way, I would witness for Jesus, but that he would have to get the ball rolling.

My initial encounter with Jehovah's Witnesses

Five years went by. One Saturday morning in 1972, my doorbell rang and I opened the door. Standing before me were a man and his wife. Immediately, I could tell by the magazines in their hands that they were Jehovah's Witnesses.

The hide-behind-the-curtains strategy was no longer an option. I could tell them that I wasn't interested, but in fact I *was* interested—not interested in becoming a Jehovah's Witness—but interested in witnessing to them. Here was my opening. They had broken the ice. They wanted to talk about religion. I wasn't about to close the door on those people or tell them "thanks but no thanks" without giving them some sort of witness for Jesus.

I invited them in, and the result was a disaster.

Why? Because they were prepared and I wasn't.

That's putting it mildly. I was *totally unprepared*. At that point, I knew next to nothing about what Jehovah's Witnesses believed. I knew that they called God "Jehovah." I knew that they went door-to-door witnessing in pairs. I knew that they offered people a magazine called *The Watchtower*. I knew that they wouldn't take blood transfusions. That's it. I didn't even know that they professed to be Christians, let alone that they believed they were the only true Christians in the world.

They asked me about my religious background. Having that invitation, I gave them a brief testimony about my conversion experience at college, about how I had received Christ into my life by faith and gained assurance of a place in heaven based on his free gift of salvation. There—I had done it. I had witnessed for Jesus, to some extent anyway. I was feeling really good about that.

Do all Christians go to heaven?

What I didn't know then was that Witnesses expect that some Christians will give their testimonies and are prepared to use them as a springboard to preach Watchtower doctrine. Unwittingly, I had set them up perfectly. The husband was ready and moved straight into his presentation.

"Actually," he said with a friendly smile, "it's a common misconception that all Christians will go to heaven."

Needless to say, I was shocked.

"Could you please turn to Acts 2:34 in your Bible and read that verse aloud?" he continued. I turned there and started to read out of my own Bible: "For David did not ascend into the heavens..." (RSV). "There, you see?" he interrupted, "Even King David didn't go to heaven, and the Bible says he was 'a man after God's own heart.'" I was stunned. I paused and tried to think of how to respond.

He went on. "The Bible says something very similar about John the Baptist. Would you please turn to Matthew 11:11 and read Jesus' own words from your Bible?" So I did: "Truly, I say to you, among those born of women there has risen no one greater than John the Baptist; yet he who is least in the kingdom of heaven is greater than he" (RSV).

"So you see," the Jehovah's Witness said to me, "John the Baptist didn't go to heaven when he died either. Also, remember, what Psalm 37:11 says. You probably know that verse from memory from the King James Version: 'The meek shall inherit...' what does it say? Heaven? No, it says, 'The meek shall inherit *the earth.*'" (KJV) Jesus quoted that promise in Matthew 5:5. Now let's go back to Psalm 37:29 to complete the thought." I read it aloud: "The righteous shall possess the land, and dwell upon it forever" (RSV).

"There!" said the Witness, "Jehovah's promise to faithful ones is that they will live on a paradise earth forever, not that they will go to heaven. Now it is true that Jesus said in Luke 12:32 that there is a 'little flock' of Christians who will go to heaven and rule alongside him. Revelation 14:3 gives us the exact number." He showed me the last part of that verse: "...the hundred and forty-four thousand who had been redeemed from the earth" (both verses, RSV).

By now, my head was reeling. I had just shared with him my testimony that I was going to heaven when I died because of what Jesus had done for me, and in a matter of minutes he had "proved" to me right out of my own Bible that it wasn't so, that even King David and John the Baptist weren't in heaven.

If I were to face those arguments today, I would note the contexts. Peter pointed out that Jesus—not David—resurrected bodily and ascended to heaven. That's *not* the same as saying David isn't in heaven in spirit form. I would also point out the context of Jesus' Matthew 11 statement. When he made that comment about John the Baptist, not only wasn't John in heaven; he was still alive and in prison. However, at the time, I didn't have a clue what to say. To be honest, I felt humiliated.

Let's pause a bit and examine what happened to me so that you can learn from my mistakes and make sure it doesn't happen to you.

LEARNING FROM MY MISTAKES

Should Christians refuse to talk with Jehovah's Witnesses?

Let's start with a fundamental question. Is it wrong for Christians to discuss religion with Jehovah's Witnesses at all?

Some Christians think so. They know that many of the teachings of the Watchtower are incompatible with biblical Christianity and are therefore heretical. For this reason, they will tell you that you should avoid all contact with Jehovah's Witnesses.

Granted, if you refuse all contact with Jehovah's Witnesses, you won't be in danger of getting sucked into their religion. But you won't win any of them to Christ that way either.

Intent on protecting their flocks from heresies, some well-meaning pastors have even instructed their congregations to turn Jehovah's Witnesses away rather than sharing the gospel with them. Some of them misapply 2 John 10-11: "If anyone comes to you and does not bring this teaching, do not take him into your house or welcome him. Anyone who welcomes him shares in his wicked work."

Why do I call this a misapplication? John was not commanding Christians to have no dialogue with people who believe and promote religious error. If we did that, unbelievers would never hear the gospel and Christianity would soon die out!

So what did he mean? In the first century, Christians met in homes rather than in church buildings. New Testament scholar F.F. Bruce states, "The injunction not to receive any one who does not bring 'the teaching of Christ' means that no such person must be accepted as a Christian teacher or as one entitled to the fellowship of the church. It does not mean that (say) one of Jehovah's Witnesses should not be invited into the house for a cup of tea in order to be shown the way of God more perfectly in the sitting-room than would be convenient on the doorstep."[1]

What would Jesus do? Can you picture Jesus hiding behind curtains when false teachers showed up at his door? Can you imagine him opening the door a small crack, saying, "Sorry, not interested. I have my own religion," and then closing the door in their faces?

Absurd? I agree. Jesus would never treat people that way.

Neither should we. We can't share the gospel with people if we refuse to talk with them. Even if you are busy when the Witnesses come, and even if you believe that 2 John 10-11 means that you shouldn't invite them into your home, you can still find a time when you can meet with them at a neutral location such as a coffee shop where you can talk about Jesus with them.

One day we will stand before God and give account for our lives (Hebrews 4:13). I don't know about you, but I don't want to have him ask me to explain why I refused to share the gospel and instead shut the door in the faces of people who came with Bibles in their hands and asked to talk with me about salvation. I certainly wouldn't want him to show me a replay of those encounters. Would you?

The importance of preparation

My mistake wasn't in inviting Jehovah's Witnesses into my home in order to share Jesus with them. My error was in trying to witness to them *unprepared*.

First, I had met with the Witnesses having no idea what they believed or why they believed it. Certainly, I didn't know that they believed in a two class system in which only 144,000 "anointed" Jehovah's Witnesses would end up in heaven and the rest would end up living forever on a paradise earth. As a result, I was totally unprepared to discuss the eternal destinations of King David and John the Baptist.

Second, although I thought we were having a spontaneous conversation, in reality I had walked unprepared into a well-rehearsed Watchtower argument. Their presentation was designed to shake my confidence in what I thought I knew of the Bible. The Watchtower had trained them to use this exact topic and line of reasoning—even down to the Bible verses to be quoted and some of the language to be used.[2] Because I was caught off guard, I was at a loss as to how to respond.

Fortunately, you don't have to remain unprepared and hide behind curtains. Granted, reaching out to Jehovah's Witnesses may require you to study the Bible like you never have before, but isn't that what Christ would have us do? 1 Peter 3:15 instructs us: "Always be prepared to give an answer to everyone who asks you to give the reason for the hope that you have."

How this book will prepare you

Let's face it. Standard gospel presentations just don't work with Jehovah's Witnesses. They're preoccupied with giving us their prepared presentations of Watchtower theology. But it's my conviction that by understanding the mindset of Jehovah's Witnesses and learning to approach discussions of Bible doctrines in ways that they won't expect, Christians *can* witness effectively to Jehovah's Witnesses.

In order to get through to Jehovah's Witnesses with the light of the gospel, you need to prepare in two distinct ways:

1. You need a clear understanding both of Christian doctrine and Jehovah's Witness teachings—what each believes and why. In this book, you will find doctrinal chapters which give you an overview of a specific area of doctrine and explain its significance to effective witnessing to Jehovah's Witnesses. This will tell you specifically *what* you need to get across to them.

2. You also need to know *how* to convey Bible truth in ways that Witnesses won't expect. To meet this need, this book also contains approach chapters related to those areas of doctrine. They will give you specific suggestions for taking Witnesses out of their prepared presentations and getting them to focus on what the Bible really teaches.

An important word of caution

When you meet with Jehovah's Witnesses, don't have this book or similar materials out where they can see them. They have no problem with you studying your own religion's doctrines in general and in learning how to articulate them, but if they see that you are studying techniques of how to witness specifically to Jehovah's Witnesses, most likely they will conclude that you aren't interested in the truth and terminate any further contact with you. So study this book as you prepare between meetings, but make your own notes to use during the meetings themselves.

GIVING AN EFFECTIVE WITNESS

I know you want to get through to Jehovah's Witnesses. That's why you're reading this book. Imagine how different the lives of the Jehovah's Witnesses in your area would be if every Christian from your church invited them in and gave them an effective presentation of the gospel. Now imagine what would happen if they received such a witness from every Christian in your community, regardless of what church they attend.

Former Jehovah's Witness Ted Dencher makes the following plea:

I am only one person, and can only do so much. But there are many thousands of you Christians, scattered throughout the many denominations of our churches in many countries. Do you love the Christ who bought you? Would you do Him a service? Then forget not my former brethren; do not pass them by. They are people just like yourselves. They have hearts and minds, consciences and souls; and above all, a Saviour who died to redeem them...

You see, it is not only a readiness on the part of the Jehovah's Witness to hear the word of God that is needed; it is also your *preparedness to give* that word. Prepared both by study and by an undergirding of the Holy Spirit, fortified by fervent prayer. If Jehovah's Witnesses continue to meet *prepared* Christians as they go from house to house, they will come face to face with Jesus Christ, and be forced to come to a decision as to what they personally think of Him.[3] (emphasis original)

Chapter 2:
My Study with
Jehovah's Witnesses

At the time we had the discussion about King David and John the Baptist, I didn't understand the contextual errors involved in the Witnesses' presentation. In fact, those Jehovah's Witnesses came across to me as very knowledgeable about the Bible, so I decided to take them up on their offer of a "free home Bible study."

Instead of beginning a verse-by-verse study of a book of the Bible, as I had expected, they presented me with a copy of the Watchtower's blue-covered book entitled *The Truth That Leads to Eternal Life*, known to Witnesses as "the *Truth* book." That was what we were going to study. You might wonder why I just passively submitted to this substitution instead of insisting on a real Bible study. In retrospect, I think there were three reasons.

First, I was genuinely interested in what the Witnesses had to say. They seemed to have great Bible knowledge, having shown me passages I had never read before—or at least had never considered in the way they presented them.

Second, I trusted the Witnesses who led the study. They were friendly, sincere people who really believed what they were sharing with me. In addition, they were donating many hours of their lives out witnessing, something I felt guilty about not doing myself.

Third, at the time I didn't understand the problems with the Watchtower's methods of "Bible study" and Bible interpretation. It is only in retrospect that I have come to see what I am sharing with you now.

THE WATCHTOWER
BOOK STUDY PROCESS

Let me give you a specific example of how the book study process worked. Each chapter and paragraph of the *Truth* book began—not with the Bible's message in its original context—but with Watchtower doctrine. Unrelated Bible passages and citations were joined together to "prove" the Watchtower dogma.

For example, the Watchtower teaches that in order to please God all true Christians must witness door-to-door, and they must refer to God by the name "Jehovah." You will not find this "truth" if you read the New Testament in context. It takes Watchtower literature to persuade you of this. In order to convince the student of these foundational Watchtower teachings, Chapter 6 of the *Truth* book contained following paragraph about the ministry of Jesus:

"For three and a half years he preached God's Word throughout the land, and he taught his disciples to do the same. (Luke 8:1) Though others in those days superstitiously avoided using the personal name of God, Jesus did not hold back from making it known. (John 17:26) He always spoke the truth, whether it was popular or not. In what he did he provided an example that we should follow if we want to please God."[1]

I was supposed to draw the conclusion that I should be emulating Jesus by going door-to-door preaching and using the name "Jehovah." In other words, I was supposed to believe that in order to be obeying God I had to become a Jehovah's Witness.

THE WATCHTOWER'S USE OF STUDY QUESTIONS

Many authors include study questions in their books in order to get their readers to think deeply about what the book has said. In contrast, the Watchtower's questions were worded in such a way as to ensure that the readers *didn't* think deeply about what the book had said. Students were expected to agree with the Watchtower writers, not to engage in independent thinking.

For example, the study questions for the above quoted paragraph asked, "Did Jesus hold back from using the personal name of God or from speaking the truth? So what should we do?"[2]

Notice the persuasion technique. "Using the personal name of God" is ranked in importance with "speaking the truth." "So what should we do?" is a rhetorical question. It's not hard to see what the "correct" answer is: Jesus used God's personal name, "Jehovah." It was superstitious people in his day who did not. If we want to please God, we have to be courageous like Jesus and follow his example. In this manner, the student was led to see the leaders of his own church as superstitious religionists who don't please God. In order to follow Jesus, the student would need to make himself unpopular with them by referring to God as "Jehovah."

The question did *not* ask if the student *agreed* that the Bible really teaches the Watchtower's dogma about door-to-door witnessing or use of the divine name. Rather, it took for granted that all of the paragraph's statements and implications were true and amply proved by the scriptures cited. In order to give the approved answer, the student was required to parrot the Watchtower's points and explain what he should do in light of this "truth."

By controlling the questions and answers in this fashion, the Watchtower controlled the conclusions that would be drawn. The student was expected to start thinking, "Let's see. What religious group is known for going throughout the land preaching? And what religious group does the unpopular thing that Jesus did and calls God by the personal name 'Jehovah'?" In this manner, the Watchtower religion was made to appear as the only true form of Christianity.

LEARNING FROM MY MISTAKES

The importance of context

2 Timothy 2:15 tells us, "Do your best to present yourself to God as one approved, a workman who does not need to be ashamed and who correctly handles the word of truth." I didn't know that verse at the time. I didn't understand what it implies— that there are correct and incorrect ways to handle the Word of truth. Merely quoting or referencing the Bible doesn't guarantee soundness of doctrine.

I didn't appreciate the critical differences between the instructional approach used by my college roommate and the teaching methods employed by the Watchtower. My friend had led me through a verse-by-verse study of a Bible book and helped me to read its message in context. The points I learned from that study were the points the apostle Paul himself was making in Romans, in the logical order in which he wrote them. In contrast, the Jehovah's Witnesses began with Watchtower dogma, pulled isolated verses out of context, and strung unrelated passages together to corroborate the Watchtower's doctrines.

The proper way to study the Bible is either to read it inductively (verse-by-verse in context to make sure you get the author's intended meaning) or topically (by gathering as many of the passages that deal with a given subject as you can and then comparing them). With either method, the key to sound Bible interpretation is context.

Context refers to four factors:

1. *The flow of thought of the book, section, paragraph, and surrounding verses in which it is contained.* Quoting a verse or part of a verse apart from this context can give us a completely erroneous understanding.

2. *The person whose viewpoint is being expressed.* Even though the Bible is God's Word, that doesn't mean that God agrees with every statement it contains. For example, Job's three friends made many statements about God. They believed what they were saying, but God declared that they were wrong (Job 42:7-8). Clearly, to take those statements as truth merely because they appear in the Bible would lead us into error.

3. *Other Bible passages that deal with the same topic.* Since God's Word, properly interpreted, will not contradict itself, we need to consider all the passages that deal with a subject before formulating doctrines.

4. *The connection or lack of connection between passages.* Beware of treating unrelated passages as if they were somehow connected. Only by carefully considering the context of each passage can we accurately determine whether there is a logical connection between them.

Example: Preaching door-to-door and using the name "Jehovah"

Let's apply these principles to the quotation from the *Truth* book which I referenced earlier. The passage cites Luke 8:1 and John 17:26, but the vast majority of students will never take the time to look up each of these verses, let alone read them in their entire contexts. They would just assume that they fully support the Watchtower's doctrines for which they have been referenced.

So what exactly is wrong with that paragraph? Where does it go off track?

First, two unrelated passages have been joined as if they were somehow logically connected. Luke 8:1 is a narrative about Jesus and his disciples going from town to town preaching. John 17:26 is one sentence out of a lengthy prayer Jesus prayed for his followers shortly before his arrest and crucifixion. The two passages are not related at all.

Second, read in its context, Luke 8:1 is *descriptive*, not *prescriptive*. That is, it describes the special traveling preaching ministry of Jesus and the twelve disciples who had given up their careers to follow him full time. It is not a command for all Christians to go and do likewise, as the *Truth* book excerpt implies, and it most certainly is not a mandate to preach out of Watchtower literature door-to-door.

Third, the Watchtower reads into—not out of—John 17:26 a connection with the name "Jehovah." In other words, it is the Watchtower that has engrafted this meaning into the text even though it isn't there. John 17:26 says nothing about people in Jesus' day being superstitious by refusing to use the name "Jehovah." The verse doesn't teach that Jesus called God "Jehovah." In fact, John 17:26 doesn't even *mention* the name "Jehovah." Here is what the verse actually says in the

Watchtower's own translation: "I have made your name known to them and will make it known, so that the love with which you loved me may be in them and I in union with them" (RNWT).

In order to gain a proper understanding, we need to consider the context by looking at the entire verse, not just the first half of it. Considering the full context is what will ensure that we are getting our understanding from the Bible itself rather than from someone else's agenda. Does the Watchtower's interpretation make sense here? How would calling God by the name "Jehovah" do anything to make known to Jesus' disciples the love with which the Father loved Jesus? How would calling God by the name "Jehovah" instill the Father's love into Jesus' disciples so deeply that this love would be "in them"? It wouldn't. Examining Jesus' entire statement in context shows that he wasn't referring to using the name "Jehovah" at all.

So what was he saying? To "make someone's name known" meant to extol and exemplify his character. So the context of the entire verse shows that when Jesus said, "I have made your name known," he was saying that during his life he had displayed to his disciples the depths of the Father's love so that they could have an intimate personal love relationship with both the Father and the Son.

Look also at the wider context, the entirety of John 17. Six times in John 17, Jesus addresses God directly. Each time he calls God "Father." Nowhere in the entire chapter does he address God as "Jehovah" or even use the name "Jehovah," not even in the Watchtower's own New World Translation. This chapter, therefore, does not teach that we must refer to God as "Jehovah" in order to please him. If anything, it proves that we do not!

I had never experienced this type of study before. It didn't occur to me then that by getting me to focus on study questions which controlled what would and wouldn't be asked the Watchtower greatly reduced the possibility that I would do what I have done here—entertain thoughts detrimental to the Watchtower's positions: "Does the fact that Jesus and his disciples went from town to town preaching prove that all Christians are required to do so? What are the main themes in Jesus' John 17 prayer? Is the name of Jehovah really under discussion there? Does Jesus actually address God as 'Jehovah' anywhere in that chapter?"

A BETTER WAY TO STUDY

Jehovah's Witnesses will expect—or at least hope—that you will be a passive student like I was, simply accepting what the Watchtower says. Instead, here are some steps you can take to make sure that you are studying what the Bible actually teaches:

1. Try to get the Witnesses to engage in a study of an actual Bible book such as Romans or Galatians. Most likely, they will not agree to do this. If they don't, simply ask, "What's wrong with studying God's Word without any outside literature? You don't believe your literature is infallible or inspired like the Bible, do you?" They will have to say no. Pray that the Holy Spirit will eventually lead them to see that they are relying on fallible Watchtower writers rather than on the Bible itself. Most likely, they will insist on using some Watchtower literature as a condition of continuing to meet with you. In that event, be an active, questioning student rather than a passive one. I will discuss how to do this in greater detail in Chapter 4.

2. Whenever you set up a meeting with the Witnesses, agree in advance on what topic you will be discussing. There is no set order that works best. In this book, I will give you approaches that you can use for any of the subjects that are likely to arise.

3. Study that topic thoroughly before you meet. Using this book, study the doctrinal chapter that explains the differences between what the Watchtower says about the subject and what the Bible actually teaches. Then examine the related approach chapters and select one to use in order to be prepared for your meeting. Jot down notes to have with you when you meet.

4. When you meet, stick to the subject you agreed to discuss. Don't let the Witnesses switch to a topic for which you aren't prepared. If at any time they try to do that, politely tell them that you will need more time to study your Bible in order to discuss that specific subject with them intelligently. If they insist on discussing the other topic, reschedule the meeting.

5. When the Witnesses cite you a Bible passage, always look it up and interpret it in accordance with the factors of context that I mentioned above. What is the entire verse? What is the entire paragraph of which it is a part? Whose point of view is being expressed? What exactly is the topic under discussion? What is the entire chapter about? Where does this chapter fit into the flow of the entire Bible book?

6. Don't base your Bible understanding on one proof text. The Watchtower makes this interpretive error repeatedly. They use isolated Bible verses (even partial verses) as mantras that seem to prove their doctrines. Those are the

quotations and phrases Jehovah's Witnesses come back to over and over. This practice leads the Watchtower to misinterpret other passages based on what they have already concluded. It also leads them to turn minor points into major ones. For example, as we have seen, in the mind of a Jehovah's Witness, "I have made your name known..." becomes proof that using the name "Jehovah" is one of the most important tests of being in the truth.

7. In comparing passages from different locations in the Bible, take your time. Don't let the Witnesses hopscotch the text, rushing you from one part of the Bible to another as they did with me when discussing heaven. When they try to jump to another part of the Bible, say, "I'll be glad to look at other passages a little later but I want to make sure I understand this one in its context before I look somewhere else." When you do go to a different part of the Bible, always examine the connection or lack of connection between the passages the Witnesses are citing you. Are they really talking about the same thing? How do we know that the passages are related?

In formulating or examining our beliefs, we need to gather, compare, and harmonize all of the Bible's teachings on the subject rather than basing our understanding on the first verse or part of a verse that someone cites to us. At the same time, however, we also need to make sure that each of the verses we use is properly understood in its own context. Striking a proper balance will be one of your biggest challenges in dealing with Jehovah's Witnesses.

Chapter 3:
Encountering the
Organizational Mindset

As I continued studying with the Witnesses, I attended several "*Watchtower* studies" at their Kingdom Hall. At least those were appropriately named, for what was studied were articles from *The Watchtower* magazine, not the Bible. The Bible was used the same way there as it was in the home book study I have just described. It was never studied inductively in context. Rather, Watchtower teachings were studied with Scripture references interspersed here and there as if they taught and emphasized exactly what *The Watchtower* was saying.

During the Kingdom Hall *Watchtower* studies, each paragraph in the study article was read aloud from the platform at the front of the hall. No questions were generated by the audience. Instead, the study conductor simply read out the corresponding study questions from the *Watchtower* article. People would raise their hands and the conductor would call on someone to answer, much as a teacher might do in school.

The only replies that were deemed correct were answers that either parroted the points in the paragraph or gave examples of why those points were correct. "That's right, Sister Smith," the study conductor would say approvingly. He would then restate the point.

The few times anyone made a "mistake" in their response—that is, failed to give the Watchtower-approved answer—the study conductor would say something like, "Well, I don't think that's exactly what the article is saying." Hands would go up again and he would call on someone else until the "correct" answer was given. Most likely, the one who made the "error" would not be called on again that evening.

At the time, I didn't see this procedure for what it was—indoctrination—so much as I found it rather mindless and boring. Nevertheless, with only the Watchtower's view being presented at the home studies and at the Kingdom Hall, I found myself thinking more and more like a Jehovah's Witness.

FRIENDS' WARNINGS BACKFIRED

As you can imagine, friends were concerned that I was being indoctrinated and urged me to break off my study with the Witnesses. I asked Christian friends to refute key Watchtower teachings point-by-point from the Bible, but for years no one even tried to do so. Possibly they didn't know Watchtower teachings and therefore didn't know how to refute them. Perhaps they assumed that as a college graduate I was too intelligent to buy into Watchtower dogma. They may not have realized that correctly understanding spiritual truth isn't just a matter of education or IQ.

In any event, as I struggled with what to believe my friends didn't help me find answers from the Bible. They just said that the Watchtower writers twisted the Scriptures, that their doctrines were unbiblical, that their religion was a cult, and that I should avoid them. These warnings didn't help me. They only seemed like personal attacks on Jehovah's Witnesses by people who had no substantive answers.

In fact, not only were my friends' warnings insufficient; they actually served to reinforce the Watchtower indoctrination. An early lesson in the *Truth* book said that the student should expect this type of opposition. It stated:

> As you examine God's Word, you will learn that your love for God will be put to the test. There may be individuals, perhaps even close friends or relatives, who will not approve of your examining the Scriptures. (1 Peter 4:4; Matthew 10:36, 37) They may try to discourage you. They may do this in all sincerity, because they do not know the marvelous truths found in the Bible. Perhaps you can help them. In other cases the opposition may come from persons who have no love for God. If this should occur, remember, having God's approval is far more important than having the approval of men. It is God, not man, who will give you eternal life if you love him above everyone and everything else.—Matthew 22:37-39.[1]

Notice how studying the Watchtower book is equated with "examining the Scriptures." Opposition to the study would come either from people who did not understand the "marvelous truths" I was learning or from "people who have no love for God." Not surprisingly, therefore, when friends told me to stop studying with the Witnesses because they were a cult, their opposition only enhanced the credibility of the Watchtower writers. Hadn't they told me to expect just this sort of opposition? I knew that my friends had a love for God, so I concluded that they just didn't understand and continued my Watchtower study.

UNDERSTANDING THE ORGANIZATIONAL MINDSET

Although I never actually became a Jehovah's Witness, I believe my experiences gave me a good understanding of how they think and feel. Again and again I saw evidence of one underlying idea that governs the life of a Jehovah's Witness: *Jehovah God works through one and only one organization today—the Watchtower Society*. Devotion to that concept is what makes a person a Jehovah's Witness. This organizational mindset dominates every aspect of their minds, hearts, and lives.

Unless they are harboring secret doubts, the Jehovah's Witnesses who come to your door are convinced of the truth of these Watchtower claims:

1. The Watchtower Society is God's sole channel of communication to mankind today.
2. Only the "faithful and discreet slave" (Matthew 24:45-47), the Governing Body of Jehovah's Witnesses, can properly interpret the Bible.
3. The Watchtower religion is "the truth," and the Watchtower organization is the only path to salvation because it is the only religion that truly adheres to the Bible.
4. All religious organizations other than the Watchtower are false and satanic.
5. Life is a loyalty and endurance test. In order to survive Armageddon (a cataclysmic divine judgment which is coming any day now), they must remain loyal to Jehovah and his organization and endure faithful until the end.
6. True servants of Jehovah can expect to be persecuted, especially since the end of the current wicked system of things is so near.

Why do Jehovah's Witnesses believe all these things? How do they come to have this organizational mindset? If they were born into or raised in a Jehovah's Witness family, it's all they know. These "truths" have been impressed on them all their lives. If they converted from a different religion or from no religion, they were taught these things through the home study and Kingdom Hall instructional processes I have described.

"Only the Watchtower Society meets the Bible's requirements" wow

How does the Watchtower attempt to prove these claims? First, it argues that God is organized, so he must have an organization. Next, it stresses that Christians should be united, not divided (1 Corinthians 1:10), and that doesn't describe the varied churches of Christendom. Jesus said in John 10:16 that his followers would be one flock with one shepherd. "Is it not obvious," the Watchtower therefore asks, "that they could not be scattered in Christendom's religions?"[2]

Having thus "proved" that God has only one organization, the Watchtower asks, "How can Jehovah's visible organization in our day be identified?" and gives the following answer (Scripture citations omitted):

(1) It truly exalts Jehovah as the only true God, magnifying his name.

(2) It fully recognizes the vital role of Jesus Christ in Jehovah's purpose—as the vindicator of Jehovah's sovereignty, the Chief Agent of life, the head of the Christian congregation, the ruling Messianic King.

(3) It adheres closely to God's inspired Word, basing all its teachings and standards of conduct on the Bible.

(4) It keeps separate from the world.

(5) It maintains a high level of moral cleanness among its members, because Jehovah himself is holy.

(6) It devotes its principal efforts to doing the work that the Bible foretold for our day, namely, the preaching of the good news of God's Kingdom in all the world for a witness.

(7) Despite human imperfections, its members cultivate and produce the fruits of God's spirit—love, joy, peace, long-suffering, kindness, goodness, faith, mildness, self-control—doing so to such a degree that it sets them apart from the world in general.[3]

These points are repeated in one form or another meeting after meeting and publication after publication. Witnesses are surrounded by people at the Kingdom Hall who believe these things and who continually reinforce each other's beliefs in them. They are even trained to teach these points themselves in the "home Bible studies" they conduct door-to-door.

In addition, Watchtower overseers are constantly exhorting Witnesses to prove their continuing loyalty to Jehovah and his organization by their performance.[4] Will they prove loyal and obedient to Jehovah even in the face of hardship and persecution as Jesus did, or will they fail the test as Adam did? If they fail the test, they will perish forever. This Watchtower worldview is what keeps Jehovah's Witnesses striving to prove worthy. It also keeps them in a state of constant uncertainty regarding their own spiritual standing before God.

"Christendom is false Christianity"

Once a person accepts the claim that the Watchtower is the only organization through which God is working, then it follows that the Watchtower religion must be the one true religion and its teachings alone must be the truth. Contrary teachings and practices of other religions must be in opposition to the truth and therefore come from Satan. The Watchtower always contrasts itself with what non-Jehovah's Witnesses consider to be Christianity. It denies that they are genuine Christians at all.

Do not other religions also follow the Bible? Many use it to some extent. But do they really teach and practice what it contains? Consider: (1) From most of their Bible translations they have removed the name of the true God thousands of times. (2) The Trinity doctrine, their concept of God himself, is borrowed from pagan sources and was developed in its present form centuries after Bible writing was completed. (3) Their belief in immortality of the human soul as the basis for continued life is not taken from the Bible; it has roots in ancient Babylon. (4) The theme of Jesus' preaching was the Kingdom of God, and he sent his disciples out to talk personally to others about it; but the churches today seldom mention that Kingdom and their members are not doing the work of preaching "this good news of the kingdom." (Matt. 24:14) (5) Jesus said that his true followers could be readily identified by their self-sacrificing love for one another. Is that true of the religions of Christendom when the nations go to war? (6) The Bible says that Christ's disciples would be no part of the world, and it warns that whoever wants to be a friend of the world makes himself an enemy of God; but the churches of Christendom and their members are deeply involved in the political affairs of the nations. (Jas. 4:4) In view of such a record, can it honestly be said that they really adhere to the Bible?[5]

IMPLICATIONS FOR GETTING THROUGH TO JEHOVAH'S WITNESSES

As much as you and I might wish that Jehovah's Witnesses didn't think and feel this way, the fact is that they do. If you are to be effective in sharing the gospel with them, it is critical that you understand this mindset and its implications thoroughly. The better you understand their thinking, the greater the likelihood that you will be able to minister to them, communicate with them effectively, and show them unconditional Christian love and compassion.

In order to get through to Jehovah's Witnesses, you must plant seeds that will lead them to question their reliance on the Watchtower organization. However, you must be careful not to come across as antagonistic. If you do, not only will they break off further contact with you, but they will go away more convinced than ever that they are "in the truth" because you have "persecuted" them.

Don't try to teach the Witnesses anything directly

Jehovah's Witnesses must be the teachers. You must be the student. This is the only way to get them to continue to have spiritual discussions with you. It's not hard to see why this is so. They believe you are in spiritual darkness. They have come to your door as representatives of "God's organization" for one reason only—to bring "the truth" to you. They don't think you have any spiritual understanding that would qualify you to teach them anything or even to share any valuable spiritual insights with them. That's why giving your testimony doesn't sway them. They think you have been deceived by Satan.

So how can you get through to them? Instead of trying to teach the Witnesses directly, assume the role of their student and ask lots of questions. Asking questions almost always works better than making statements. If you make a declaration of what is true and what is false, they will see you as trying to take over the teaching role, and they will resist you. Making the same point by asking questions is much more effective. Keep the questions respectful rather than accusatory or sarcastic.

Go out of your way to avoid triggering their persecution mindset

When discussing the Bible with Jehovah's Witnesses, conflict is inevitable. Key Watchtower teachings are simply not compatible with the doctrines of biblical Christianity. The Bible doesn't tell us to avoid such conflict. In fact, Jude 3 instructs Christians "to contend for the faith that was once for all entrusted to the saints."

However, this doesn't mean that we are to be contentious in our manner. We should do what we can to avoid unnecessary conflict, matters that stir up ill will without advancing the message that we are trying to get across. 1 Peter 3:15-16 admonishes us to answer those who question us "with gentleness and respect, keeping a clear conscience, so that those who speak maliciously against your good behavior in Christ may be ashamed of their slander."

Don't attack their organization

Don't attack the character or motives of past or current Watchtower overseers, and don't accuse Jehovah's Witnesses of being in a cult. It is perfectly acceptable for you to question the teachings of the Watchtower organization in a respectful manner. However, a verbal assault on the Watchtower, its Governing Body, or its elders will be seen as an attack on God and his chosen channel of communication. The Witnesses will be likely to call off any further meetings. Even if they do return, the hostile atmosphere will poison your attempts to witness.

Because the Witnesses expect to be persecuted, go out of your way to make clear that your questions and expressions of disagreement over various doctrines are in no way intended as a personal attack or insult. Be sure to convey to them that you love them and want the best for them because Jesus loves them and died for them.

Don't invite them to your church

Asking Witnesses to come to church with you can actually be a relational barrier rather than a bridge. Remember that they are indoctrinated in the belief that all the churches of Christendom are satanic. They view attendance at a church as participation in false religion which is opposed to the true worship of Jehovah. Even if you reach the stage where they see serious problems with the Watchtower, they will still have these fears.

In addition, it is critical that you make sure they understand that you do not believe that your church or denomination is the only true Christian organization on earth. Emphasize that the key to salvation is a personal relationship with Jesus Christ, not affiliation with the right religious organization.

Don't offer them literature

Because they consider all religious organizations but the Watchtower to be satanic, Jehovah's Witnesses usually will not read any Christian literature. If you offer it to them, they may refuse to take it. Even if they do take it in order to be polite, they probably will throw it away without reading it as soon as they are out of your sight. In the event that they ask you to help them find such resources, be willing to do so but make sure they understand that you are not trying to force anything on them.

Don't offer them literature written by ex-Jehovah's Witnesses except in the rare situation where they ask you to do so. Unless they have already developed serious doubts about the Watchtower, Jehovah's Witnesses will not read writings of or listen to testimonies of ex-Jehovah's Witnesses. They consider such people to be traitors to Jehovah. Witnesses can be disfellowshipped (excommunicated) by Watchtower elders if they are even caught possessing such materials.

If you want to confront them with something an ex-Jehovah's Witness has written, the best way to do it is to tell them that you have read something written by a former Jehovah's Witness that troubles you and to state that you think it's only fair to hear the Witnesses' side of it. Give them the choice as to whether to look at the item or not.

Don't let them provoke you

It has been my experience that if Jehovah's Witnesses get frustrated and realize that they have no answers for some of the points you are making, they sometimes get antagonistic and verbally abusive. If that happens, don't take it personally and don't retaliate. Psychologically, they may be trying to provoke you into doing something they can construe as persecution so as to justify to themselves ending your discussions without having to think any further about what you have said.

How did Jesus himself act when people reviled him? The Holy Spirit can enable you to have the same attitude as the Lord did: "When they hurled their insults at him, he did not retaliate; when he suffered, he made no threats. Instead, he entrusted himself to him who judges justly" (1 Peter 2:23).

Accept it as a given that Jehovah's Witnesses think that all of Christendom, including your church or denomination, is deceived by Satan. Take it in stride if this attitude comes through to you. Love them anyway. Now you understand how they have been led to believe what they do. Remember that the Lord Jesus himself extended love and grace to people who branded him a false Messiah.

OVERCOMING THE ORGANIZATIONAL MINDSET

If Witnesses are to come to saving faith in the Lord Jesus Christ, their organizational mindset and reliance on the Watchtower organization must be overcome. You have to ask questions that challenge Watchtower dogma, but at the same time you have to go out of your way to avoid coming across as trying to take over the role of teacher. Moreover, because of the level of trust Witnesses place in their organization and its overseers, you have to walk on eggshells so as not to come across as a persecutor. That would only serve to drive them deeper into the Watchtower.

Getting through to Jehovah's Witnesses is an art, not a science. It's not always easy to know when to press a point and when to back off. Despite your best efforts, your motives and your tone can be misconstrued. You also need to guard your own heart throughout the process to make sure that you maintain a proper balance of Christian confidence and Christian humility.

All of the approaches I will share with you in this book take these realities into account. They are designed to help Witnesses break free and come to Jesus. Ultimately, of course, only the Holy Spirit can bring a person to saving faith, and any approaches you use must be undertaken at his direction and in reliance on him.

Chapter 4:
Witnessing Principles
I Learned

We can't get through to every Jehovah's Witness, but we can get through to some of them.

It's tempting to seek a "quick fix"—one Bible passage that will convince Witnesses that the Watchtower is wrong or some "smoking gun" evidence that will conclusively prove to them that the Watchtower can't be trusted.

It doesn't work like that.

There's no such thing as a "can't miss" witnessing method.

My own spiritual journey involved a four year agonizing struggle. One week, I would attend an evangelical Christian church. The next week, I would skip church and read Watchtower literature. One minute I thought like an evangelical Christian. The next minute, I thought like a Jehovah's Witness. I couldn't decide what to believe and I couldn't understand why I couldn't make up my mind.

Despite being that deeply swayed by Watchtower thinking, I never became a baptized Witness, nor did I ever go door-to-door with them as an "unbaptized publisher." I wanted to be completely sure I was doing the right thing before I started promoting the Watchtower religion or committing myself to it.

My breakthrough came when I reached the point where I gave up and acknowledged to God that I was totally incapable of figuring things out. I pleaded with him to straighten me out, to give me a proper understanding. Shortly thereafter, a Christian friend shared with me doctrinal tapes by Walter Martin that had been specifically prepared to explain and refute Watchtower teachings.

I listened to those tapes and studied all the scriptures cited by both sides. I did my best to make sure that I was getting all aspects of the Bible's teaching on the topics, not just a limited sample of quotations handpicked to support someone's doctrinal agenda. I tried to be as unbiased as possible—not believing or disbelieving something because of which side was saying it. In the end, I concluded that the Watchtower organization is wrong about many of its key doctrines and that evangelical Christian teachings are correct.

I harbor no ill will against Jehovah's Witnesses. In fact, because of all I went through, I love them. I don't see them as stupid or wicked. I see them as very sincere and zealous. I understand what they believe and why they believe it.

My experiences have taught me a great deal about what to do and what not to do. I've written this book to share with you what I learned. In this chapter, I'm going to give you witnessing principles that apply to all the approaches presented in this book.

PRINCIPLE #1:
PREPARE YOUR HEART

Take personal inventory

Before you begin to witness, make sure that you yourself are saved, that you have been born again. If you are unsure of your salvation, then your own spiritual condition needs to be your first priority. You can't tell someone else how to find a relationship with God unless you have such a relationship yourself.

Have you come to the point of repentance for your own sins? Are you relying on Christ and Christ alone for your own salvation? Have you given up on generating your own righteousness and trying to earn God's acceptance through good works? Have you humbled yourself and asked Christ to forgive your sins and save you based solely on his atoning sacrifice on the cross? If not, I urge you to take that step now. If you have questions about what you need to do or why, then find someone who can help you and get your own standing with God secured.

As part of your personal inventory, make sure that you have a submissive spirit toward God. If you know that you are saved, how is your walk with the Lord? I'm not saying that you need to be walking in sinless perfection before you try to help someone else. By that standard, none of us would qualify. What I am saying is that you need to be walking in reliance on the Holy Spirit if you are going to be effective in reaching out to others.

Likewise, make sure that you have a godly motive. Are you itching to win a spiritual argument with some Jehovah's Witnesses? Are you hoping to stump them with clever questions? Are you planning to impress them with your Bible knowledge and understanding? Do you long to add some spiritual scalps to your belt? Are you hoping to have a success story to relate to your inner circle of Christian friends? Attitudes like this are easy to fall into, but they are nothing but sinful pride that will hinder your witness.

Pray earnestly

When you share the gospel with someone—particularly someone in a false religious system—you are engaging in spiritual warfare. Ultimately, it is the Holy Spirit that has to get through to them because only God can impart spiritual understanding (Ephesians 1:16-19). It is not by our cleverness but by God's

Spirit that we are able to share the gospel effectively. Pray as you read this book. Pray when you first see the Witnesses at your door. Pray silently while they are with you. Pray again after they leave. Pray as you study and prepare for the next meeting. Even continue to pray if they break off contact with you. Pray that the Holy Spirit will continue to work with them even if you can't.

Establish safeguards

Don't get overconfident and think that you know far too much about the Bible and about the Watchtower to get sucked in. Be sure to pray about how to proceed. Have one or more trusted Christian friends debrief you after each session with the Witnesses to make sure that you are not lapsing into the role of a passive student.

If anything the Witnesses say causes you to doubt your own beliefs, be open with your Christian friends about it and seek answers. Call off future meetings with the Witnesses until such time as you have clearly resolved any such issue in your own mind.

PRINCIPLE #2:
BUILD RELATIONAL BRIDGES

It is critical that we exhibit unconditional Christian love—not merely as a technique for sharing the gospel—but as a way of life. Part of extending this type of love is building relational bridges. I'm not suggesting that you pretend to agree with erroneous Watchtower teachings or water down the gospel message. I am saying that you must see and treat Jehovah's Witnesses as people for whom Christ died, as people whom he loves and to whom he is offering salvation. Don't have a spiritual chip on your shoulder.

Remember that it is only by the grace and mercy of God that any of us can understand any spiritual truth at all (2 Corinthians 4:4).

Begin at your doorstep

Jehovah's Witnesses experience a great deal of rejection as they go door-to-door. Most people aren't interested in their message. Many are openly hostile. A former Witness elder once told me that over a period of fifty years he had doors slammed in his face, got doused with water, was set on by dogs, and had a gun pointed in his face.

Several well-intentioned people who were trying to witness to him told him directly that he was in a cult, that he was in league with the devil, that he was a false prophet, and that he was going to hell. Do you think any of this hostility won this man to Christ? Of course not. It only served to convince him that he was indeed in the true religion and was being persecuted because of his loyalty to Jehovah.

It is true that Jehovah's Witnesses come to you with a false gospel and a great deal of misunderstanding of the Bible. It is also true that they believe that they are in the light and that you are in darkness. Love them anyway. Treat them with respect. Be gracious to them. Be patient with them. Remember how Christ treats you. Even if they aren't impressed with a thing you say, your Christlike attitude can be a powerful witness to the reality of the new birth and the transformed life.

If you greet them in a friendly manner when you open the door, most likely they will use a conversation starter they have learned from the Watchtower. Don't interrupt them. They will be brief. Smile and thank them for coming. Isn't that how you would want to be treated if you were witnessing door-to-door?

If you have time available right then, invite them to come in. This may be your only chance to talk with these particular individuals. If they accept your invitation, offer them something to drink and invite them to sit down and talk with you. If you do nothing but extend to them this kind of common courtesy, you will have given them a better witness than they get from most Christians.

What if the time is not convenient? They may be carpooling with other Witnesses or nearing the end of the time they have allotted for their field service that day. Your children may be fussing or you may be late for work. Tell them you are interested in hearing what they have to say and set up a time for another visit.

If you are having trouble with scheduling, you can suggest meeting with just one of them. It is rare that a Jehovah's Witness will agree to meet with you without another Witness present, but I have had it happen. I am always happy with such an arrangement because a Witness is sometimes more open with you if there's no witnessing partner present to hear what is being said. Be accommodating, but not overeager.

Because you have been friendly, the Witnesses are almost certain to set up an appointment to come back to meet with you for an extended discussion. Ask for their names and phone numbers so you can notify them in the event that something unexpected comes up. If they don't want to give out their phone numbers, that's fine. At least you showed them courtesy.

What if they want to leave a copy of *The Watchtower* magazine or other material with you in the meantime? Should you accept it? I recommend that you take their literature as long as you won't be contributing money to their cause. You don't want to create a barrier needlessly.

If you are concerned about some impressionable person in your household reading it and being misled, you can make sure that doesn't happen. If nothing else, you can throw away the magazine after the Witnesses leave. Before you do, though, I recommend that at least you make a mental note of the general topics of the articles. That may give you a good clue as to what the approach they will take when they return. It may also give you ideas as to what approach might be best for you to take with them.

Some Christians have a conviction against accepting any cult literature even on that basis. If that describes you, the best way to decline so as not to give offense is to say, "Thank you for the offer. I make it a practice not to accept any religious literature from anyone until I first have the chance to talk with them and find out more about their organization and its teachings. I hope you understand."

Continue in your living room

When you first meet with Jehovah's Witnesses inside your home, find out as much about them as you can. Invite them to tell you a little bit about themselves. How long has each of them been a Jehovah's Witness? Are they converts or were they born into the Watchtower religion? Do they enjoy the door-to-door witnessing? How many years have they been doing it? How many hours a month do they average? Are they married? Do they have children? Are all their relatives Jehovah's Witnesses or are they perhaps the only one in their family? What line of work are they in?

Don't ask these questions as if you were the Grand Inquisitor. Ask them casually and in a friendly way. Answer similar questions about your own religious background, family, and career. Gathering this type of information should help you relate to them as your meetings progress. If nothing else, obtaining such information will help you to see those Jehovah's Witnesses as individuals rather than as representatives of an organization. It will also help you pray for them more intelligently.

As your discussions progress, if you sense at any point that you are making headway with one of the Witnesses more than the other, address your comments and questions primarily to the one on whom you are having the impact.

Often more experienced Witnesses such as elders or pioneers serve as mentors for less experienced Witnesses. When this happens, the more experienced of the two tends to jump in and take over completely the moment their partner runs into difficulty. Don't allow this to happen. Be polite, but as soon as you can, draw the partner back into the conversation.

In order to make sure that they aren't wasting their time, sometimes early in the discussions they will ask if you would be willing to become a Jehovah's Witness if they show you that they alone have the truth. I recommend that you tell them, "Yes, I would, but I have a lot of questions I would need answered before I would reach that point." You can be sincere in saying that. You know they won't be able to persuade you that the Watchtower religion is the truth, but *if* they could prove to you that they were right, wouldn't you join them? That answer also gives them fair notice that if they proceed, there will be a lot of questions you will be expecting them to answer.

In order to build relational bridges between you and the Witnesses, make clear to them areas on which you agree: (1) God exists. (2) The Bible is his inerrant and inspired Word. (3) Jesus Christ is the Messiah. (4) As descendants of Adam, human beings are sinners who need to be saved. (5) Christians should maintain high moral standards.

I am not suggesting that you gloss over the differences. I am saying that it is easier to have a positive impact on people if you are aware of values and beliefs you hold in common. When you do get into areas of disagreement, do so respectfully. Treat them the way you want them to treat you.

After you have met with them several times, go out of your way to let them know that you care about them and consider them your friends even though you don't see eye to eye on everything. This should surprise them because it doesn't match the Watchtower's us-versus-them and persecution paradigms. Whether you make substantial progress with them or not, at least you will have shown them genuine Christian love.

PRINCIPLE #3:
COMMUNICATE EFFECTIVELY

Be an active, questioning "student"

In your first session, establish your right to ask the Witnesses questions. You can do this in a friendly way by saying something like, "I find that I learn a lot more if I am an active participant in discussions and ask a lot of questions when I don't understand something. Is it all right if I interrupt your presentation from time to time if I have questions?" Of course, they will say yes. In fact, they will probably encourage you to do so. Students are supposed to ask questions, and as teachers the Witnesses will have to try to come up with answers.

Asking questions almost always works better than making statements. I'm not talking about "gotcha" questions such as a hostile attorney might ask during cross-examination. I'm talking about asking questions in such a way that will get them to focus on what the Bible is really saying while still keeping the dialogue going.

I am not saying that you should never make direct statements about what you believe. However, when you do make such a statement, it is very helpful to follow it immediately with a question like, "Do you see why I would think that?" or "Can you give me your take on that?" In that manner, you can get your point across without them feeling that you are trying to usurp their "rightful" role as teachers. They will be more likely to continue to meet with you.

An important word of warning—*don't become a passive student.* Even after you get their permission to ask your own questions, the Witnesses will still try to get you into the type of programmed learning I described earlier in which the Watchtower literature asks the questions and you parrot back their answers. They have a definite strategy for changing active questioners into passive students. At first, they will address your questions as soon as you raise them. But soon you will notice them suggesting that you defer your questions until later, promising that most of them will be covered during the course of the study. They will assure you that if you have additional questions, you can always raise them later.

Although this suggestion sounds reasonable, based on my experience I can tell you that if you agree to such a procedure, you will soon find yourself answering the Watchtower's study questions and forgetting to ask your own. The Witnesses will be the ones setting the agenda. The Watchtower literature will provide both the questions and the approved answers, and you will become a passive student who hears only what the Witnesses are comfortable telling you.

Don't allow this to happen. Don't argue with them or confront them with what they are doing. Instead, when they try to get you to defer specific questions, simply make it clear that you learn best by getting your questions answered at the time they arise. Tell them that you want to address the present issue before moving on to anything else.

Use language they will understand

As you listen to Jehovah's Witnesses talk, you will find them using Watchtower lingo—phrases like "the ransom sacrifice" and "Jehovah's arrangement for salvation." After you get them to define their terms, it often helps to use the Watchtower expressions yourself, so long as you aren't agreeing to doctrinal error by doing so. For example, you might have them read aloud a passage of Scripture and then ask, "How do you think that verse relates to Jehovah's arrangement for salvation?" By doing that, you are helping them to read the Bible in context using terms that they identify with and understand.

It is also important to avoid the use of Christian lingo unless you are careful to explain exactly what you mean. In church services and in our conversations with fellow Christians, we become so accustomed to hearing and using Christian terms that we sometimes forget that people outside the faith have no idea what we are talking about. Unfortunately, in such situations our well-intentioned efforts to witness can come across as gibberish.

For example, author Ted Dencher says that Christian testimonies made no sense to him when he was a Jehovah's Witness: "They used expressions like, 'I know Christ as my personal Saviour.' That orbited over my head! What did they mean—*knowing* the Lord? What did they mean by *personal*

Saviour? No one ever bothered to explain, so I concluded they did not know!"[1] (emphasis original)

There are two ways to avoid this error. First, think in advance about how your words will come across to someone from a totally different religious background. Will they be understandable or would it be better to say things differently? Second, if you do decide to use a Christian expression, solicit the Witnesses' feedback by saying something like, "I'm not sure if that came across very well. Was what I said clear or confusing?" In this way, you can make sure that you are getting your points across.

Be aware of Bible translation differences

You can use your favorite Bible translation in your discussions with Jehovah's Witnesses (I use the NIV in this book unless otherwise noted), but the only Bible they are likely to use is the 2013 revised edition of the Watchtower's New World Translation (RNWT). Where I quote Watchtower literature, you will often find that their Bible quotations come from an earlier edition of their own New World Translation (NWT).

I consider both the NWT and the RNWT to be faulty and deceptive translations. Many verses have been rendered in a manner that supports Watchtower doctrines rather than in a way that best accords with the Hebrew and Greek manuscripts. However, the Watchtower has convinced Jehovah's Witnesses that its version of the Bible is the best and most accurate translation available, so they will be using it throughout your time together.

When there is a significant difference between recognized versions and the RNWT, I will give you the wording of the Watchtower version. That way you will know what it says and won't be caught off guard. When you ask the Witnesses to read a particular passage, you will be prepared to make your points without fear that you will be taken by surprise.

One example will suffice to show you what I mean. If you are like most Christians, one of your favorite texts that proves the deity of Christ is John 1:1: "In the beginning was the Word, and the Word was with God, and the Word was God." Imagine sharing that verse with Jehovah's Witnesses only *then* to learn that their translation renders that verse as follows: "In the beginning was the Word, and the Word was with God, and the Word was *a god*" (RNWT, emphasis added).

I can tell you from my own experience that being caught unaware in such a fashion puts the Christian at a tremendous disadvantage. You have no idea what to say, and the Witnesses proceed to take over the discussion and overwhelm you with all their Watchtower texts that "prove" that Jesus is "a god," a mighty one, but not God Almighty.

As you study this book, you will learn what those problem passages are and how the Watchtower version renders them. I will also give you recommendations as to how to handle those situations.

Clarify terminology

The Watchtower uses Bible words and phrases but often attaches very different meanings to them. In talking with Jehovah's Witnesses, therefore, it is critical that you get them to define the terms they are using. Likewise, define the terms you are using. Unless you clarify definitions at the outset, you will think you are communicating while in fact you will be talking about totally different concepts.

Don't take anything for granted. For example, Hebrews 9:27 says that "man is destined to die once, and after that to face judgment." To the Christian, this proves that there is no second chance to receive Christ as Savior after we die. In fact, to us that conclusion may seem so obvious that we find it hard to believe that anyone could dispute it.

The Watchtower, however, teaches a totally different meaning of the word "judgment." To Jehovah's Witnesses, Hebrews 9:27 means that after death those who are resurrected will have a testing period during Christ's millennial kingdom in which to learn about Jehovah's ways, progress to perfection, and thereby prove worthy of everlasting life.

If you suspect that you have conflicting definitions of words or phrases, explain your understanding of the terms and ask them to explain theirs. Make clear which definition is being used at various points in the conversation. That way, you will avoid the pitfall of appearing to communicate when in reality you are *mis*communicating.

In situations in which you want to help the Witnesses see the problems with the Watchtower's definition of a key term, one way to do it is to place the Watchtower's definition into a related Bible text to see if it makes sense. For example, the Watchtower teaches that a person's spirit is not a conscious part of the person that will survive death. Instead, they teach that it is an impersonal "active life-force."[2] Substitute that definition for the word "spirit" in 1 Corinthians 2:11 and see if it makes sense: "For who among men knows the thoughts of a man except the man's *impersonal, active life-force* within him? In the same way no one knows the thoughts of God except the *impersonal, active force* of God." Your point will be clear; an impersonal force can't know anyone's thoughts but our spirits and God's Spirit can.

Clarify differing positions

I have found that one effective way to explain the Christian position is to start by summarizing your understanding of the Watchtower teaching on that issue and then describing what you believe in terms of its similarities and differences.

As an example, you might say, "It's my understanding from what you have said that the Watchtower believes that the name 'Jehovah' only applies to the Father. What I believe is that the name 'Jehovah' applies to the Father but that it also applies to the Son and the Holy Spirit as well."

Often, a light bulb will go on. They may not agree that you are right, and they may ask you to explain further, but at least they will understand what you have been saying.

Another way to make sure that you are truly communicating is to ask the Witnesses to restate your position on the topic under discussion so you can be sure you have communicated your point effectively. A friend of mine once explained to a Jehovah's Witness the doctrine of justification by faith. He asked the man to restate what he had just said in order to make sure he understood. He was shocked when the Witness replied, "Sure. You believe that everyone will be saved." He was able to correct the misunderstanding, although it took several tries before the Witness actually comprehended the Christian teaching. Had my friend not asked for this feedback, he would have had no idea that there had been a serious miscommunication.

In order to make this a fair process, you can also take the time to clarify what the Witnesses have told you until they are satisfied that you have understood them. In this way, you do them the honor of showing that you are listening and avoid having a fruitless discussion in which no one truly understands what the other person is saying. Making it clear that you are seeking to understand them will increase the likelihood that they will listen to you and begin to think for themselves about something you have said.

PRINCIPLE #4: CONSISTENTLY MODEL GOOD BIBLE STUDY TECHNIQUES

In addition to examining only one verse or passage at a time and being careful to examine the context of the verse or passage you are studying (as described in Chapter 2), there are several other ways you can encourage good Bible study techniques.

Ask them to read the text aloud

When you are about to examine a Bible passage with the Witnesses, I recommend that you ask one of the Witnesses to read it aloud. That's the best way to get them to focus their attention on what the Bible is really saying. Why aloud? If you ask them to read it silently, they can just skim through it or simply assume that they know what it says.

Why ask them to read it aloud instead of doing the reading yourself? If you are the one who reads aloud, the Witnesses will often tune you out while they are thinking of the next point they want to make. I don't say that you should never take your turn doing the reading, but the more crucial a passage you are examining, the more important it is to make sure they are fully engaged. One way to get them to do the reading is to ask them how the Watchtower translation renders the passage.

Former Jehovah's Witness elder David Reed suggests the following procedure: "Have the Witness break down the verse into clauses, phrases, and individual words. Ask him or her to comment on what each means. The Watchtower interpretation of the whole may disintegrate when the parts are examined separately."[3]

Respectfully question erroneous Watchtower assumptions

Although Jehovah's Witnesses are not allowed to question Watchtower teachings, you are free to do so. After all, you aren't expected to understand. Just be careful that you don't trigger the Watchtower persecution mindset by coming across as disrespectful.

For example, I shared with you in Chapter 1 how a Jehovah's Witness informed me that when Jesus used the term "little flock" in Luke 12:32 he was referring to the group of 144,000 that is mentioned in Revelation 14:3. Jehovah's Witnesses have read and heard that so often that it never occurs to them to question that assumption.

If you were to tell them outright that the Watchtower has misled them by hopscotching the Bible, they would be offended and deny it vigorously. However, as their "student" you can tell them respectfully that you don't see the connection between the two passages. One was a statement Jesus made to his disciples while he was alive on this earth. The other was a description of a vision John had more than 50 years later. Ask them to demonstrate to you that they are talking about the same thing. For example, why couldn't the "little flock" be the original 12 disciples? In order to answer you, they will be forced to consider alternative possibilities and think about whether the Watchtower teaching really makes sense.

Ask follow-up questions to stimulate thinking

Frequently, Jehovah's Witnesses will answer your questions reflexively with a standard Watchtower reply they have been trained to give. When this happens, they aren't really thinking about your question. They are simply on autopilot, giving you a programmed response.

When you sense that happening, you need to ask follow-up questions in order to get them genuinely to think about what you are saying. The best way I have found to do this is to tell them, "I'm sorry. I don't get that. I'm puzzled (or confused) by what you said. Please help me understand." If necessary, rephrase or expand on your question.

Follow-up questions are also often helpful in dealing with the Witnesses' practice of changing the subject when you ask a question for which they have no good answer. This technique gets them off the hook and onto a topic they feel more comfortable discussing. The best way to stop that is to say, "I'm sorry. I guess I didn't phrase my question very well. What I'm asking is..." Then simply rephrase the question.

Because of Jehovah's Witnesses' resistance to thinking independently of the Watchtower, you may need to ask your questions several different ways. Don't use the same words each time, but keep pressing for a better answer. By posing such questions, you will be modeling critical thinking skills, asking questions they would never think to ask and helping them to think independently of the Watchtower organization.

Be careful not to come across as rude, sarcastic, or condescending. If you reach an impasse, tell them, "I'm sorry. I just don't get what you are saying" or "I guess we're just not on the same wavelength on this. Maybe we should just move on for now and come back to this later."

PRINCIPLE #5:
BE FLEXIBLE

The approaches in this book are intended to be guidelines rather than recipes or formulas that must be followed to the letter. When I suggest points you should make to Jehovah's Witnesses, I have put them in an order that I hope you will find to be both logical and helpful. However, in actual conversations with the Witnesses you will need to be flexible. They will make their points in whatever order seems best to them, and you will need to adjust.

When I say things like, "Ask the Witnesses this," or "tell the Witnesses that," please understand that I am not trying to put words in your mouth. If you prefer to phrase things differently or skip certain points, that's fine. In other words, these approaches are not presented as scripts that should be memorized and recited verbatim. Rather, they are intended to be helpful suggestions from someone who has engaged in many such discussions with Jehovah's Witnesses.

When you use one of my approaches, don't feel that you have to cover every subtopic or Scripture passage in the chapter. Be sensitive to the Holy Spirit. It is better to discuss a few items effectively with Jehovah's Witnesses than to rush conversations along in an attempt to cover everything.

If you sense that you are getting through to the Witnesses on a particular point, stop and let that point sink in. Don't rush ahead to press your advantage or to cover more ground. Silence can be a very effective witnessing tool. Give the Holy Spirit time to work.

APPLYING THESE PRINCIPLES
TO SPECIFIC TOPICS

In the remaining sections of this book, I will be applying the lessons and principles of Section 1 to the discussion of specific Bible topics. I will explain the differences between Watchtower and Christian teachings on those matters. I will also give you approaches for discussing those issues in ways the Witnesses will not expect in order to help you get them to focus on what the Bible really says rather than simply reciting their prepared presentations.

Settle in advance on the topic that will be discussed, and then use relevant chapters of the book to prepare for that meeting. Remember not to have this book or any other books about Jehovah's Witnesses visible when the Witnesses arrive. Rather, make your own notes of the questions you will want to raise in your time together.

SECTION 2: DISCUSSING SALVATION

Chapter 5: Irreconcilable Differences

Christians and Jehovah's Witnesses both believe that as descendants of Adam we are born under condemnation. Christ's sacrificial death is the key to our salvation; without it, we would have no hope. So far, it sounds like we believe the same thing.

Not so. The Bible's way of salvation and the Watchtower salvation system are totally incompatible.

THE CONTRAST IN A NUTSHELL

The Bible teaches that sinners are justified (declared righteous) and saved by grace through faith in Christ and his atoning sacrifice. God does have righteous works for us to do, but these works have no role in saving us. Rather, it is only by becoming new creations in Christ through the new birth that we are capable of doing them.

These principles are set out in Ephesians 2:8-10: "For it is by grace you have been saved, through faith—and this not from yourselves, it is the gift of God—not by works, so that no one can boast. For we are God's workmanship, created in Christ Jesus to do good works, which God prepared in advance for us to do."

In contrast, the Watchtower teaches that there are two classes of Christians (by which they mean Jehovah's Witnesses)—the anointed 144,000 and the "great crowd" of "other sheep."

It does not believe that the new birth (John 3:3) has anything to do with an inner transformation of redeemed sinners by the

55

Holy Spirit. Rather, the Watchtower says the new birth is an experience by which God's spirit designates a person to be one of the 144,000. This designation is what gives a person the opportunity to be resurrected in spirit form and reign with Christ from heaven—provided they prove worthy in this life by their works.[1]

According to the Watchtower, all other Jehovah's Witnesses have the prospect of being resurrected in bodily form and living on a paradise earth. The faithful ones of this group will progress to moral perfection by their obedience during the 1,000 years of Christ's kingdom. They do not need to be born again or justified by faith. They will merit everlasting life without it.

The Watchtower explains: "The 'great crowd' will not undergo a change of nature from human to spiritual and so do not need the justification by faith and the imputed righteousness that the 144,000 'chosen ones' have required. Not imputed human perfection by faith in Christ's blood, but *actual human perfection in the flesh* by the uplifting, cleansing help of God's Messianic kingdom—this is what the 'great crowd' will need and what they will attain by Christ's kingdom of a thousand years"[2] (emphasis added).

Let's look at the Watchtower salvation system and the Bible's way of salvation in more detail.

THE WATCHTOWER SALVATION SYSTEM

Because nearly all Jehovah's Witnesses you will meet consider themselves to be members of the great crowd (earthly class), I'll focus on what the Watchtower's salvation system says about them.

Faith in Christ's "ransom sacrifice" doesn't give them everlasting life. Instead, it gives them a *chance* for everlasting life. In order to obtain this salvation, they have to "exercise faith" in this opportunity during this life. In order to prove worthy to make it into Christ's millennial kingdom on earth, they "must do their utmost to measure up to Jehovah's requirements of holiness."[3]

If they are deemed worthy to make it into the millennial kingdom, their slate will be wiped clean. Their past sins in this life will never be held against them.[4] However, they will enter the millennium with the same sinful inclinations and personality they had at the end of their life in this old system.[5]

They don't need to be justified by faith. Instead, Christ's millennial kingdom will be a 1,000-year testing period in which they will have an opportunity to overcome these sinful inclinations and progress to actual moral perfection.[6] How will this happen?

1. Satan and demons will be bound for 1,000 years and no longer able to tempt them.[7]
2. Christ's rule will be completely righteous and just.[8]
3. They will have the benefits of Christ's "ransom sacrifice" applied to them as they submit to Christ's righteous rule.[9]
4. "...as the result of the dripping and trickling down of righteousness from the 'new heavens,' the human soil of the 'new earth' will respond and become fruitful in a corresponding way."[10]
5. Jesus as High Priest will "help them get out of their weaknesses and inclinations to badness."[11]
6. There will be "new scrolls" containing Jehovah's detailed requirements.[12]

7. Earthly overseers—"princes," including the ancient Israelite worthies and Jehovah's Witness elders—will help them learn about Jehovah and his ways and progress to perfection.[13]

At the end of the 1,000 years, Satan will be loosed and have a final opportunity to test their loyalty and dedication to Jehovah.[14] An indefinite number will fail this test, rebel against Jehovah, and be summarily executed by him because they failed to prove worthy to be justified, that is, declared righteous.[15] The rest God will justify (declare righteous) "on the basis of their own merit" since they will have passed this final, decisive test.[16]

Those who pass the final test will be adopted by Jehovah and acknowledged as his sons through Jesus Christ.[17] This will get them back to where Adam was originally—living in paradise on earth without sinful inclinations but still capable of choosing to rebel against Jehovah. In the unlikely event that any become rebels by sinning deliberately, Jehovah will then annihilate them.[18]

THE BIBLE'S WAY OF SALVATION

All human beings (except Jesus) are born with unrighteousness within us which we inherited from Adam and are therefore under condemnation (John 3:18; Romans 3:23). We are born as slaves to the power of sin. Unless God transforms us through the new birth, it is impossible for us to be truly righteous or to live the righteous kind of life God desires (Romans 7:14-24; 8:8-9). God sent Christ to give his life as an atoning sacrifice for our sins (Romans 3:22-25), thus making it possible for us to be born again.

Although there will be a group of 144,000 chosen for a special mission in the end times (Revelation 7:4), they are not a separate class of Christians with a separate destination and a separate path to salvation. Christ has only one flock (John 10:16).

There is no second chance after death (Hebrews 9:27). In order to be saved, we need to come to Christ by faith (John 5:39-40), repent of our sins (Luke 13:3), and thereby receive salvation as a free gift (Ephesians 2:8). When we repent of ours sins and place faith in Christ's atoning sacrifice, the following immediately happens:

1. All our sins are covered by Christ's blood and we are completely forgiven (1 John 2:12).
2. The old man (the person we were in Adam) is crucified with Christ (Galatians 2:20). This doesn't mean we are incapable of sinning. It means we are no longer slaves to sin (Romans 6:6).
3. We receive a new birth and thereby become a new creation (John 3:3; 2 Corinthians 5:17; Galatians 6:15).
4. We are justified (declared righteous) by our faith. Our works have no role in saving us (Romans 3:28; Galatians 2:16; 3:24; Ephesians 2:8-9).
5. The Holy Spirit indwells us (Romans 8:9-11). He places us in Christ (2 Corinthians 5:17) and Christ in us (Colossians 1:27).

After this spiritual rebirth, we are now capable of doing righteous works which God has prepared in advance for us to do (Ephesians 2:10). We do this by allowing Christ to live through us by faith (Galatians 2:20).

When Christians die, we will go in spirit form to be with Christ (2 Corinthians 5:8; Philippians 1:23-24). At the resurrection, we will receive glorified, immortal bodies of flesh and bones and our spirits will be reunited with our bodies (Luke 24:39; 1 John 3:2).

All Christians will be wherever Christ is, whether in heaven or on earth (1 Thessalonians 4:17). During the millennium, Christians will reign with Christ over those in the nations who survived the great tribulation (Revelation 2:26-27). After the millennium, the heavenly Jerusalem will come to earth and God will dwell with us there. At that time, the distinction between heaven and earth will be abolished (Revelation 21:1-4).

FOR FURTHER STUDY

In order to get through to Jehovah's Witnesses with the light of the gospel, you will need to lead them to see that the Watchtower's salvation system is not the way of salvation which God sets out in the Bible. Here is how the next five chapters will help you do this:

- Chapter 6, "The Righteousness Approach" explains how to help Jehovah's Witnesses see that the Watchtower's salvation system does not work.
- Chapter 7, "The Come to Jesus Approach" explains how to convey to Jehovah's Witnesses their need for coming to Jesus for salvation and gives suggestions for explaining to them how to do so.
- Chapter 8, "The Faith and Works Approach," explains how to show Jehovah's Witnesses the biblical relationship between faith and works.

- Chapter 9, "The Bodily Resurrection Approach," explains how to challenge the Watchtower's two-class, two-paths-to-salvation system by showing that the Bible teaches that all Christians will have a physical resurrection body like the one Jesus displayed to his disciples.
- Chapter 10, "The New Birth Approach," explains how to show Jehovah's Witnesses that the new birth involves an inner transformation of a person by the Holy Spirit and is the only way by which anyone can obtain eternal life.

.

Chapter 6:
The Righteousness Approach

"Since they did not know the righteousness that comes from God and sought to establish their own, they did not submit to God's righteousness" (Romans 10:3).

The objective of this approach is to help Jehovah's Witnesses see that striving to become righteous enough to prove worthy of everlasting life is an impossible task.

Jehovah's Witnesses think that if they will just work harder, attend more meetings, study Watchtower literature more thoroughly, do more door-to-door witnessing, and obey God's laws more faithfully, then Jehovah may deem them worthy to be resurrected or to survive Armageddon into the "new system," Christ's millennial kingdom. They think this is the way to obtain peace with God and a sense of his approval.

What they fail to understand is that we can never by self-effort become righteous enough to meet God's standards. If we try to generate sufficient righteousness by self-effort and dedication, we are thwarted at every turn by the power of sin that dwells within us as descendants of Adam (Romans 7:14-24; 8:8).

While Ephesians 4:1 and Philippians 1:27 do instruct Christians to prove worthy of their calling, these are exhortations to live in accordance with the righteousness God gave them when they were saved by grace through faith, not directives to establish their own righteousness in order to obtain salvation.

The more we try to become righteous in God's eyes through keeping rules and laws, the more we just become aware of our repeated sins and failures. This explains why so many Jehovah's Witnesses feel unworthy and fear that God will reject them. Because they are basing their quest for God's approval on the Watchtower's performance-based salvation system rather than on God's Jesus-based acceptance provision, they don't experience the rest Jesus promised to his followers in Matthew 11:28 or the peace with God described in Romans 5:1.

Despite these problems, most Witnesses are not ready to accept God's way of salvation—justification by faith apart from works. Before they will come to Jesus to receive as a gift the righteousness that comes from God, they first have to see that the Watchtower's salvation system is not God's way of salvation. Trying to attain moral perfection simply doesn't work, even if you have 1,000 years to try. Until they are challenged to face this reality, they will be able to get by with wishful thinking. They will assume that things will all somehow work out for them as long as they follow all the Watchtower's directives.

How can we get them to see that this assumption is wrong? Telling it to them point blank would backfire. Lecturing them or arguing with them would be counterproductive. They would just dig in their heels and insist that the Watchtower religion is the truth.

Instead of arguing with them, do the unexpected by drawing them out. Ask them to describe the Watchtower's salvation process in detail. Have them explain exactly how good we have to be in order for Jehovah to deem us worthy of everlasting life.

Establish that he will require us to be morally perfect and completely righteous by the end of Christ's 1,000-year kingdom. Ask them to explain step-by-step just how they expect to get there.

YOU CAN'T MAKE YOURSELF WORTHY BY YOUR WORKS

Begin by asking this question: "Exactly what do I need to do to become acceptable to God?"

If they talk about having faith in Jesus' ransom sacrifice, you can tell them that you do have faith in his sacrifice and ask what else you need. They may tell you about the need to vindicate Jehovah's sovereignty and prove loyal to him and to his organization. They may come up with an extensive list of works you supposedly need to perform.

Continue asking, "What else would I need to do to be sure that I will be acceptable to God? How will I know when I have done enough?" If necessary, ask, "Would you say that Jesus' ransom sacrifice was the down payment but that we need to keep up the installments?" No matter how they respond, ask, "So how much depends on Jesus and how much depends on me?"

Jehovah's Witnesses often don't examine the details of the Watchtower's salvation system, so what they tell you may or may not correspond to the Watchtower teachings that I documented for you in Chapter 5. Don't tell them directly that their answers make no sense or that they are inconsistent with the Bible or even that the Watchtower has actually said something different. Instead, direct the course of the discussion by continuing to ask questions.

Express your confusion over what they are telling you and ask more questions for clarification. In their effort to explain things to you, they will have to think about problems with Watchtower doctrine that they ordinarily would never consider. The greater the difficulty they have in coming up with satisfactory answers to your questions, the better the chance that they will see for themselves the fatal flaws in the Watchtower salvation system.

You want them to see for themselves that they are on an endless treadmill of works. They will never arrive at their desired destination. They can never be sure that they have done enough or that what they have done is good enough. All of their efforts to prove worthy are doomed to failure. As you lead them to see these deficiencies in the Watchtower system, you will be helping them to see that God's arrangement for their salvation must be something far better.

FOLLOW-UP QUESTIONS TO ASK

When they finish their initial explanation, tell them you would like to back up a bit and get their answers to some specific questions that are causing you confusion about what they have told you. As you go through these questions, you may reach a point where their only answer is "I don't know" or "It doesn't matter." At that point, you may need to back off and focus on the answers they have already given you.

1. What alienates us from God in the first place?

They will talk about Adam's disobedience in Eden that brought the condemnation of death on all his descendants. Tell them you have a question about the power of sin that resides in us as descendants of Adam. Ask them how Romans 7:14-20 relates to this problem. Have them read it aloud:

> For we know that the Law is spiritual, but I am fleshly, sold under sin. For I do not understand what I am doing. For I do not practice what I wish, but I do what I hate. However, if I do what I do not wish, I agree that the Law is fine. But now I am no longer the one doing it, but it is the sin that resides in me. For I know that in me, that is, in my flesh, there dwells nothing good; for I have the desire to do what is fine but not the ability to carry it out. For I do not do the good that I wish, but the bad that I do not wish is what I practice. If, then, I do what I do not wish, I am no longer the one carrying it out, but it is the sin dwelling in me (RNWT).

Ask, "How can we be totally acceptable to God as long as we are unable to do what is right because of the power of sin that resides in us?"

The point you want to get them to see is that not only do we have a problem with our *sins*, for which we need forgiveness, but that we also have a problem with our *self* that renders us incapable of living the righteous life that God desires unless he transforms us through a new birth.

2. How do we prove righteous enough to enter the millennial kingdom?

After you have listened to their answer, ask, "On what basis will God decide whether you and I have proved righteous enough to make it into the millennial kingdom? In other words, what is his standard?"

No matter how much they say, they will never be able to give an exhaustive answer, and that is the point of your question. The more difficulty they have in articulating exactly what is required, the more it becomes clear that under the Watchtower's salvation system, there is no way they can know where they stand.

Ask, "How do you feel about this personally? I mean, if you were to die right now, how confident are you that Jehovah will deem you worthy of resurrection?"

This will be a tough question for them. They won't want to come across as presumptuous and boastful, but neither will they want to come across as people who won't be able to prove worthy themselves. Most likely they will tell you that they believe they will be resurrected but that the Bible cautions us about being overconfident or thinking of ourselves more highly than we ought.

Ask, "If Jehovah were to tell you that you are going to die tonight and gave you a chance to tell him why you think you have proved worthy to be resurrected, what would you tell him?" When they run out of things to say, ask what they think they could have done differently in order to be more certain. The purpose of these questions is to show them that their works will never be as good as they should be.

Ask both Witnesses to comment on their opinions of the meaning of Romans 5:1. Have them read it aloud. In their Bibles, it reads as follows: "Therefore, now that we have been declared righteous as a result of faith, let us enjoy peace with God through our Lord Jesus Christ..." (RNWT).

Specifically, ask them what being "declared righteous as a result of faith" means. If they tell you that this applies only to the anointed 144,000, don't argue with them about their two-class system. Instead, ask them to explain the differences between how the 144,000 are declared righteous and what everyone else has to do to get there.

Ask, "How can we enjoy peace with God if we don't know where we stand with him?" I recommend using the term "we" here so as to identify with them. "How can we...?" sounds far less confrontational than, "How can you...?"

3. What happens to our sin debt when we enter the millennial kingdom?

Tell them you would like clarification about how entry into the millennial kingdom will work. If Jehovah decides we are worthy of being resurrected or surviving Armageddon, what will happen to our sin debt when we enter that new system? If they answer in accordance with Watchtower doctrine, they should tell you that the sins we committed during this old system will not be held against us in the new system.

Ask, "What exactly pays our sin debt? Is it Jesus' sacrifice alone? Is it our own deaths? Is it proving worthy through our works?" The purpose of these questions is to help the Witnesses to see that they are not relying on Jesus but on themselves.

Next, ask them to explain the purpose of the millennial kingdom. If God decides we are worthy of a resurrection or of surviving Armageddon, why not just grant us everlasting life right then? Why a 1,000-year kingdom? They should tell you that this kingdom gives people a chance to learn how to obey Jehovah completely. At the end of the 1,000 years there will be a final loyalty test by Satan.

4. Will we be freed from the power of sin within us? If so, how and when?

Ask the Witnesses if we will be freed from the power of sin that resides within us immediately upon our entering the new system.

The Watchtower's answer is no. If they don't know what the Watchtower teaches about this and give you the opposite answer, you can show them the Watchtower's position indirectly by asking if this means that there will be no sin during the millennial kingdom. They know the Watchtower teaches that there will be sin during that period, and this should force them to reconsider their answer.

Ask them, "Will we ever be freed from the power of sin within us? If so, how will that happen and when?"

They will not have a good answer for this. They may talk about the benefits of the ransom being applied to us, having new instructional scrolls to guide us, Satan being restrained, and the like. But then what about this final test by Satan? Will everyone pass the test? They will say no. If that is correct, then our propensity to sin hasn't been removed even by the end of the 1,000 years, has it? And what will happen to people who succumb to it? Jehovah will annihilate them.

That brings up the question as to just how good we will have to be by the end of the 1,000 years in order to be deemed worthy so that we will not be annihilated but instead be granted everlasting life. What will Jehovah's standard be then? Whatever standard they give you, ask them to explain how sinful descendants of Adam are supposed to accomplish that.

5. Will we ever be 100% secure?

Ask the Witnesses, "If we prove worthy enough to make it into the millennial kingdom and then prove worthy at the end by passing the final test by Satan, will we then be 100% secure or will we still be capable of sinning?"

The Watchtower's answer is that we will be free moral agents like Adam was originally—unfettered by a sinful power within us but still capable of choosing to rebel. What happens if we do rebel? We will be annihilated on the spot by God. So according to the Watchtower teaching, we will never be 100% secure.

When they have explained this, say something like this: "That troubles me. Maybe it's just me, but I really don't see how we can ever have true peace with God if we know that he still might find sin in us and annihilate us."

CONCLUSION

This approach has a limited objective. It doesn't explain God's true plan of salvation. Instead, it focuses on showing the Witnesses that the Watchtower's salvation system doesn't work because it is nothing more than the flesh (all that we are in Adam apart from an inner transformation by the Holy Spirit) trying to overcome the flesh. It says that we will be required to attain to moral perfection by the end of the millennial kingdom but doesn't satisfactorily explain how we can accomplish it. In other words, the Watchtower gospel is impossible.

The approach highlights the fact that the Watchtower system can never give the Witnesses what they want most—forgiveness, victory over sin, rest, peace, and assurance of God's approval. Since Jehovah promises all these things to people who trust him, he must have a different—a better—way of salvation.

This foundation will open the door for you to lead the Witnesses to see that God's real solution to our sin problem is for us to come to Jesus to receive forgiveness and to receive a transformed, new heart which enables us to live righteously.

Chapter 7:
The Come to Jesus Approach

"You diligently study the Scriptures because you think that by them you possess eternal life. These are the Scriptures that testify about me, yet you refuse to come to me to have life" (John 5:39-40).

The objective of this approach is to help Jehovah's Witnesses see their need to come to Jesus Christ personally in order to obtain salvation.

People often ask Jehovah's Witnesses if they have accepted Jesus Christ as their personal savior. Some of them will say yes because they do believe that Jesus is "the savior," but truth be told, they have no idea what you are talking about.

Jehovah's Witnesses have no personal relationship with the Lord Jesus Christ. They don't claim to. They don't think such a thing is desirable or even possible. Rather than coming directly to Jesus for salvation, Witnesses rely on their dedication and service to the organization they think he has chosen to represent him on earth—the Watchtower Society.

If anything, Witnesses consider it sinful and idolatrous for a person to try to develop a personal relationship with Jesus today. Why? The Watchtower teaches them that only the Father is God, that only he is Jehovah. They believe that Jesus Christ is not God but that he is really Michael the archangel, the first creation of Jehovah God.[1] Think of the alarm bells that would go off inside you if someone told you that you need to have a personal relationship with the archangel Michael, that you need to pray to him and ask him to forgive your sins. This is the obstacle that you have to overcome with Witnesses.

For years, I tried to address this challenge by tackling head-on the Watchtower's misunderstandings concerning the identity of Jesus. The problem was that the need to come to him personally for salvation got lost amidst controversy over the Trinity, the nature of Jesus' divinity, and the Watchtower's claim that Jesus is Michael. Then I heard a talk by Arnold Hoffman in which he recommended a separate devotional approach which bypasses discussion of these identity issues in order to focus attention on the Witnesses' need for a personal relationship with Jesus Christ. I am indebted to him for many of the ideas in this chapter.

The key to the approach is to show the Witnesses that Jehovah God wants them—in fact commands them—to come to Jesus personally in order to obtain salvation and forgiveness of sins.

SALVATION REQUIRES COMING TO JESUS

Jehovah's Witnesses need to see that Jehovah wants them to come to Jesus to get their sins forgiven. They need to know that they are *obeying Jehovah God* if they come to Jesus for forgiveness and that they are *disobeying Jehovah God* if they don't. This concept will surprise them. The Watchtower has not trained them to deal with it.

Don't overwhelm them. I will be giving you a number of scriptures you can use. You don't have to use all of them. To the contrary, if you sense that you are making substantial progress, slow down and give the Witnesses time to think. Pray silently for the Holy Spirit to speak to them.

Jehovah has delegated to Jesus the authority to forgive sins

Jehovah's Witnesses believe that it is Jehovah who saves and forgives, not Jesus. Although they may want to argue whether Jesus is God or a created being, with this approach it is best to sidestep the identity issue. If necessary, agree to discuss that topic later. For the present, focus instead on helping them come to understand that in Jehovah God's arrangement, it is Jesus who actually has the authority to forgive their sins and give them eternal life.

You can introduce this concept by saying something like this: "We all sin; we can never do enough to measure up to God's holy standards. To whom can we go to get those sins forgiven?" Have one of the Witnesses read aloud Jesus' words in Matthew 9:6: "'But so that you may know that the Son of Man has authority on earth to forgive sins...' Then he said to the paralytic, 'Get up, take your mat and go home.'"

Ask, "According to this verse, who has authority to forgive our sins?" Make sure that they acknowledge that the answer is Jesus. They probably will ask, "Who gave him that authority?" Rather than getting sidetracked into an argument about who Jesus really is, simply answer, "Jehovah gave him that authority. That's my point. It seems to me that this passage says that's Jehovah's arrangement. He has delegated to Jesus the authority to forgive sins. That's why I believe we need to come to Jesus if we want our sins forgiven."

Have one of the Witnesses read aloud John 5:22-23: "Moreover, the Father judges no one, but has entrusted all judgment to the Son, that all may honor the Son just as they honor the Father. He who does not honor the Son does not honor the Father, who sent him."

Ask, "According to this passage, who will pass judgment on our lives—the Father or the Son? What was the Father's reason for arranging things this way?" The point you should make is that focusing on Jesus and his authority doesn't rob his Father of honor; it brings his Father honor! You can also ask, "Do you honor the Son just as you honor the Father? Isn't that what this passage says the Father wants us to do?"

Jesus commands us to come to him

One of the most effective passages I have found with regard to coming to Jesus for forgiveness is John 5:39-40. Have one of the Witnesses read aloud Jesus' statement to the Pharisees: "You diligently study the Scriptures because you think that by them you possess eternal life. These are the Scriptures that testify about me, yet you refuse to come to me to have life."

Ask the Witnesses to explain to you what mistake Jesus said the Pharisees were making. Pray silently that they will realize that they are making the exact same mistake. Jehovah's Witnesses search the Scriptures to find the way to everlasting life, but they refuse to come to Jesus to get it.

Because Witnesses consider Jehovah to be the ultimate authority, sometimes it is helpful to stress that whenever Jesus gave a command or a teaching, he was saying exactly what his

Father told him to say. In other words, Jesus was expressing Jehovah's will for our lives. You can make this point by saying something like this: "John 8:28 says that Jesus only spoke the words that his Father gave him to speak, so when Jesus says we need to come to him for life, isn't he expressing the will of Jehovah? Don't we need to comply with that command by coming to Jesus?"

You can also have the Witnesses read aloud the Father's own words in Matthew 17:5: "While he was still speaking, a bright cloud enveloped them, and a voice from the cloud said, 'This is my Son, whom I love; with him I am well pleased. Listen to him!'"

Having established that when Jesus tells us to do something, it is a command that comes from Jehovah, you can show the Witnesses additional passages where Jesus instructs people to come to him for salvation. Ask them to read one or more of them aloud (as many as are necessary to get the point across):

- Matthew 11:28: "Come to me, all you who are weary and burdened, and I will give you rest." "Come to me..." is a command, not a request. You can say, "If Jesus says, 'Come to me,' then what does God want us to do?"
- John 6:37: "All that the Father gives me will come to me, and whoever comes to me I will never drive away."
- John 6:44-45: "No one can come to me unless the Father who sent me draws him, and I will raise him up at the last day. It is written in the Prophets: 'They will all be taught by God ["Jehovah"—RNWT].' Everyone who listens to the Father and learns from him comes to me." If you sense that they don't get the point of this passage, ask, "According to that passage, if we listen to the Father, to whom must we come?"

- John 7:37: "On the last and greatest day of the Feast, Jesus stood and said in a loud voice, 'If anyone is thirsty, let him come to me and drink.'"

Jesus personally gives eternal life

Jehovah's Witnesses believe that it is Jehovah who gives eternal life, not Jesus. Help them to see that the Bible teaches that in Jehovah's arrangement, Jesus personally gives life to his sheep. Have one of the Witnesses read aloud John 10:27-28, where Jesus said, "My sheep listen to my voice; I know them, and they follow me. I give them eternal life, and they shall never perish; no one can snatch them out of my hand."

Ask, "According to this passage, who gives us eternal life?"

You can also have one of the Witnesses read aloud John 17:1-2 and comment on who, in Jehovah's arrangement, actually gives eternal life: "After Jesus said this, he looked toward heaven and prayed: 'Father, the time has come. Glorify your Son, that your Son may glorify you. For you granted him authority over all people that he might give eternal life to all those you have given him.'"

Say, "If the Bible told us that God had delegated to Moses the authority to forgive sins and give us life, then the only way to obtain forgiveness and eternal life would be to come to Moses. Instead, it says that he has delegated this authority to Jesus. So if we want forgiveness of our sins and if we want eternal life, it seems to me that we have to obey Jehovah and come to Jesus to get it. I have done this. Have you? Have you obeyed this commandment of Jehovah?" This often shocks the Witnesses, since they believe they are the only ones who are obeying God.

Have one of the Witnesses read aloud John 10:7-9: "Therefore Jesus said again, 'I tell you the truth, I am the gate for the sheep.

All who ever came before me were thieves and robbers, but the sheep did not listen to them. I am the gate; whoever enters through me will be saved. He will come in and go out, and find pasture.'"

Ask, "How can we enter *through* a gate unless we first come *to* the gate?"

OVERCOMING BARRIERS

Why is it so difficult for Jehovah's Witnesses to come to Jesus? Their Watchtower training has created three significant barriers, and you need to know how to address them.

Barrier #1: Most Witnesses see Jesus' sacrifice as historical, not personal

Ask Jehovah's Witnesses to explain their understanding of Jesus' sacrifice. Most of them will focus on Adam's sin rather than on their own sins.

The Watchtower says, "By sacrificing, or giving up, his perfect human life in flawless obedience to God, Jesus paid the price for Adam's sin. Jesus thus brought hope to Adam's offspring."[2]

This comes across as very impersonal, almost like an entry in an accountant's ledger. Adam was a perfect man. Jesus was a perfect man. Adam disobeyed Jehovah. Jesus obeyed Jehovah. Adam' sin cost us perfect human life. Jesus' sacrifice paid the ransom price to give Adam's offspring a chance to obtain everlasting life. Jesus counterbalanced Adam.

That's what I mean when I say that most Witnesses see their relationship to Jesus as historical, not personal. Rarely will you hear Jehovah's Witnesses say, "Jesus died for *me*."[3] Such a comment would seem proud and arrogant to them. In order to help them understand the personal nature of Jesus' "ransom sacrifice," have one of the Witnesses read aloud 1 Peter 2:24 and explain it to you phrase by phrase: "He himself bore our sins in his body on the tree, so that we might die to sins and live for righteousness; by his wounds you have been healed." In discussions with Witnesses, use the term "the tree" rather than "the cross.' You don't want to get distracted by arguing over the shape of the instrument on which he died.

Ask follow-up questions if necessary to make sure they cover the following points:

- Whose sins did Jesus bear? (Ours)
- What sins are those—our personal sins or Adam's sin? (Our personal sins)
- Where did he bear those sins? (In his own body)

Arnold Hoffman recommends illustrating 1 Peter 2:24 to Jehovah's Witnesses visually by drawing a figure of a man and putting marks on it to represent Jesus taking our sins into his own body.[4] Ask the Witnesses if this is how they visualize what Jesus did for us.

If they think this is talking about Adamic sin only, there are three passages you can use to reinforce that Jesus died for their personal sins as well. Isaiah 53:5 clearly refers to personal sins: "But he was pierced for our transgressions, he was crushed for our iniquities; the punishment that brought us peace was upon him, and by his wounds we are healed." Also have them read 1 Corinthians 15:3: "that Christ died for our sins according to the Scriptures..." and Galatians 1:4: "who gave himself for our sins..."

A good follow-up question at this point is, "Are there any sins that you and I can commit in this life that weren't paid for by Jesus' sacrifice?"

The Watchtower teaches that Jesus made the "ransom sacrifice" primarily out of loyalty to his Father, to vindicate Jehovah's sovereignty, his moral right to run the universe. Consequently, Jehovah's Witnesses don't see Jesus' sacrifice in terms of his personal love for them as individuals. In order to make the personal connection, have one of the Witnesses read aloud what Jesus said about the personal nature of salvation. Luke 15:4-5: "Suppose one of you has a hundred sheep and loses one of them. Does he not leave the ninety-nine in the open country and go after the lost sheep until he finds it? And when he finds it, he joyfully puts it on his shoulders..."

Ask, "Doesn't that mean that if you had been the only sinner who needed saving, Jesus still would have come and died to save you?"

Barrier #2: Witnesses think they need to come to Jehovah through an organization

Witnesses think that the way to come to Jehovah is to come to the "faithful and discreet slave" organization that he has chosen to represent him on earth—the Watchtower Society. They really don't see that they have allowed an organization run by fallible human beings to usurp the role that rightfully belongs to Jesus Christ alone. If you accuse them point blank of allowing the Watchtower organization to supplant Jesus, they will deny it vigorously and most likely will call off any further meetings with you.

The best way I have found to deal with this barrier is to discuss it in the context of a different religious organization. I give them my personal testimony in which I say something like this, "When I was a young man, I was brought up in a Protestant church. They had a training booklet for teens called, 'I Choose the Church.' The teaching was that the way to put faith in Jesus' sacrifice was to join the church and let the church help you obey all of God's commandments. I tried hard to do all those things, but I knew I fell short and I had no peace and no assurance of salvation. It took me years to realize that I was seeking salvation through my own performance and through affiliation with an organization run by fallible men rather than coming to God through Christ himself.

"I came to a point where I realized that I owed God a sin debt I could never pay. I had thought that salvation was a matter of faith plus works plus finding the right church. I never knew if I had done enough. Finally, I understood from the Scriptures that Jesus paid the entire price for my sin. I came to understand that salvation is not, 'Jesus made the down payment, but we have to keep up the installments and join the right organization.' Once I understood that, I believed God's Word and I did exactly what he told me to do in those scriptures—I came to Jesus and asked him to forgive my sins. Then I finally had a sense of God's approval on my life because I knew that I had done exactly what God commanded me to do. I found that I was trusting Jesus Christ completely for my salvation rather than my own performance or affiliation with other fallible men."

If you had a similar journey to faith, you can share with them those aspects of your own testimony. If you never fell into those errors, then feel free to tell them my story. Don't cite this book by name or show it to them. Instead, using your own notes, get into my testimony by telling them that you recently read about a man who tried in vain to find peace with God through joining the "right" religious organization and by keeping all of the Bible's commandments. Go from there.

In order to address the "right organization" issue directly from the Scriptures, have one of the Witnesses read aloud Mark 9:38-40: "'Teacher,' said John, 'we saw a man driving out demons in your name and we told him to stop, because he was not one of us.' 'Do not stop him,' Jesus said. 'No one who does a miracle in my name can in the next moment say anything bad about me, for whoever is not against us is for us.'"

Ask, "What does this passage say as far as whether we have to be affiliating with the right organization or group in order to be serving Jesus and his Father?"

If you sense the Holy Spirit prompting you to press the matter, you might add, "Does the Bible say that an organization is the door to God or does it teach that Jesus himself is the door? Does it say that some organization is the way, the truth, and the life or does it teach that Jesus himself is the way, the truth, and the life? Does it say that Jesus is the one who showed us the way or does it say that Jesus *is* the way?"

The Watchtower actually applies John 6:67-68 to itself in order to convince Jehovah's Witnesses that there is nowhere to go but the Watchtower organization in order to gain eternal life. To counter that false interpretation, have one of the Witnesses read that passage aloud: "'You do not want to leave too, do you?' Jesus asked the Twelve. Simon Peter answered him, 'Lord, to whom shall we go? You have the words of eternal life.'"

Ask simply, "Who did Peter say we have to go to in order to obtain eternal life—to an organization or to Jesus personally?"

Have one of the Witnesses read aloud 1 John 5:11-13: "And this is the testimony: God has given us eternal life, and this life is in his Son. He who has the Son has life; he who does not have the

Son of God does not have life. I write these things to you who believe in the name of the Son of God so that you may know that you have eternal life."

Ask them to explain their understanding of these verses. Ask, "According to this passage, is gaining eternal life and knowing that you have eternal life dependent on associating with the right organization or on having a personal relationship with Jesus himself?"

Barrier #3: Witnesses believe that it is wrong to pray to Jesus

One reason Jehovah's Witnesses substitute an organization for Jesus is that they think it is idolatrous to pray to him directly. For this reason, they believe that we can only come to Jehovah by coming to someone else who represents him. The Witnesses with whom you are meeting may take the initiative in telling you that it is wrong to pray to Jesus. If they don't, you can get them to discuss this barrier by asking them one or more of the following questions:

- "Do you ever pray to Jesus?"
- "Have you ever asked Jesus for anything?"
- "Have you ever thanked Jesus for anything?"[5]
- "Have you ever thanked Jesus for loving you so much that he paid the penalty for your sins?"

Christians in the Bible prayed to Jesus

You don't have to get into an argument about the deity of Jesus at this point. Just show them examples in the New Testament where early Christians *did* pray to Jesus.

Have one of the Witnesses read aloud 1 Corinthians 1:2 and explain to you whose name Paul said Christians were calling on: "To the church of God in Corinth, to those sanctified in Christ Jesus and called to be holy, together with all those everywhere who call on the name of our Lord Jesus Christ—their Lord and ours..."

If need be, ask them what it means to call on someone's name in prayer. Doesn't that mean you are addressing your prayer directly to that person?

You might note that some chain reference Bibles link 1 Corinthians 1:2 with Acts 4:12: "Salvation is found in no one else, for there is no other name under heaven given to men by which we must be saved." Point out to them that the name being referred to is "Jesus." Ask, "Doesn't this indicate that God's arrangement for salvation is that we call on the name of his Son in order to obtain forgiveness of sins? We are not dishonoring the Father when we call on the name of Jesus. We are obeying him."

Have one of the Witnesses read aloud Acts 7:59: "While they were stoning him, Stephen prayed ["made this appeal"—RNWT], 'Lord Jesus, receive my spirit.'" The Witnesses may say that he only did this because Jesus was appearing to him in a vision. However, you can point out that this prayer occurred well after the vision ended and after the people had dragged him out of the city to stone him.

Have one of the Witnesses read aloud Acts 9:20-21, which tells us that immediately after Paul's conversion, "At once he began to preach in the synagogues that Jesus is the Son of God. All those who heard him were astonished and asked, 'Isn't he the man who raised havoc in Jerusalem among those who call on this name? And hasn't he come here to take them as prisoners to the chief priests?'"

Ask, "According to these verses, whose name were these Christians calling on?"

Have one of the Witnesses read aloud to whom Paul says he prayed concerning his "thorn in the flesh." 2 Corinthians 12:8-9: "Three times I pleaded with the Lord to take it away from me. But he said to me, 'My grace is sufficient for you, for my power is made perfect in weakness.' Therefore I will boast all the more gladly about my weaknesses, so that Christ's power may rest on me." Clearly, Paul was praying to Jesus.

Dealing with the Lord's Prayer

Jehovah's Witnesses will tell you that we are not to pray to Jesus. Rather, we are to pray to Jehovah God in Jesus' name. They almost always cite Jesus' instructions in the Lord's Prayer as proof: "'Our Father in the heavens, let your name be sanctified.' Jesus thus reminded his followers that all prayers should be directed to his Father, Jehovah."[6]

In reply, point out that Jesus taught that method of prayer to his disciples, people who had already come to him in faith and were therefore able to address God as "Father." Also, at the time Jesus taught that prayer, he was still on earth. His disciples did not need to pray to him; they could just talk to him face-to-face. Even though he is now in heaven, 1 Peter 2:4 says that we are still supposed to come to him. That requires prayer.

CONCLUSION

If the Witnesses follow you and are receptive to the seeds you are planting and are prepared to come to Christ for salvation, by all means lead them through that process. But don't be discouraged if they aren't ready to do that. If you sense that you are at an impasse, pray silently for wisdom as to how to proceed. Perhaps it is best to move on to a different point. It might be better to back off altogether and return to that point later after more groundwork has been laid.

Unfortunately, given the depth of Watchtower indoctrination, Witnesses are very unlikely to be ready to come to Christ so quickly. Be encouraged by any progress you do make. Define success as by faith letting God present his message through you and leaving the results to him.

If they are not ready to proceed further in this direction, leave them with this thought: No matter how many good works we do, no matter how much preaching we do, no matter how many meetings we attend, we can only be saved if we comply with God's arrangement and come to his Son, Jesus, for forgiveness based on his sacrifice. It is only by obeying God by coming to Jesus that we can have the peace with God that we all want and need.

Chapter 8:
The Faith and Works Approach

"For it is by grace you have been saved, through faith— and this not from yourselves, it is the gift of God—not by works, so that no one can boast. For we are God's workmanship, created in Christ Jesus to do good works, which God prepared in advance for us to do" (Ephesians 2:8-10).

The objective of this approach is to correct Jehovah's Witnesses' false view that "justification by faith" is a license to sin and to show them the biblical relationship between faith and works in the Christian life.

The usual discussion between Christians and Jehovah's Witnesses regarding faith and works follows a completely predictable pattern. The Christian starts with verses which teach that salvation is by grace through faith apart from works. The Witnesses counter by talking about "exercising faith" and quoting passages which stress the importance of obedience, endurance, and good works. The dialogue often results in an impasse in which both sides are frustrated and little, if any, productive communication takes place.

The crux of the problem is that when you tell Jehovah's Witnesses that salvation comes by faith apart from works, they completely misunderstand what you are saying. They think you are claiming that all you have to do is muster up some sort of intellectual belief in Jesus without genuine repentance of sin and Jesus saves you, giving you a ticket to heaven while leaving you free to indulge in immorality. They also think you are saying that obedience, endurance, and good works are irrelevant to the Christian life. Of course, that isn't what you are saying at all.

In addition, the Watchtower teaches Jehovah's Witnesses that all of Christendom is a counterfeit Christianity controlled by Satan. They view it as being infested with clergymen who talk about Jesus one day and hire prostitutes the next, all the while raking in money from gullible followers. The highly publicized fall of prominent televangelists reinforces this impression. When they hear you saying that you believe salvation comes by "faith without works," they think this is what you are defending.

Jehovah's Witnesses also take pride in the fact that they volunteer hundreds or even thousands of hours each year going door-to-door "sharing the good news of Jehovah's kingdom." They think that you, on the other hand, believe in a faith-without-works "Christianity" in which you spend your life in a spiritual rocking chair, going to church every now and then but not doing much of anything else. They see any good works that non-Jehovah's Witness "Christians" do as mere Pharisaical window dressing, hypocritical acts being done for the praise and adulation of men.

Therefore, if you begin by showing Jehovah's Witnesses passages that talk about justification by faith apart from works, they will immediately counter with James 2:26: "...faith without works is dead..." (KJV). That verse is almost a mantra to them.

What I recommend is that you reverse the process. Bring up James 2:26 first yourself. Acknowledge up front the importance of good works, obedience, and godly behavior in the Christian life. Decry the false Christianity that says godliness is unimportant. By starting this way, you will correct many of the Witnesses' false views of what justification by faith is all about.

SHOWING THE RELATIONSHIP BETWEEN FAITH AND WORKS

Begin by saying something like this: "I'd like to talk with you about the role of faith and works in the Christian life. I want to start by saying that I believe what James 2:26 says, that faith without works is dead. So if a person says, 'I'm saved! I'm saved!' but then he runs off and gets drunk and cheats on his wife, that isn't biblical Christianity. When I read about preachers who talk about Jesus one day and hire prostitutes the next, I'm just as appalled at that as you are. When someone tells me, 'I'm saved!' but then he sits back in his easy chair and lives a self-absorbed life and never shows any concern for his neighbors, that's not biblical Christianity.

"So I do believe that works are an important part of the Christian life. But, you know, Paul says some things in Romans about the relationship of faith and works that are hard to reconcile with what James says. I wonder if we could look at some of those verses together. I'd really like to get your take on them."

Whenever the Witnesses try to steer the discussion toward the importance of works, instead of arguing with them, you can agree that God calls Christians to abandon immorality and to do good works. Then steer the conversation back to Paul's statements that these works—though important—have nothing whatever to do with saving us. They are the *products of* salvation, not the *prerequisites to* salvation.

Romans 4:1-8

Ask one of the Witnesses to read Romans 4:1-8 aloud. Tell them that afterwards you will want to go over the passage and ask questions because you really want to hear what they have to say about it. Then ask them to go through that passage with you step-by-step. By doing this, you'll be modeling proper Bible study methods. Stress that you are not arguing with them, that you want to understand the passage properly and you are asking for their understanding of it.

Read through those verses aloud again with the Witnesses, this time in smaller bites. As you do that, ask them questions to get them to think about what Paul is really saying:

"1 What then shall we say that Abraham, our forefather, discovered in this matter? 2 If, in fact, Abraham was justified by works, he had something to boast about—but not before God."

Ask, "According to Paul, did God declare Abraham righteous as a result of his works?" You are looking for the answer no, that God declared Abraham righteous because of his faith.

At this point, they may bring up James 2:21, which says that Abraham was declared righteous by works when he offered Isaac on the altar. If so, tell them that's a good point and that you want to discuss that with them also but that right now you'd like to focus on what Paul says in Romans 4 to make sure you understand what he is trying to get across. Then you'll be happy to look at James because you know God's Word doesn't contradict itself.

"3 What does the Scripture say? 'Abraham believed God, and it was credited to him as righteousness.'"

Ask, "When did that happen? What exactly did Abraham have faith in?" Their chain reference directs them to Genesis 15, where then childless Abraham believed God's promise that he would have a son as an heir.

Ask, "How is being declared righteous because of faith different from being declared righteous as a result of works?" Listen to their explanation. The answer you are looking for is that one of them is being declared righteous by trusting Jehovah's promise; the other is being declared righteous as a result of one's own good behavior.

"4 Now when a man works, his wages are not credited to him as a gift, but as an obligation. 5 However, to the man who does not work but trusts God who justifies the wicked, his faith is credited as righteousness."

Ask, "What point is Paul making about the difference between the man who works (verse 4) and the man who does not work (verse 5)?" The answer you are looking for is that the man who obtains something by his works isn't receiving a gift. He is entitled to what he receives; they are wages he has earned.

With regard to verse 5, ask, "Does the man who doesn't work end up being declared unrighteous or righteous?" You are looking for the fact that he ends up being declared righteous despite the fact that he doesn't work.

Ask, "In verse 5, who is the one who justifies the wicked and declares the ungodly man righteous?" You are looking for them to say "Jehovah."

Ask, "Why would Jehovah declare an ungodly man—a man who doesn't work—righteous?" You are looking for them to say that it's because of his faith. Summarize by noting that this man doesn't work and he's ungodly, but Jehovah declares him righteous because of his faith.

Ask, "If Jehovah has declared him righteous, is he righteous or is he unrighteous?" Establish that such a man is righteous even though he has not yet produced any good works to prove it.

"6 David says the same thing when he speaks of the blessedness of the man to whom God credits righteousness apart from works:"

Ask, "Since 'faith without works is dead,' how can God count this man righteous apart from works? That seems puzzling to me." They should have trouble coming up with an answer. Don't rush in to give them your answer—that first comes salvation by faith and with it an inner transformation that produces good works. Let them wrestle with it. The goal is to get them to engage with what the scripture is saying.

"7 'Blessed are they whose transgressions are forgiven, whose sins are covered.'"

Ask, "On what basis did Jehovah forgive the man's transgressions and cover his sins?" You are looking for them to say that it is by faith.

Follow up by asking, "According to Paul, what did the man's works have to do with getting him this forgiveness and covering?" The answer is that works had nothing to do with it.

Ask, "Can we know for certain that our own transgressions have been pardoned and that our sins have been covered because of our faith or does that depend on our works?" This question may also give them trouble. We can know that our transgressions have been pardoned and our sins covered because we have faith in Christ, but Witnesses don't believe that.

"8 'Blessed is the man whose sin the Lord will never count against him.'"

Ask, "According to this verse, can we by faith know that Jehovah will not take our sins into account or does that depend on our works?" Most likely they will want to take you over to James. Again, tell them you will be glad to look at James a little later, but first you want to understand what Paul is saying about this.

The point of the entire passage is that Paul contrasts the righteousness that comes by faith with the righteousness that comes as a result of works. He says that Abraham was declared righteous by God *apart* from works. He says that this results in our being blessed because Jehovah has pardoned our transgressions and covered our sins. Jehovah's Witnesses have no such assurance because they think their salvation depends on constant works and endurance.

Ephesians 2:8-10

Ephesians 2:8-10 is another great passage to show the proper relationship between faith and works. Have the Witnesses read it aloud and note the order that describes the relationship between faith and works:

"8 For it is by grace you have been saved, through faith—and this not from yourselves, it is the gift of God—"

Say, "Paul speaks in the past tense. He says his readers *have been* saved." Ask, "Can you say that? Can you say that you *have been* saved, or are you just hoping one day that you will prove worthy enough to become saved?"

Next ask, "According to this verse, what role does Paul say works played in his readers' obtaining their salvation?" See if their answer is the same as Paul's answer in the next verse, namely, that works have nothing to do with it. First comes salvation by faith apart from works. God credits us with righteousness as a gift purchased by Jesus Christ.

"9 not by works, so that no one can boast."

If the Witnesses gave a faith-plus-works answer, ask, "According to this verse, what role does Paul say works played in his readers' obtaining their salvation?"

Ask, "If our works were involved, what would we be able to do?" We could boast about our loyalty and endurance, but Paul says that no one can boast because our works don't contribute to our salvation. This is the same point he made in the passage we just looked at from Romans 4.

Because of this scripture, Jehovah's Witnesses may tell you that they agree that salvation is a gift and that we can't earn it by our works. If they do, say, "I'm confused. Please explain to me the difference between meriting salvation by our works—which you just said we can't do—and proving worthy of everlasting life by our works."

"10 For we are God's workmanship, created in Christ Jesus to do good works, which God prepared in advance for us to do."

Ask, "According to this verse, what has to happen to us before we can do the works God wants us to do?" We first have to become God's workmanship, created in Christ Jesus by God. Explain that, in your understanding, this is what the new birth is all about. As Paul says, God does have good works for us to do, but they are the result of the inner transformation God works in us once we have been saved by faith. They are not how we obtain salvation.

In an online instructional video, Evidence Ministries founder Keith Walker illustrates the difference by way of two equations. They can be helpful in dealing with Jehovah's Witnesses because they are easy to visualize and remember:

It is NOT "Faith + Works = Salvation."
Rather, it is "Faith = Salvation + Works."[1]

You can sum up the biblical relationship between faith and works this way: "I believe that a Christian does not work *for* salvation. A Christian works *from* salvation. A Christian does not work *for* God's approval. A Christian works *from* God's approval. It is God who does the works through the Christian."

ANSWERING WATCHTOWER ARGUMENTS

Discussing James 2

The Witnesses will insist on looking at what James 2 says about faith and works. Here is how to deal with that chapter.

James 2:21 states, "Was not Abraham our father declared righteous by works after he offered up Isaac his son on the altar?" (RNWT). Acknowledge that at first appearance, James seems to be saying the opposite of what Paul said, but since the Bible doesn't contradict itself, it must be possible to reconcile the passages.

Ask, "Which came first for Abraham—the righteousness by faith or the righteousness of works?" Faith. That happened in Genesis 15. He didn't offer Isaac on the altar until Genesis 22, more than 25 years later.

Ask, "Was Abraham righteous all those 25-plus years before he did the work of offering Isaac on the altar?" Yes. How? By faith. Even though he sinned in between those events, such as by siring Ishmael by Hagar, God still considered him righteous and continued to work in his life.

James 2:22-24 says: "You see that his faith was active along with his works and his faith was perfected by his works, and the scripture was fulfilled that says: 'Abraham put faith in Jehovah, and it was counted to him as righteousness, and he came to be called Jehovah's friend.' So you see that a man is to be declared righteous by works and not by faith alone" (RNWT).

If the Witnesses ask you how you reconcile Paul's statements with those of James, you can comment that it was the righteousness Abraham had by faith that led to his further trust of God, and that led to his righteous obedience and works. In other words, it was the inner righteousness that he obtained by faith in Genesis 15 that produced the righteous works and obedience in Genesis 22.

The point you need to convey to Jehovah's Witnesses is that genuine Christian faith does produce righteous works, but the works have nothing to do with saving us or with making us righteous. We begin as unrighteous. Then comes justification by faith, where God declares an ungodly person righteous in Jesus Christ. At that moment, the person becomes God's workmanship, created in Christ Jesus. Later, this inner righteousness that came apart from works is what enables the person to do the good works that God prepared in advance for him to do (Ephesians 2:10). In this manner, God displays to us and to others the righteousness that he has given us and that he is producing in us.

James' comments address the fact that although God can see the faith that is in our hearts without seeing works as proof—as he did with Abraham in Genesis 15—human beings cannot. Although we are justified by faith alone before God, we are justified before men through works that they can see. That is, the only way people can see that someone has actually had this inner transformation by God based on his faith is by that person's changed attitudes and behavior (James 2:18).

Jehovah's Witnesses think that their works prove that they are "exercising faith" and are therefore "in the truth." Don't accuse them of anything, but do point out that when we think about works, we need to be cautious in our evaluation. People who have not experienced an inner transformation by God can, through self-effort, produce religious works that *appear* righteous to themselves and to others, but those works will be rejected by God because merely human-generated righteousness is like filthy rags in his sight (Isaiah 64:6). The Pharisees are a prime example of this. Because of their zealous attempts to obey God's laws, they considered themselves to be righteous, as did others who saw their outward behavior and dedication. Yet their apparent righteousness was an illusion (Matthew 23:27-28).

Jehovah's Witnesses are constantly trying to prove their sincerity, dedication, and loyalty to Jehovah. For that reason, as you discuss James 2, make clear to them that righteous works of which James speaks—works which truly please God—are not works generated by human effort and dedication in order to obtain divine approval or salvation, else they would be something of which we could boast (Ephesians 2:9).

Rather, genuine Christian works must be the product of the righteousness that God previously imparted to us as a gift. We receive that gift of righteousness solely by faith before we have any works—as Abraham did in Genesis 15—and we are saved at that time. The Holy Spirit then comes inside us to empower us to live righteously. Our good works are then God's works which he does through us rather than our works done to gain his approval. In this way, righteous Christian works are produced by God and not by our own efforts to make ourselves worthy (Romans 8:9-14).

Discussing Matthew 10:22

Often Witnesses will quote Matthew 10:22 to the effect that "the one who has endured to the end will be saved" (RNWT). Point out that the context of this verse is surviving the persecution of the coming tribulation. It is not talking about how we become righteous before God. In his statement about how we become righteous in God's sight, Paul didn't mention endurance at all. Neither did James.

Discussing Philippians 2:12-13

Jehovah's Witnesses often quote from Philippians 2:12: "...work out your own salvation with fear and trembling..." By using that partial quotation, the Watchtower gives the impression that we have to prove worthy of our salvation by our works and tremble in fear lest we fall short and get destroyed. But that is not what the passage is saying at all.

Have the Witnesses look at Philippians 2:12-13 in full context: "Therefore, my dear friends, as you have always obeyed—not only in my presence, but now much more in my absence—continue to work out your salvation with fear and trembling, for it is God who works in you to will and to act according to his good purpose."

Ask, "Are Christians to be in fear and trembling because they might not prove worthy of salvation by their works? Or are Christians to be in awe and tremble because they know God has transformed them from the inside out and that he himself is working inside them to produce righteous works that they could never produce on their own? I believe Paul is not saying that we have to work *for* our salvation and be afraid that we might not make it. He is saying that we need to work *from* our salvation that we receive solely by faith (as Abraham did) and be in awe knowing that God himself is now working in us to give us the desire and the power to live righteously."

CONCLUSION

Make clear that the relationship between faith and works is not a matter of mere semantics. People who rely on faith plus works for their salvation are not relying on Christ. They are really relying on themselves, and that produces condemnation, not salvation. It is only when we humble ourselves, give up on ourselves, and trust in Christ's sacrifice alone that God saves us.

A good diagnostic question to ask Jehovah's Witnesses is this: "If Jehovah were to speak to you tonight and give you an opportunity to make a case to him as to why you are worthy of everlasting life, what would you tell him?"

Would they say, "Because I am not immoral like those television preachers and because I do good works such as door-to-door witnessing"? Or would they say, "Because I have received as a free gift the righteousness from God that comes by faith in Jesus' sacrifice and I know because of that he is working inside me"?

The first answer is self-exaltation. The second answer is the way of salvation.

If you sense that the Witnesses are making progress in understanding salvation by faith, you may want to discuss with them their need for coming to Jesus to receive it. I explained how to do this in Chapter 7, "The Come to Jesus Approach."

Chapter 9:
The Bodily Resurrection Approach

"See my hands and my feet, that it is I myself; feel me and see, for a spirit does not have flesh and bones just as you see that I have'" (Luke 24:39, RNWT).

The objective of this approach is to refute the Watchtower's two-class, two-paths-to-salvation system by showing that all Christians will be raised from the dead—as Jesus was—in a glorified physical body of flesh and bones.

Although this approach deals with the topic of whether resurrected bodies are spirit or physical, its primary purpose is *not* to quibble over the composition of the resurrected form. The importance of the approach lies deeper—in the Watchtower's claim that there are two different classes of Christians who have two different resurrection forms, two different destinations, and two different paths to becoming righteous enough to merit everlasting life.

If you can demonstrate from the Scriptures that all resurrections are physical, you will also have shown that the new birth is not what the Watchtower claims it to be, a selection of a person to be, one of a special class of 144,000 destined permanently to have incorporeal spirit bodies. You will then have an opening to show the Witnesses what the new birth really is. I will explain how to do that in the next chapter.

Because Christians believe that we will go to heaven in spirit form immediately when we die, Jehovah's Witnesses mistakenly think that this is our view of the resurrection. They have a long list of proof texts ready to show you in order to prove that—except for the 144,000—everyone whom God raises from the dead will be resurrected in physical form and live on earth during Christ's 1,000-year kingdom.

To correct their false impression, after they tell you this concept of the resurrection you will surprise them by agreeing that you will be raised from the dead in physical form and live on earth during Christ's millennial reign. From there, you will go on to discuss the nature of Jesus' own resurrection.

ALL RESURRECTIONS ARE PHYSICAL

Begin this approach by asking the Witnesses, "If God chooses to resurrect me, do you believe I will be resurrected in physical form or as a spirit?" They will tell you that you will be raised in a physical body and live on the earth. Tell them you agree with that and that you are looking forward to it. This should surprise them greatly. Tell them that you believe this because of what the Bible says about Jesus' own resurrection.

All Christians will be like Christ

Ask one of the Witnesses to read aloud 1 John 3:2: "Dear friends, now we are children of God, and what we will be has not yet been made known. But we know that when he appears, we shall be like him, for we shall see him as he is."

Ask, "Is there anywhere in this epistle where John says this applies only to 144,000 people and not to all Christians?"

This question is of great significance, for if all Christians will have a resurrection body like Jesus' body, then the Watchtower's two-class system is wrong. There will not be two types of Christians with two different paths to salvation. All Christians, not just 144,000, "will be like him, for we shall see him as he is."

The Witnesses may ask, "Do you believe that immediately when you die, you will be resurrected as a spirit and go to heaven?" You should answer them this way: "I do believe that all Christians will go to heaven in spirit form to be with Christ the moment they die, but this event is not the same as the resurrection. The resurrection will take place in the end times, and it is a reuniting of soul and spirit into a glorified body of flesh and bones. Because we will be with Christ wherever he goes (John 12:26; 1 Thessalonians 4:17), our resurrection bodies will be in a physical form suited for life both in heaven and on earth."

That said, don't get sidetracked into a discussion about the soul and spirit. All you are trying to establish at this point from 1 John 3:2 is that John said nothing about there being two different classes and two different types of resurrections. Despite what this verse says, expect the Witnesses to defend the Watchtower position that only the 144,000 will have "spirit resurrections like Jesus did."

Jesus rose from the dead in a physical body

Tell the Witnesses that you are puzzled when they tell you that Jesus' physical body was never raised from the dead, because there are a number of scriptures that seem to say otherwise. Tell them you would like to show them these passages and hear their explanation.

Jesus' prophecy in John 2

Ask them to read aloud John 2:18-22: "Then the Jews demanded of him, 'What miraculous sign can you show us to prove your authority to do all this?' Jesus answered them, 'Destroy this temple, and I will raise it again in three days.' The Jews replied, 'It has taken forty-six years to build this temple, and you are going to raise it in three days?' But the temple he had spoken of was his *body*. After he was raised from the dead, his disciples recalled what he had said. Then they believed the Scripture and the words that Jesus had spoken" (emphasis added).

Don't just summarize the passage by saying, "Jesus said he would raise his own body from the dead." Rather, make sure they read the text aloud so they will see for themselves what the Bible actually says.

Ask:

- What temple did the Jews think Jesus was talking about? (The temple building in Jerusalem)
- What temple does John say Jesus really was talking about? (His body)
- What did Jesus say he would do with his body if the Jews destroyed it? (He would raise it up in three days)
- So did Jesus raise his body on the third day as he said or was his body never raised from the dead?

The Witnesses may argue that Jesus was dead, so he couldn't raise anything. The Father performed the resurrection.[1] Actually, that is a good argument against the Watchtower's view of death as nonexistence until the resurrection, but that's not the point you are making here. You are talking about what Jesus said would happen to his body if they destroyed it.

They may try to say that Christ was speaking about his spiritual body, the Christian congregation. However, the passage shows he was talking about a body the Jews could kill, a body that would be raised up three days later. Verse 22 shows that he was talking about his own resurrection.

Jesus' demonstration in John 20

Have the Witnesses read aloud John 20:20, where the resurrected Christ appeared to some of his disciples: "After he said this, he showed them his hands and side. The disciples were overjoyed when they saw the Lord."

Ask, "What specifically was he showing them?" Establish that it was his execution wounds from the nails and the spear (John 19:34). (I recommend that you avoid using the word "cross" lest they try to change the subject by arguing that it was an upright stake with no crossbeam.)

Have them also read aloud the second such encounter in John 20:24-28:

Now Thomas (called Didymus), one of the Twelve, was not with the disciples when Jesus came. So the other disciples told him, "We have seen the Lord!" But he said to them, "Unless I see the nail marks in his hands and put my finger where the nails were, and put my hand into his side, I will not believe it." A week later his disciples were in the house again, and Thomas was with them. Though the doors were locked, Jesus came and stood among them and said, "Peace be with you!" Then he said to Thomas, "Put your finger here;

see my hands. Reach out your hand and put it into my side. Stop doubting and believe." Thomas said to him, "My Lord and my God!"

Ask, "Since Jesus showed them his physical execution wounds on two separate occasions, was his resurrection in spirit form or physical form?"

They will tell you that Jesus was raised as a spirit creature and that he only materialized in physical form in order to instill faith in the disciples. They will point out that, in the past, angels had materialized in physical form when appearing to humans.[2]

Ask, "Did Jesus want them to believe they were seeing and touching his execution wounds?" They will have to say yes. That was his way of proving to them that he had been resurrected.

Ask, "Were those *real* execution wounds or *fake* execution wounds that he was showing them?" They cannot say that they were real execution wounds because that would mean it was Christ's own resurrected body that they were seeing and touching.

Follow up by saying, "If the Watchtower is right, then Jesus deliberately deceived his disciples, didn't he?" When they ask you what you mean by that, explain it this way: "Well, when the disciples examined Jesus' hands and his side, they thought that those were really the nail holes and spear holes in Jesus' own body caused by Jesus' execution, didn't they? They didn't know that Jesus was showing them make-believe wounds on a manufactured body."

Witnesses will say that Jesus had to do this because Thomas said it was the only way he would be persuaded. To that, you can reply, "Jesus displayed his wounds to the other disciples when doubting Thomas wasn't even there, so Thomas' statement had nothing to do with it. Surely the Son of God was not forced to present false evidence. Despite what Thomas said, Jesus had many other ways of proving his resurrection to his disciples. He could have spoken to them in a vision as he did with Stephen in Acts 7 or addressed them from heaven with a blinding light as he did with Paul in Acts 9. In short, Jesus could have demonstrated the reality of his resurrection in any number of ways. Why would he deliberately mislead them into thinking what they were seeing and touching was actually his own body? Would God's Son really resort to that type of deception?"

Jesus' declaration in Luke 24

In Luke 24, Jesus specifically denies that he has been resurrected as a spirit. Ask the Witnesses to read aloud Luke 24:36-39: "While they were speaking of these things he himself stood in their midst and said to them: 'May you have peace.' But because they were terrified and frightened, they imagined that they were seeing a spirit. So he said to them: 'Why are you troubled, and why have doubts come up in your hearts? See my hands and my feet, that it is I myself; feel me and see, *for a spirit does not have flesh and bones just as you see that I have*'" (RNWT, emphasis added).

How does the Watchtower explain this? "Humans cannot see spirits, so the disciples evidently thought they were seeing an apparition or a vision. (Compare Mark 6:49, 50.) Jesus assured them that he was no apparition; they could see his body of flesh and could touch him, feeling the bones; he also ate in their presence. Similarly, in the past, angels had materialized in order to be seen by men; they had eaten, and some had even married and fathered children. (Gen. 6:4; 19:1-3)"[3]

Ask, "If the Watchtower view is correct, why didn't Jesus just tell them the same thing you are telling me? 'I have been raised an invisible spirit creature but I am materializing in physical form like angels did in order to give you faith.'" He could have changed from one body to another right before their eyes in order to prove it to them.

Have them read aloud once again what Jesus said instead in verse 39: "See my hands and my feet, that it is I myself; feel me and see, for a spirit does not have flesh and bones just as you see that I have" (RNWT). Add, "I believe what Jesus said, that it was really his own hands and feet they were touching. Isn't that what Jesus both told them and demonstrated to them?"

Paul's teaching in Romans 8

Ask the Witnesses to read aloud Romans 8:11: "And if the Spirit of him who raised Jesus from the dead is living in you, he who raised Christ from the dead will *also* give life to *your mortal bodies* through his Spirit, who lives in you" (emphasis added).

Ask them what happened to Jesus' mortal body that will also happen to our mortal bodies. It says that God will also give life to our mortal bodies. But the Watchtower teaches that God did *not* give life to Jesus' mortal body when he raised him from the dead, nor will he give life to the mortal bodies of any people who have God's spirit residing in them. Those are the ones the Watchtower says will have a spirit resurrection. Tell the Witnesses you are confused by this and ask them to explain.

The Watchtower says that the Greek word translated "resurrection" literally means "a standing up again."[4] In order to have a resurrection, then, doesn't something have to die and then come back to life again? Ask the Witnesses regarding Christ's resurrection, "What died and then was raised back to life?" They say it wasn't his body. They say that he did not have a separate soul that could be raised. They say that a person's spirit is only an impersonal, animating force analogous to electricity. So what exactly died and then stood up again, raised back to life?

ANSWERING WATCHTOWER ARGUMENTS

In addition to making a positive case for the bodily resurrection of Christ, you will also need to be able to anticipate and answer Watchtower proof texts and arguments. I will set out the arguments Witnesses most often present, along with recommendations for responding to them.

Argument #1: There must be two different kinds of resurrection bodies because flesh and blood cannot inherit God's kingdom

Remember that the Watchtower frequently quotes verses isolated from their contexts in order to prove their doctrines. They do this with two passages in 1 Corinthians 15. Witnesses often quote the following two proof texts in rapid succession in order to try to prove the Watchtower teaching that Jesus and the 144,000 are resurrected in immaterial, spirit bodies.

Their first proof text is 1 Corinthians 15:44-45: "...it is sown a natural body, it is raised a spiritual body. If there is a natural body, there is also a spiritual body. So it is written: 'The first man Adam became a living being'; the last Adam, a life-giving spirit." They say this shows that the great crowd are resurrected with physical bodies, while Jesus and the 144,000 are resurrected with spirit bodies.

Their second and principal proof text is 1 Corinthians 15:50, which says, "I declare to you, brothers, that flesh and blood cannot inherit the kingdom of God, nor does the perishable inherit the imperishable." They say that this shows that the great crowd cannot go to heaven and rule with Christ. Only the 144,000 can do so because they don't have "flesh and blood" in their "spirit resurrection."

To understand what a Bible passage is really saying, we need to look at the entire context, not just isolated quotations. In order to model that method of Bible study, ask the Witnesses to go through the entire passage with you step-by-step.

Natural bodies vs. resurrection bodies

1 Corinthians 15:35-37: "But someone may ask, 'How are the dead raised? With what kind of body will they come?' How foolish! What you sow does not come to life unless it dies. When you sow, you do not plant the body that will be, but just a seed, perhaps of wheat or of something else."

At this point ask, "Where do these verses say they are contrasting two different types of resurrection bodies? Aren't they rather contrasting the natural bodies we have now (the seed that gets planted) with the Spirit-empowered bodies Christians will have in the resurrection (the body that comes from it after the seed dies)?"

You can add, "It seems to me that this passage is saying that after the present body dies, a new type of body will come from it in the resurrection. The present body is the seed from which the resurrection body is made. Christians' resurrection bodies will not be identical to their current ones, but they will still be physical because the resurrection bodies will come from the current bodies like plants that come up from a seed."

Verses 38-39: "But God gives it a body as he has determined, and to each kind of seed he gives its own body. All flesh is not the same: Men have one kind of flesh, animals have another, birds another and fish another."

Ask, "Doesn't this say that the kind of body that is planted determines the kind of body that it produces and that all human beings have the same kind of flesh or seed? Do you see from this why I believe that all Christians who are resurrected will have the same kind of resurrection body?"

Perishable bodies vs. imperishable bodies

Verses 40-41: "There are also heavenly bodies and there are earthly bodies; but the splendor of the heavenly bodies is one kind, and the splendor of the earthly bodies is another. The sun has one kind of splendor, the moon another and the stars another; and star differs from star in splendor."

Ask, "Is Paul contrasting two different types of resurrection bodies here or is he contrasting our current perishable bodies and the imperishable bodies Christians will have in the resurrection? Let's look at his own explanation in the next few verses."

Verses 42-45: "So will it be with the resurrection of the dead. The body that is sown is perishable, it is raised imperishable; it is sown in dishonor, it is raised in glory; it is sown in weakness, it is raised in power; it is sown a natural body, it is raised a spiritual body. If there is a natural body, there is also a spiritual body. So it is written: 'The first man Adam became a living being'; the last Adam, a life-giving spirit."

Ask, "Are these verses talking about the composition of the resurrection body of Adam and contrasting it with the composition of the resurrection body of Jesus? When it says, 'the first Adam became a living being,' it can't be talking about the resurrection of Adam because Adam hasn't been resurrected. It seems to me instead that these verses are contrasting the different power sources of the natural body which Adam had and of the resurrection body Jesus has. Isn't it saying that the life we get from Adam is a life solely empowered from the elements of earth and that, in contrast, the resurrection life which Christians will get from Christ will be empowered by the Holy Spirit from heaven?"

Verses 46-49: "The spiritual did not come first, but the natural, and after that the spiritual. The first man was of the dust of the earth, the second man from heaven. As was the earthly man, so are those who are of the earth; and as is the man from heaven, so also are those who are of heaven. And just as we have borne the likeness of the earthly man, so shall we bear the likeness of the man from heaven."

Ask, "Isn't this describing two different sources or origins of life? The life we get from Adam comes first. The source of that is the dust of the earth. The resurrection life Christians will get from Christ comes second. The origin of that life is from heaven."

Verse 50: "I declare to you, brothers, that flesh and blood cannot inherit the kingdom of God, nor does the perishable inherit the imperishable."

Although asking questions of the Witnesses is usually the recommended method, sometimes you have to make direct statements in order to get your point across. I have found that the most effective way to get Witnesses to listen to you is to preface your remarks by saying something like this: "I'd like to tell you how I see this and when I'm done I'd like to get your response. Is that okay?"

Here, you can say, "It seems to me that 'flesh and blood' here means our limited, perishable, earthly bodies that we inherited from Adam. Those bodies can't inherit God's kingdom because they are perishable. But the resurrection bodies Christians will receive from Christ *can* inherit God's kingdom because they will be imperishable. They must be changed into imperishable bodies, empowered by the Spirit and no longer subject to decay and death. Can you see how I would believe that based on this passage?"

You can also say to the Witnesses, "Every time the phrase 'flesh and blood' appears in the New Testament, it is used as a figure of speech meaning 'natural man,' and I would certainly agree that natural, perishable man can't inherit God's kingdom."

If they ask you for examples, you can show them Matthew 16:17 where Jesus uses a figure of speech by telling Peter that "flesh and blood" (RNWT) did not reveal to him that Jesus is the Son of God. Rather, the Father revealed it. Jesus wasn't talking about literal flesh and literal blood revealing things. He was saying that Peter did not learn Jesus' identity from fallible men but from God himself.

In Ephesians 6:12, Paul says that we are not wrestling against "flesh and blood" but against evil spiritual forces. Once again, he is using "flesh and blood" as a figure of speech to mean natural man.

In Galatians 1:16, Paul says that he did not confer with "any human (Lit. 'with flesh and blood')" (RNWT and accompanying footnote). As the Watchtower's own translation and footnote acknowledge, he isn't speaking about conferring with literal flesh and literal blood. Once again, he is using the phrase figuratively to refer to natural man.

You can tell the Witnesses, "I believe that the reason why our flesh and blood bodies cannot inherit the kingdom is because natural man is perishable, corrupted by sin. We all need to receive imperishable bodies like Jesus did in order to be able to inherit the kingdom."

All Christians vs. 144,000 Christians

Pg 24 77

Verses 51-53: "Listen, I tell you a mystery: We will not all sleep, but we will all be changed—in a flash, in the twinkling of an eye, at the last trumpet. For the trumpet will sound, the dead will be raised imperishable, and we will be changed. For the perishable must clothe itself with the imperishable, and the mortal with immortality" (emphasis added).

Ask, "Does Paul say here that this is only for 144,000? Does he say that some Christians will be changed when their perishable bodies are clothed with immortality or that all Christians will be transformed in this manner?"

Argument #2: There will be two different resurrections so there are two different classes

John 5:28-29 and Revelation 20:4-6 speak of two different resurrections. One will occur at the beginning of the millennium, the other at the end (Revelation 20:5). The Watchtower teaches that the 144,000 take part in the first resurrection, which has already begun. They will be resurrected invisibly in spirit bodies and go to heaven. Later, the great crowd will be resurrected in physical bodies suited for life on earth and will not fully come alive in a spiritual sense until the end of the 1,000 years.

The best response is to agree that the Bible teaches that there will be two separate resurrections, but to emphasize that they are not spirit and physical resurrections of two different classes of Christians. The first resurrection is of believers, those whom God has justified (declared righteous) by faith. This will occur when the millennial kingdom begins. During the millennium, resurrected believers will rule as kings and priests with Christ over people who survived the great tribulation and their descendants.

The second resurrection is of the rest of the dead, unbelievers who died without having been justified by faith. This will occur at the end of the 1,000 years of the millennial kingdom.[5] The purpose of the latter resurrection is not a second chance at salvation, but a meting out of punishment proportionate to their sins in this life. At this point, Witnesses may tell you that Romans 6:7 says that those who are resurrected to life on earth will not be judged on what they did in this life but rather on what they do during the millennial kingdom. The short answer is that Romans 6 isn't talking about death freeing people from punishment for sins. It's talking about death freeing them from the controlling power of sin.

Argument #3: Jesus was "made alive in the spirit" rather than in the body

One of the Watchtower's favorite proof texts is 1 Peter 3:18, which it renders as follows: "He [Christ] was put to death in the flesh, but made alive in the spirit" (RNWT). The Watchtower interpretation is that Jesus died in the flesh but rose from the dead as an invisible spirit creature.

Say to the Witnesses, "The King James Version and several modern versions render it that Christ was made alive 'by the Spirit' rather than 'in the spirit.' Which translation is more consistent with Jesus' own statement in Luke 24:39: 'See my hands and my feet, that it is I myself; touch me and see, for a spirit does not have flesh and bones just as you see that I have'?" (RNWT).

Argument #4: If Jesus had taken back his body, he would have nullified the ransom sacrifice

The Watchtower makes the following argument: "If a man pays a debt for a friend but then promptly takes back the payment, obviously the debt continues. Likewise, if when he was resurrected, Jesus had taken back his human body of flesh and blood, which had been given in sacrifice to pay the ransom price, what effect would that have had on the provision he was making to relieve faithful persons of the debt of sin?"[6]

In response, have them read aloud John 10:17-18, where Jesus said, "The reason my Father loves me is that I lay down my life—only to take it up again. No one takes it from me, but I lay it down of my own accord. I have authority to lay it down and authority to take it up again. This command I received from my Father."

Ask, "By allowing Jesus to take back the life he had surrendered, was God somehow nullifying the sacrifice of Jesus' life?" Of course not!

Add, "I am not saying that Jesus took back his identical body of flesh and blood. He poured out his blood for the sins of the world. As Paul said, his earthly body was like a seed. Jesus was resurrected in a transformed, glorified, immortal body of flesh and bones. There was continuity, but the bodies were not identical."

Argument #5: Jesus could not have appeared in a locked room if he had a physical body

The Watchtower asks, "But how was it possible on that occasion for him suddenly to appear in their midst even though the doors were locked? (John 20:26, 27) Jesus evidently materialized bodies on these occasions, as angels had done in the past when appearing to humans."[7]

The best way I have found to respond to this argument is to point out that even before his resurrection, Jesus walked on water, as did Peter when Jesus gave him permission (Matthew 14:25-32). Ask, "Did Jesus and Peter have to dematerialize into spirit bodies in order to walk on water, or can Jesus overcome natural laws while still in physical form?"

Argument #6: Jesus could not be "the exact representation of God's very being" if he had a physical body in heaven

The Watchtower says, "If the disciples had actually seen Jesus in the body that he now has in heaven, Paul would not later have referred to the glorified Christ as being 'the exact representation of [God's] very being,' because God is a Spirit and has never been in the flesh. – Heb. 1:3; compare 1 Timothy 6:16."[8]

In response, say, "I believe that is talking about his character, not his form." Then have them read aloud Colossians 2:9: "For in Christ all the fullness of the divine quality dwells bodily" (RNWT). Even though this is a mistranslation ("divine quality" instead of "deity"), you can still use it by asking the Witnesses, "Does this verse say that Christ now dwells in *spirit* form or in *bodily* form?"

Argument #7: Jesus wasn't recognized because he materialized in different bodies

The Watchtower asserts, "Following his resurrection, Jesus did not always appear in the same body of flesh (perhaps to reinforce in their minds the fact that he was then a spirit), and so he was not immediately recognized even by his close associates. (John 20:14, 15; 21:4-7) However, by his repeatedly appearing to them in materialized bodies and then saying and doing things that they would identify with the Jesus they knew, he strengthened their faith in the fact that he truly had been resurrected from the dead."[9]

Let's look one-by-one at the post-resurrection appearances where Jesus' friends failed to recognize him.

Jesus appeared "in a different form"

Mark 16:12 says that Jesus appeared "in a different form" to the disciples on the road to Emmaus. If the Witnesses cite you this verse, ask how it reads in their translation. It isn't there. The Watchtower's Revised New World Translation states in a footnote that the verses after Mark 16:8 do not appear in the reliable early manuscripts of the Bible. You can tell the Witnesses, "Since some Bible versions, including the Watchtower version, don't recognize this passage as belonging in the canon of Scripture, I don't think we should draw any conclusions from it."

The Emmaus disciples didn't recognize him

Luke 24:15-32 is a more detailed account of Jesus' encounter with the disciples on the road to Emmaus. It's true that they didn't initially recognize him. However, verse 16 says that this was because "their eyes were kept from recognizing him" (RNWT). When Jesus was ready, verse 31 says, "At that their eyes were fully opened and they recognized him, and he disappeared from them" (RNWT).

Ask, "Don't these verses actually prove that Jesus didn't materialize in a different body? If he had a different body, why would it be necessary for their eyes to be kept from recognizing him?" Verse 31 concludes by saying that Jesus disappeared from their sight. Note that it does *not* say that he dematerialized.

Mary Magdalene didn't recognize him in the garden

John 20:14-16 is the account of Mary Magdalene at the tomb: "At this, she turned around and saw Jesus standing there, but she did not realize that it was Jesus. 'Woman,' he said, 'why are you crying? Who is it you are looking for?' Thinking he was the gardener, she said, 'Sir, if you have carried him away, tell me where you have put him, and I will get him.' Jesus said to her, 'Mary.' She turned toward him and cried out in Aramaic, 'Rabboni!' (which means Teacher)." Does this encounter prove that Jesus was appearing in a different body? Not at all.

Ask, "According to John 20:1, how much light was there when this happened?" That verse tells us that it was dark. Also ask, "Given that this happened in a garden in the dark, she was crying, and she thought Jesus was dead, is it any surprise that she would mistake him for the gardener?"

The disciples who were fishing didn't recognize him

In John 21:4-7, the risen Lord stood on a shore at daybreak and called to his disciples, who were out fishing in their boat. It was only after they obtained a huge catch of fish at his instructions that they realized it was Jesus.

Say, "This incident occurred at daybreak, and they were a great distance away, so it's not surprising that they didn't immediately recognize him. It is certainly not evidence that he had manufactured a different body."

You can also ask, "If the disciples' confusion proves that Jesus materialized in a different body, then, by the same logic, doesn't that mean that Jesus must also have materialized a different body before he died? In Mark 6, the disciples on the Sea of Galilee didn't recognize Jesus at first when they saw him walking on the water." Of course, no one actually contends that this wasn't Jesus' own body, not even the Watchtower.

Argument #8: Jesus appeared to some people but not to others

The Watchtower also notes that Acts 10:41 says, "He was not seen by all the people, but by witnesses whom God had already chosen—by us who ate and drank with him after he rose from the dead." Based on this, they ask, "Why did not others see him too? Because he was a spirit creature and when, as angels had done in the past, he materialized fleshly bodies to make himself visible, he did so only in the presence of his disciples."[10]

Ask, "Does this passage say anywhere that Jesus went around invisibly throughout Israel and materialized in manufactured physical bodies only in front of his disciples? Doesn't it just mean that after his resurrection, Jesus did not show up at the temple or another public place or walk into a meeting of the Sanhedrin in order to authenticate his resurrection to the Israelites at large or to skeptics and enemies?"

Argument #9: Jesus appeared fully clothed, not in grave linens

The Watchtower says, "Interestingly, although the physical body was not left by God in the tomb (evidently to strengthen the conviction of the disciples that Jesus had actually been raised), the linen cloths in which it had been wrapped were left there; yet, the resurrected Jesus always appeared fully clothed. – John 20:6, 7."[11]

If the Witnesses raise this argument with you, ask, "What does that prove? Of course the risen Christ didn't continue to wear the blood-stained shroud in which his body had been buried. But how does the fact that he was clothed tell us anything about whether he appeared to his disciples in a different body materialized for the purpose or in his own risen, glorified body of flesh and bones?"

Notice that in the Watchtower's view, Jesus' resurrection had nothing to do with his body. Jesus could still have been resurrected in spirit form even if his lifeless body had remained in the grave! Why, then, was his body missing from the tomb? According to the Watchtower, God evidently removed it in order to help convince the disciples that Jesus had come back from the dead. If the Witnesses present this argument to you ask, "If the Watchtower is right, then didn't God's strategy backfire by misleading Thomas and the other disciples into the misconception that Jesus' own body had risen from the dead?"

Also ask, "If Jesus' resurrection had nothing to do with his physical body, why did God bother to have angels disable the tomb guards and roll away the stone so the disciples could go inside? Why not leave the body in the sealed tomb undisturbed and simply have Jesus manufacture a duplicate body and appear to his disciples in the upper room?"

That brings up a related point. Ask, "If the disciples, like the Watchtower, went about preaching that Jesus' resurrection was in spirit form rather than physical, why did the authorities claim that the disciples had stolen Jesus' body? Their ability or inability to produce his body wouldn't in any way have proved or disproved a *spirit* resurrection claim. Only if the disciples were proclaiming a *bodily* resurrection would the authorities have needed an alternative explanation as to why they were unable to produce Jesus' body."

Argument #10: Jesus disappeared when he ascended to heaven

What about the fact that Jesus ascended to heaven? Acts 1:9-11 states: "After he said this, he was taken up before their very eyes, and a cloud hid him from their sight. They were looking intently up into the sky as he was going, when suddenly two men dressed in white stood beside them. 'Men of Galilee,' they said, 'why do you stand here looking into the sky? This same Jesus, who has been taken from you into heaven, will come back in the same way you have seen him go into heaven.'" Because he disappeared from their sight into a cloud, the Watchtower concludes that he will return in like manner—invisibly!

Note that the passage doesn't say that Jesus dematerialized. It says that a cloud hid him from their sight. Ask, "If you see an airplane take off and disappear into a cloud, do you conclude that it has dematerialized? Do you expect that when it returns in the same way in which you saw it go, it will come back invisibly?"

Jehovah's Witnesses sometimes argue that Jesus could not have had a physical body, given that he ascended into the sky. Point out that he did have a physical body because the Bible says that the people saw him until he entered the cloud. Follow up by asking, "Given that Jesus was able to walk on water before his death without dematerializing, why would his ascension require dematerialization? God also miraculously carried up Elijah (2 Kings 2:11) and Philip (Acts 8:39), and no one suggests that they had to be turned into spirit creatures in order for him to accomplish this."

The Witnesses may ask you how it would be possible for a man with a physical body to exist in heaven. You can answer, "Heaven is not outer space, so the issue is not whether a man could exist in the cold and vacuum of space. Where does the Bible say that a man with a physical body cannot exist in heaven?"

Have them read aloud 1 Timothy 2:5, which says that there is now a *man* who is the mediator between God and men. Have them also read aloud Acts 17:31, which says that one day God will also judge the world in righteousness by a *man*. Jesus is still a man, not an archangel in a spirit body.

Argument #11: Paul didn't learn the gospel from a man but from Jesus

A Jehovah's Witness recently made the following argument to a friend of mine: In Galatians 1:12, Paul says that he did not learn the gospel from any man, that he learned it instead from Jesus Christ. Therefore, the resurrected Christ is not a man.

As usual, the answer lies in showing the Witnesses the context of the verse being quoted. The subject under discussion in Galatians 1 is not whether Jesus is now an exalted man or an archangel. The first chapter of Galatians is a warning against false gospels made up by mere men.

In verse 1, Paul states he was sent by God the Father and by Jesus Christ. That is, unlike the false teachers, Paul was not a representative of some mere man or group of men. In verse 10, Paul says that he is not trying to please men. In verse 11, he says that the real gospel is not something contrived by man. In verses 12 through 20, Paul states that he did not learn the gospel from any man or group of men, not even Peter or James or any of the other apostles. He learned the gospel directly from Jesus Christ. He is distinguishing Christ from all of those ordinary men, not trying to explain the nature of Jesus' resurrection body.

The language Paul uses in Galatians 1 is simply his way of saying that his message comes from the highest sources possible—Jesus Christ and God the Father. In fact, in verse 8, he specifically indicates that a contrary gospel proclaimed by an angel from heaven would not have the authority that Paul has behind the gospel he has been preaching. Doesn't this mean that Jesus Christ is superior to any angel from heaven? If so, the resurrected Christ can't be an archangel from heaven.

CONCLUSION

When we discuss the nature of the resurrection, we can get so engrossed in disputing with Jehovah's Witnesses the meaning of various proof texts about the resurrection body that we lose sight of the big picture. Discussion of the composition of resurrection bodies—both Jesus' and ours—is not an end in itself. Rather, that topic needs to be the springboard that leads Witnesses to question the Watchtower's entire plan of salvation.

Sum up this topic by saying to the Witnesses, "Do you see why I consider this issue to be so important? If what I believe about the resurrection is correct, then there aren't two different classes of Christians. All Christians will raised in bodily form. All of us need to have Christ's righteousness imputed to us through faith in order to become Christians and obtain eternal life. This inner transformation is what the new birth is all about. I believe that 1 John 3:2 teaches that all true Christians will be like Jesus: 'we shall be like him, for we shall see him as he is.'"

Chapter 10:
The New Birth Approach

"In reply Jesus declared, 'I tell you the truth, no one can see the kingdom of God unless he is born again'" (John 3:3).

The objective of this approach is to show Jehovah's Witnesses that the new birth involves an inner transformation of a person by the Holy Spirit and is the only way by which anyone can obtain eternal life.

If the Watchtower's two-class salvation system were only a matter of location—whether all Christians will go to heaven or whether most of them will live forever in paradise on earth—the topic would be of little practical significance. However, because of the Watchtower's erroneous teachings, the vast majority of Jehovah's Witnesses believe the new birth and the new covenant are not for them.

The Watchtower does not believe that the new birth is an inner transformation of a repentant sinner by the Holy Spirit. Nor does it believe that being born again is necessary for salvation. Instead, the Watchtower claims that when Jesus revealed to his disciples that he was instituting a new covenant, he was telling them that a "little flock" of Christians (Luke 12:32) would one day go to heaven to be with him and share in ruling his kingdom.

According to the Watchtower, this is a destiny available only to Jesus and 144,000 anointed Jehovah's Witnesses chosen by God throughout all the centuries of the Christian era. Old Testament believers will not be included. In fact, none of them had any expectation of going to heaven.

In Watchtower theology, "born again" means being "begotten by holy spirit."[1] This is how God designates someone to be one of the anointed, heaven-bound group. All other Christians and believers from the Old Testament era will be saved without being born again and without having Christ's righteousness imputed to them. They benefit from the new covenant by virtue of their association with the anointed 144,000, but they themselves are not a part of that new covenant.

This approach is designed to help you show Jehovah's Witnesses that the Bible presents only one way of salvation, not two, and that God's offer of the inner transformation of a new birth and entry into the new covenant are essential to their own salvation.

Witnesses will expect you to show them Jesus' statement to Nicodemus that he must be born again. You will discuss that passage with them, but you will do so in a way the Witnesses won't expect. You will ask them why Jesus expressed surprise that Nicodemus didn't already understand all of this. If the Watchtower explanation is right, there is no way Nicodemus *could* already have understood it. In this way, you will open the door to showing the Witnesses that the new birth and the new covenant are something quite different from what the Watchtower teaches.

THE NEW BIRTH PROVIDES
AN INNER TRANSFORMATION

Ask the Witnesses to tell you what they understand the new birth to be. After they give you their explanation, tell them that their definition is very different than your understanding and ask them to help you by examining Jesus' conversation with Nicodemus in John 3.

John 3:1-10

Have one of them read aloud John 3:1-10. Focus on Jesus' key question to Nicodemus in John 3:10: "You are Israel's teacher,' said Jesus, 'and do you not understand these things?'"

Ask, "If Jesus' statement about the need to be born again was a totally new teaching that 144,000 people would receive spirit bodies when they die and go to heaven, why would he be surprised that Nicodemus didn't already understand that? Why would he expect a man raised and educated solely under the Mosaic Law Covenant to know such a thing?"

Don't let them hopscotch to other Bible passages. You are asking specifically about what Jesus expected *Nicodemus* to understand. They believe that a Jewish scholar would have expected to live on a paradise earth.

After you have listened to their response, ask if you can tell them what you think Jesus meant and why you think that makes more sense than the Watchtower interpretation. Say, "I believe Jesus was indicating that all human beings need a spiritual rebirth, an inner transformation by the Holy Spirit, in order to meet Jehovah's righteous standards. That's something he would expect an Old Testament scholar like Nicodemus to understand." Then take them to two Old Testament passages that teach this.

Jeremiah 31:31-34

Ask one of them to read aloud Jeremiah 31:31-34:

"Look! The days are coming," declares Jehovah, "when I will make with the house of Israel and with the house of Judah a new covenant. It will not be like the covenant that I made with their forefathers on the day I took hold of their hand to lead them out of the land of Egypt, my covenant that they broke, although I was their true master," declares Jehovah. "For this is the covenant that I will make with the house of Israel after those days," declares Jehovah. "I will put my law within them, and in their heart I will write it. And I will become their God, and they will become my people. And they will no longer teach each one his neighbor and each one his brother, saying, 'Know Jehovah!' for they will all know me, from the least to the greatest of them," declares Jehovah. "For I will forgive their error, and I will no longer remember their sin" (RNWT).

Ask, "Wouldn't Jesus have expected Nicodemus to understand from this passage that human beings had no way of meeting Jehovah's righteous demands or proving worthy of everlasting life except by allowing God to put them into this new covenant that would give them an inner righteousness that they couldn't otherwise attain as sinful descendants of Adam?"

Ezekiel 11:19-20

Ask one of them to read aloud Ezekiel 11:19-20: "I will give them an undivided heart and put a new spirit in them; I will remove from them their heart of stone and give them a heart of flesh. Then they will follow my decrees and be careful to keep my laws. They will be my people, and I will be their God."

Ask, "Based on this, do you see why I believe that the need for inner transformation by God is what Jesus meant by being born again? He expected Nicodemus to understand that sinful descendants of Adam need a new spirit and a new heart in order to make them *able* to live according to Jehovah's righteous standards. In other words, being born again isn't about designating a special group of people to go to heaven in spirit form. It's an inner transformation we all need in order to experience salvation and eternal life."

Have one of the Witnesses read aloud Romans 8:8-9: "So those who are in harmony with the flesh cannot please God. However, you are in harmony, not with the flesh, but with the spirit, if God's spirit truly dwells in you. But if anyone does not have Christ's spirit, this person does not belong to him" (RNWT).

Ask, "According to this passage, can we please God and belong to Christ unless we have God's spirit dwelling within us?" Wait for their answer. Then ask, "How do we get God's spirit dwelling within us except by the inner transformation of the new birth?"

ALL CHRISTIANS ARE IN THE NEW COVENANT

Because of the Watchtower teaching that only the anointed 144,000 are born again into the new covenant, at their annual Memorial service (their version of communion) only those who profess to be in this class are allowed to partake of the bread and wine. Others attend and watch, but the Watchtower says that the new covenant in Christ's blood is not for them.

To show the Witnesses that this practice is unscriptural, I recommend that you draw their attention to the following passages. Ask them to read them aloud.

Matthew 26:26-28

"While they were eating, Jesus took bread, gave thanks and broke it, and gave it to his disciples, saying, 'Take and eat; this is my body.' Then he took the cup, gave thanks and offered it to them, saying, 'Drink from it, all of you. This is my blood of the covenant, which is poured out for many for the forgiveness of sins.'"

Ask, "Didn't Jesus command all those present to eat and drink? Did he say that some should partake and that some should not?" Most likely they will say that all of the apostles were of the 144,000. If so, ask, "Don't you believe that Jesus' ransom sacrifice applies to you? Don't you believe that Jesus' blood was poured out for the forgiveness of your sins as well as for the sins of the 144,000?"

John 6:53-56

"Jesus said to them, 'I tell you the truth, unless you eat the flesh of the Son of Man and drink his blood, you have no life in you. Whoever eats my flesh and drinks my blood has eternal life, and I will raise him up at the last day. For my flesh is real food and my blood is real drink. Whoever eats my flesh and drinks my blood remains in me, and I in him.'"

Ask, "Why aren't you included in *whoever*?"

Add, "I believe that Jesus is speaking of an inward experience of which partaking of the bread and wine is only a symbol. But when you pass the bread and wine along without partaking, aren't you testifying that you have never had this inward experience which Jesus said was essential in order to have eternal life?" If they insist that this experience is only for the 144,000, say, "Jesus says that people who don't eat his flesh and drink his blood have no life in themselves. Don't you have life in you?"

1 Corinthians 10:16-17

"Is not the cup of thanksgiving for which we give thanks a participation in the blood of Christ? And is not the bread that we break a participation in the body of Christ? Because there is one loaf, we, who are many, are one body, for we all partake of the one loaf."

Ask, "According to this passage, how many bodies are there? Why aren't you included in *all*?"

Responding to Watchtower objections

Expect the Witnesses to make the following argument to "prove" that only 144,000 go to heaven. 1 Peter 1:3-4 says that those who are born again have an inheritance in heaven. Revelation 14:3 says those in heaven are the 144,000 who have been redeemed from the earth. Luke 12:32 says God will give the kingdom to a "little flock." Revelation 20:6 says they will rule as kings and priests. If all Christians were born again and ended up in heaven, there would be no one on earth for them to rule over and no millennial kingdom.

I recommend that you make the following points in response:

1. Heaven and earth are not mutually exclusive. Angels are able to exist in either place and to travel back and forth. There is no reason why Jehovah couldn't enable born again people to do likewise. If the Witnesses ask you if they will have physical bodies or spirit bodies, I recommend that you tell them you would like to devote an entire session to discussing the nature of the resurrection because of its importance. Prepare for that by studying Chapter 9, "The Bodily Resurrection Approach."

2. Revelation 14:4 calls the 144,000 "firstfruits," not the only ones who are born again and not the only ones who have access to heaven.

3. There is nothing in the Bible that equates the "little flock" with the 144,000. Ask, "Why couldn't the 'little flock' to whom the Father gave the kingdom simply be the apostles to whom Jesus made that statement? He told them that in the end times they would sit on 12 thrones judging the 12 tribes of Israel (Matthew 19:28).

4. There will be a millennial kingdom on earth. Those whom born again people serve as kings and priests will be the people of the nations who survive the tribulation, as well as their children who are born during the millennium. Witnesses may deny that any unbelievers will survive the tribulation. Show them Revelation 20:7-8, which says that when Satan is released after the 1,000 years he will again mislead the nations and gather to him "as many as the sand of the sea" for his final rebellion. They will encircle the holy city. Clearly, these particular subjects of the millennial kingdom are not true believers and their number is too large to count.

THE NEW BIRTH IS
AVAILABLE TO EVERYONE

Once you have built this foundation, direct the Witnesses' attention to scriptures which show that Jesus' invitation and promises are for everyone who will receive him, not just a select group of 144,000.

John 17:20, 24

Have one of the Witnesses read aloud John 17:24, where Jesus prayed, "Father, I want those you have given me to be with me where I am, and to see my glory, the glory you have given me because you loved me before the creation of the world."

If they claim that he was just referring to his 12 disciples or to his first century followers, take them back to verse 20: "My prayer is not for them alone. I pray also for those who will believe in me through their message..." The point is that Jesus wants all Christians to be with him where he is, not just 144,000 of them.

John 12:26

Ask them to read aloud John 12:26: "Whoever serves me must follow me; and where I am, my servant also will be. My Father will honor the one who serves me..."

Ask what Jesus means by "whoever" and "my servant." Are those words restricted to a limited group of 144,000?

Ephesians 4:4-6

Have one of them read aloud Ephesians 4:4-6: "There is one body and one Spirit—just as you were called to one hope when you were called—one Lord, one faith, one baptism; one God and Father of all, who is over all and through all and in all."

Ask, "Does this passage speak of two hopes or just one?" They may say that the one hope is of your calling and that means there is a heavenly calling and an earthly calling. But the phrase is defined by the context of the passage—one body, one spirit, one hope, one Lord, one faith, one baptism, one God and Father of all. That's not consistent with there being two different hopes and two destinies. Nor is it consistent with there being a born-again way and a non-born-again way of salvation.

CONCLUSION

Don't allow the discussion to turn into mere wrangling about what will or won't happen in the end times or which Christians will end up in what location. Stay focused on the objective and end with a positive note of witness, asking them if they see why you believe that all of the invitations and promises of Jesus are available to them and that the key to salvation for any of us is to receive the inner transformation of the new birth that Jesus described to Nicodemus.

SECTION 3: DISCUSSING THE NATURE OF GOD

Chapter 11:
Who Exactly Is God?

THE TRINITY

Christianity

Christians believe that within the nature of the one true God there are three distinct Persons—Father[1], Son[2], and Holy Spirit.[3] Each of these Persons is fully God, yet there is only one God.[4]

Jehovah's Witnesses

Jehovah's Witnesses believe that the Trinity teaching is a pagan, God-dishonoring doctrine.[5] The Watchtower teaches that only the Father is Jehovah God[6] and that Jesus Christ is Michael the archangel, God's unique Son, the first and greatest creation of Jehovah God—"a god," but not Almighty God.[7] They also believe that "holy spirit" (they usually omit the definite article and use lower case type) is neither Jehovah God nor a person; rather, it is Jehovah's impersonal, active force.[8] They contend that the Trinity is derived from pagan sources[9] and was forced onto Christendom by Emperor Constantine at the Council of Nicea in 325 A.D.[10]

They often point out that the word "Trinity" doesn't appear anywhere in the Bible. Of course, the fact that a word or phrase doesn't appear in the Bible doesn't mean that it's wrong to use it. For example, Witnesses themselves meet in a building called a "Kingdom Hall" and claim that the Watchtower is "God's theocratic organization." Neither of those phrases can be found in the Bible. So the question isn't whether the word "Trinity" appears in the Bible. Admittedly, it doesn't. Rather, we need to examine whether the *concept* is taught there.

THE IDENTITY OF JESUS CHRIST

Christianity

Christians believe that Jesus is fully God and fully man. As God, the Word (who became Jesus) existed from all eternity.[11] The Word became flesh at the incarnation (John 1:1, 14). Jesus was miraculously conceived in the Virgin Mary's womb by the Holy Spirit (Matthew 1:18-25), who is God.[12] Unlike other human beings, Jesus was born without unrighteousness inherited from Adam.[13] Jesus Christ is God in human flesh.[14] As such, he was and is greater than Adam. Jesus lived a sinless life.[15] For this reason, Jesus did not need to be born again.[16]

Dependence on the Father

The Bible is clear that when he became a man and lived on earth, Jesus voluntarily gave up the independent exercise of his divinity (Philippians 2:5-8). That is, he relied completely on the Father for his divine power and teachings (John 5:19-23; 14:10).

Accordingly, there were times when he displayed supernatural knowledge (Matthew 9:4; 17:27; Luke 10:18), and times when there were things he did not know (Matthew 24:36; Mark 5:30-32). He was able to walk on water and enable Peter to do so (Matthew 14:25-33), yet most of the time he walked from place to place just as we do (Matthew 4:18). He was able to feed thousands of people miraculously at one time (Matthew 14:15-21; 15:32-38) and offer a woman living water (John 4:10), but he himself grew hungry (Mark 11:12) and thirsty (John 19:28). Several times, he demonstrated power over death by raising people from the dead (Mark 5:22-43; Luke 7:11-15; John 11:11-44), yet Jesus himself died (Mark 15:37).

Subordination to the Father

Because Jesus is fully human, made lower than the angels for the suffering of death (Hebrews 2:9), the Father is greater positionally than Jesus (John 14:28). While on earth, Jesus addressed his prayers to his Father (Matthew 26:39). As a man, Jesus worshipped his Father as God (John 4:21-22). In heaven today, Jesus is still a man (1 Timothy 2:5, Acts 17:31) with the Father as his head (1 Corinthians 11:3). In the future, Christ will deliver the kingdom to his Father and will be in subjection to him (1 Corinthians 15:24-28). None of these facts negates the deity of Christ. They simply confirm his humanity and explain the relationship of Father and Son.

Jehovah's Witnesses

Jehovah's Witnesses also believe that Jesus was miraculously conceived in the womb of a virgin named Mary[17] and that he was born without unrighteousness inherited from Adam.[18]

Jesus is Michael the archangel

However, they believe that God's Son was Jehovah's first and greatest creation, the archangel Michael; as such he had a beginning.[19] When Jesus was conceived in Mary's womb, "Jehovah transferred the life-force and the personality pattern"[20] of Michael the archangel into Jesus.

A perfect man, nothing more, nothing less

Despite this, Witnesses do not believe that Jesus was an archangel and a man at the same time. Rather, the Watchtower teaches that when he was on earth Jesus was an exact equivalent to Adam.[21] "As a perfect man—nothing more, nothing less—and the exact counterpart of the once-perfect Adam, Jesus could 'give himself a corresponding ransom for all,' that is, for all of sinner Adam's imperfect offspring."[22]

Sinless, but born again

They agree that Jesus lived a sinless life,[23] but they also believe that Jesus was born again following his water baptism.[24] They do not believe that "born again" involves spiritual regeneration of people who are dead in their trespasses and sins (Ephesians 2:1), but rather that it means that the person obtains a conditional right to life in the heavens if he remains faithful to Jehovah through testing.[25]

Resurrected as Michael

After Jesus' death, he was resurrected in spirit form, thereby no longer being a man and once again becoming Michael the archangel.[26]

THE IDENTITY OF THE HOLY SPIRIT

Christianity

Christians believe that the Holy Spirit is a person, not an impersonal force. In fact, he is Jehovah God himself, the third person of the Trinity.[27] He gives both physical life and spiritual life, reveals spiritual truth, teaches and illumines, empowers

Christians for service, unifies the church, and gives genuine Christians assurance of salvation.[28]

Jehovah's Witnesses

Jehovah's Witnesses believe that "holy spirit" is not God and is not even a person. Rather, they believe that "holy spirit" is an impersonal "active force" that emanates from and is used by Jehovah God to accomplish various purposes.[29]

FOCUS YOUR DISCUSSION ON THE BIBLE

If Witnesses present you with arguments about pagan "trinities," Constantine, or the Council of Nicea, say, "All I really care about is what the Bible actually teaches because only the Bible is inspired by God. Can we just look together at the Scriptures?" They should agree to that procedure.

The next three chapters give you specific approaches you can use in discussing the identity of Jesus and the identity of the Holy Spirit with Jehovah's Witnesses. I strongly recommend that you discuss these two topics separately. I have found that when Jehovah's Witnesses get in trouble regarding who Jesus is, they often try to switch the conversation to the Holy Spirit. When they run into difficulty regarding the identity of the Holy Spirit, they often want to confront you with one of their proof texts about Jesus. Be polite, but insist on staying focused on the topic at hand.

Remember throughout your discussions that your purpose is not to win an argument but to open the minds of the Witnesses to the possibility that Jesus and the Holy Spirit are much more than the Watchtower claims they are. You want to plant the seeds that may eventually make it possible for them to come to Jesus, through the Holy Spirit, for salvation.

FOR FURTHER STUDY

- Chapter 12, "The Jesus Isn't Michael Approach" explains how to help Jehovah's Witnesses see that, contrary to Watchtower doctrine, Jesus is not Michael the archangel.
- Chapter 13, "The Jesus Is the God-Man Approach" explains how to help Jehovah's Witnesses see that Jesus is fully God and fully man.
- Chapter 14, "The Holy Spirit Is God Approach" explains how to show Jehovah's Witnesses that the Holy Spirit is both a person and God himself, not an impersonal, "active force."

Chapter 12:
The Jesus Isn't Michael Approach

"For to which of the angels did God ever say, 'You are my Son; today I have become your Father'? Or again, 'I will be his Father, and he will be my Son'?" (Hebrews 1:5).

The objective of this approach is to help Jehovah's Witnesses see that, contrary to Watchtower doctrine, Jesus is not Michael the archangel.

The identity of Jesus Christ is of critical importance to our salvation (John 8:24). Among the cardinal doctrines of the Watchtower religion are the assertions that God is not a Trinity and that Jesus is not God Almighty. Although the Watchtower claims to exalt Jesus as king, in fact it has demoted him by teaching that he is a created being, Michael the archangel.[1] Because of this false teaching, Jehovah's Witnesses don't have a personal relationship with Christ. They don't think such a thing is desirable or even possible. Opening their minds to the possibility that Jesus is more than what the Watchtower portrays him to be can be a major step in leading them out of that organization to a saving knowledge of the Lord.

Witnesses expect you to claim that Jesus is fully God and that God is a Trinity. They are prepared to put you on the defensive by making you try to prove these claims and then attacking what you present. However, with this approach you will turn the tables by claiming merely that Jesus isn't Michael and putting the burden on them to show that he is.

When to use this approach

At some point, Jehovah's Witnesses will initiate a discussion of the nature of God or the identity of Jesus. Perhaps they will do so by explicitly condemning the Trinity doctrine as a fourth century heresy of Christendom. If you sense the Holy Spirit leading you to address those issues head-on, you can do so. I will give you many suggestions for doing that in Chapter 13, "The Jesus Is the God-Man Approach."

However, you may sense that the limited approach presented in this chapter would be a better and more helpful first step. Whereas discussing the Trinity may take several sessions, this limited approach can be accomplished in one session, two at most.

THE BIBLE DOESN'T IDENTIFY JESUS AS MICHAEL

I recommend that you begin this approach by establishing that the Watchtower teaches that Jesus is the archangel Michael. If they have already told you this, just tell them you want to make sure you understood them correctly. If they haven't said it yet, say something like, "It's my understanding that the Watchtower organization teaches that Jesus is Michael the archangel. Is my understanding correct on that point?"

If they try to get you into an argument about the deity of Christ or the Trinity, tell them that you have always been taught that Jesus is God but that instead of arguing with them, you want to know what they believe and why because you find it confusing.

Ask them to show you where the Bible says specifically that Jesus is Michael. If they tell you there is no direct statement to that effect (which there isn't), then ask them to show you from the Scriptures why they believe that this teaching is true.

They may tell you that "Michael" means "Who is like God?"[2] and that Jesus is said to be "the image of the invisible God, the firstborn of all creation" (Colossians 1:15, RNWT). They may add that Michael's name "evidently designates Michael as the one who takes the lead in upholding Jehovah's sovereignty and destroying God's enemies."[3]

Tell them that you would like them to go through each of the passages that mention Michael by name to see exactly what the Bible says about him. There are five such passages. There is a sixth passage that mentions "archangel" and "Jesus" together but doesn't use the name "Michael." Go through them with the Witnesses one-by-one. If they don't bring up some of these passages, make sure you do so.

1 Thessalonians 4:16

The principal proof text they use doesn't mention Michael by name at all. Rather, it speaks of "the voice of the archangel." 1 Thessalonians 4:16: "For the Lord himself will come down from heaven, with a loud command, with the voice of the archangel and with the trumpet call of God, and the dead in Christ will rise first." Here is the Watchtower's explanation: "At 1 Thessalonians 4:16 (RS), the command of Jesus Christ for the resurrection to begin is described as 'the archangel's call,' and Jude 9 says that the archangel is Michael. Would it be appropriate to liken Jesus' commanding call to that of someone lesser in authority? Reasonably, then, the archangel Michael is Jesus Christ. (Interestingly, the expression 'archangel' is never found in the plural in the Scriptures, thus implying that there is only one.)"[4]

Ask, "Where does it say that Jesus is the one making the 'commanding call'? Couldn't it just mean that an archangel accompanies him as a forerunner or herald for the king?"

Also ask, "If being accompanied by an archangel's voice makes the Lord an archangel, couldn't someone by the same logic say that his having God's trumpet means that Jesus is God?"[5]

Daniel 10:13

Daniel 10:13 reads as follows: "But the prince of the Persian kingdom resisted me twenty-one days. Then Michael, one of the chief princes, came to help me, because I was detained there with the king of Persia."

Say, "This passage calls Michael *one* of the chief *princes*. Wouldn't that make him one of a group of such princes? But the Bible says that Jesus is unique, not one among many princes that are equal in rank."[6]

Daniel 10:21

Daniel 10:21 states, "...but first I will tell you what is written in the Book of Truth. No one supports me against them except Michael, your prince."

This verse does not indicate that it is speaking about the Messiah. In fact, isn't Jesus God's chosen *king*, not a prince?

Daniel 12:1

Daniel 12:1 says, "At that time Michael, the great prince who protects your people, will arise. There will be a time of distress such as has not happened from the beginning of nations until then. But at that time your people—everyone whose name is found written in the book—will be delivered."

The Watchtower argues as follows: "Daniel 12:1 (RS) associates the 'standing up of Michael' to act with authority with 'a time of trouble, such as never has been since there was a nation till that time.' That would certainly fit the experience of the nations when Christ as heavenly executioner takes action against them. So the evidence indicates that the Son of God was known as Michael before he came to earth and is known also by that name since his return to heaven where he resides as the glorified spirit Son of God."[7]

Point out that all Daniel 12:1 indicates is that Michael will rise up for God's people during the tribulation in the end times. Nowhere in the passage does Daniel identify Michael as being the Messiah, the "Son of Man."

Jude 9

Jude 9 reads, "But when Michael the archangel had a difference with the Devil and was disputing about Moses' body, he did not dare to bring a judgment against him in abusive terms, but said: 'May Jehovah rebuke you'" (RNWT).

With regard to this verse, point out that in contrast to Michael's deference and restraint, Jesus confronted Satan directly. On multiple occasions, he ordered demons to leave people, and they obeyed. When Jesus was tempted by Satan, he did not hesitate to rebuke Satan to his face. Three times he countered Satan's temptations with scripture. The final time he told him directly, "Away from me, Satan!" and Satan obeyed (Matthew 4:10).

When Peter tried to dissuade Jesus from going to his death, rather than address Peter, Jesus directly rebuked the devil, saying, "Get behind me, Satan!" (Matthew 16:23).

Ask, "If Michael did not dare rebuke Satan directly but Jesus both rebuked Satan and issued commands to him, doesn't that show that Jesus is greater than Michael?"

Revelation 12:7-9

Revelation 12:7-9 states, "And there was war in heaven. Michael and his angels fought against the dragon, and the dragon and his angels fought back. But he was not strong enough, and they lost their place in heaven. The great dragon was hurled down—that ancient serpent called the devil, or Satan, who leads the whole world astray. He was hurled to the earth, and his angels with him."

Say, "Michael and his angels defeat Satan and his angels. I see that, but I don't see anything there that identifies Jesus with Michael." Let them try to prove to you a connection.

The Watchtower argues as follows: "Revelation 12:7-12 says that Michael and his angels would war against Satan and hurl him and his wicked angels out of heaven in connection with the conferring of kingly authority on Christ. Jesus is later depicted as leading the armies of heaven in war against the nations of the world. (Rev. 19:11-16) Is it not reasonable that Jesus should also be the one to take action against the one he described as 'ruler of this world,' Satan the Devil? (John 12:31)"[8]

If they make this argument, have them actually read aloud Revelation 19:11-16 and say, "It seems to me that the book of Revelation clearly distinguishes between two different leaders

(Michael in Revelation 12 and Jesus in Revelation 19) leading their armies into battle against two different enemies (the dragon and his angels and the nations of the world) at two different times. I don't see anything in either of these Revelation passages which says that Michael and Jesus are the same person."

You can also point out that when John refers to Christ in Revelation, he describes him in much more exalted terms than he uses to describe Michael. In Revelation 12, Michael is not given any title, but in Revelation 19 Jesus wears a robe and is called "King of kings and Lord of lords."

Ask, "Doesn't this show that they are two different persons and that Jesus is more highly exalted in heaven than Michael?"

WATCHTOWER TEACHINGS ABOUT JESUS CONTRADICT EACH OTHER

Two Watchtower teachings about Jesus' identity contradict each other. The Watchtower does claim that Jesus is the archangel Michael, but it also teaches that because what Adam's sin lost was a perfect human life, it took "a ransom equal in value to what was lost"[9] in order to buy back what was lost. The Watchtower concludes, therefore, that Jesus was "a perfect man—nothing more, nothing less—and the exact counterpart of the once-perfect Adam..."[10] Through a judicious use of questions, you can help the Witnesses see that these two Watchtower doctrines contradict each other.

Ask, "Do you believe that Jesus was Michael the archangel in human flesh or that when he was on earth he was just a man?"

This question puts them on the horns of a dilemma. If they tell you that Jesus was Michael in human flesh, then ask, "If Jesus was Michael on earth as a man, wouldn't that mean that Jesus was far more than just a perfect man like Adam?" They should realize that this contradicts what the Watchtower teaches about the "ransom sacrifice."

More likely, they will tell you that Jesus was just a perfect man when he was on earth because Michael gave up his heavenly life in order to become human. Likewise, Jesus gave up his human life in order to return to heaven as Michael.

They may cite you Hebrews 2:17-18: "For this reason he had to be made like his brothers in every way, in order that he might become a merciful and faithful high priest in service to God, and that he might make atonement for the sins of the people. Because he himself suffered when he was tempted, he is able to help those who are being tempted."

If that is what they tell you, say, "It sounds like you are saying that Michael was an archangel and not a man and that Jesus wasn't an archangel but only a man like Adam. So then Jesus really wasn't the archangel Michael, was he? Do you see why I'm confused?"

THE BOOK OF HEBREWS SHOWS THAT JESUS IS SUPERIOR TO ANY ANGEL

The entire first chapter of the book of Hebrews is written to show the superiority of Christ to the prophets and to the angels. Have the Witnesses read each of these passages aloud, one at a time.

Hebrews 1:2-3

Hebrews 1:2 says that God has appointed his Son "heir of all things" and tells us that it was through his Son that God created the world. Hebrews 1:3 proclaims Christ as the "radiance of God's glory and the exact representation of his being." It also says that Christ is "sustaining all things by his powerful word."

Ask, "How could an angel create and sustain the universe?"

Hebrews 1:4-5

Ask one of them to read aloud Hebrews 1:4-5, which says of Christ, "So he became as much superior to the angels as the name he has inherited is superior to theirs. For to which of the angels did God ever say, 'You are my Son; today I have become your Father'? Or again, 'I will be his Father, and he will be my Son'?"

Ask them to answer the question set out in verse 5. Clearly, the answer is that God never called any angel his Son. Christ has a more excellent name than the angels. Jehovah's Witnesses may try to get around this by saying that Jesus was an archangel, not just an angel, but an archangel is an angel just as the Chief of Police is a police officer, and this passage tells us that God never called *any* angel his Son.

Hebrews 1:13-14

Hebrews 1:13-14 finishes the chapter, once again demonstrating that Christ is not an angel: "To which of the angels did God ever say, 'Sit at my right hand until I make your enemies a footstool for your feet'? Are not all angels ministering spirits sent to serve those who will inherit salvation?"

Ask, "Doesn't this passage show that Christ is not any sort of angel?"

Hebrews 2:5

Hebrews 2:5 says, "It is not to angels that he has subjected the world to come, about which we are speaking."

Ask, "Doesn't this verse show that Christ the king is not any kind of angel?"

CONCLUSION

In summary, you can tell the Witnesses that you find the Watchtower's claim that Jesus is Michael the archangel to be confusing. The Bible doesn't identify Jesus as Michael, and the Watchtower's teaching that he is Michael contradicts its teaching that while he was on earth he was only a man like Adam. In addition, the Bible shows that Jesus is greater than Adam and all of the angels.

Remember that you are trying to open their eyes to the possibility that Jesus is far more than the Watchtower teaches, not trying to win an argument. Take your time with this. Don't allow them jump into their proof texts for Jesus not being God before you have finished discussing whether or not he is Michael. When you do think the time is right, you can continue on to discuss Jesus as being both fully human and fully God.

Chapter 13:
The Jesus Is the God-Man Approach

"Thomas said to him, 'My Lord and my God!' Then Jesus told him, 'Because you have seen me, you have believed; blessed are those who have not seen and yet have believed'" (John 20:28-29).

The objective of this approach is to help Jehovah's Witnesses see that Jesus is fully God and fully man.

Jehovah's Witnesses love to argue about the Trinity doctrine and about the identity of Jesus in particular. They have been well-trained in how to try to prove to you that Jesus was the first and greatest creation of Jehovah God—an exalted being to be sure, but not God himself.

If the Watchtower view of Jesus were correct, they would be right not to worship him[1] or seek to have a personal relationship with him. But if Jesus is truly Jehovah God himself, then a personal relationship with him is not only possible, but essential to our salvation.

The Witnesses will expect you to focus on trying to prove to them that Jesus is God. Instead, you will begin in a way that will build bridges—by stressing your belief in the *humanity* of Jesus.

By starting with this balanced Christology, you will be preempting many of their arguments and referring to proof texts they had expected to be showing to you.

Even though you try to limit the discussion to the identity of Christ, Jehovah's Witnesses may well suddenly say something like, "The Trinity is three. The Father and the Son are only two. What about the Holy Spirit?" When they say that, I rejoice. I consider that to be an indication that they have found my presentation about Jesus to be far more difficult to handle than they expected, and they hope to distract me.

If that happens to you, I recommend that you say, "That's a good point, and I'll be happy to look with you at what the Bible says about the Holy Spirit in a later meeting after we have finished discussing the scriptures that deal with the identity of Jesus." If they persist in trying to switch to the Holy Spirit topic prematurely, ask, "Are you agreeing that I am right about who Jesus is?" They are almost certain to say no—emphatically. Then say, "No problem. Why don't we stick to the identity of Jesus for now and save the issue of the Holy Spirit for another day?"

THE HUMANITY OF CHRIST

In their efforts to disprove the deity of Christ, Jehovah's Witnesses are prepared to show you many Bible passages that stress Jesus' human limitations. You can preempt many of these arguments by making clear to them that you believe in a fully human Jesus. Acknowledging the humanity of Jesus and his positional subordination to the Father is not a denial of the doctrine of the Trinity. It is an integral part of that doctrine. Jehovah's Witnesses often do not understand that we believe Jesus is both fully God *and* fully man.

Tell the Witnesses, "I believe in a fully human Jesus." Then you can cite the following scriptures relatively quickly. You won't need to dwell on them because Jehovah's Witnesses have no problem with them. In fact, many are verses they normally bring up themselves:

- When he was young, Jesus was subject to the authority of Mary and Joseph (Luke 2:49).
- Jesus experienced both hunger and thirst (Matthew 4:2; John 4:7; 19:28).
- He needed sleep (Matthew 8:24).
- He was tempted (Matthew 4:1-11; Hebrews 4:15).
- He didn't know who had touched him in a crowd (Mark 5:30-32).
- He didn't know either the day or the hour of his return (Matthew 24:36).
- He worshipped his Father as his God (John 4:21-22).
- He prayed to his Father in heaven (Matthew 26:39).
- He learned obedience through the things he suffered (Hebrews 5:8).
- He temporarily was made lower than the angels and died (Hebrews 2:9).
- He depended on the Father totally for his teachings (John 14:24) and works (John 10:37).
- The Father is greater positionally than Jesus (John 14:28).
- The Father is the head of Christ (1 Corinthians 11:3).
- One day, Jesus will deliver the kingdom to his Father and will be subject to him (1 Corinthians 15:24-28).

The Witnesses will agree with you wholeheartedly because you have stressed the humanity of Jesus and his positional subordination to the Father. As soon as you tell them that you also believe Jesus is God, though, they will see that as a contradiction and the battle will begin. You will want to make this transition in as smooth and respectful a way as possible.

Overcoming the language barrier

In formulating a basic statement of the Christian position, it is critical for you to understand that in the mind of a Jehovah's Witness, "Almighty God" or "Jehovah" means only one thing—the Father. So if you say that you believe Jesus is God, they may think you are claiming that Jesus is his own Father or that when he prayed, he was praying to himself. They will ask who you think ran the universe when Jesus died. Answer, "The Father." Then continue by correcting their misconceptions.

Say, "I understand that you will disagree with this, but what I believe is that within the nature of the one true God, Jehovah, there are three distinct persons—the Father, the Son, and the Holy Spirit. So when you see the name 'Jehovah,' you think one thing—the Father. When I see the name 'Jehovah,' I look to the context to see which person or persons it is referring to."

If they start trying to show you proof texts, tell them that you will be glad to get into those scriptures in a moment but that first you want to make sure you've adequately conveyed to them what you believe. Ask them to state it in their own words.

They may tell you that they don't understand what you mean because it makes no sense to them. How can God be three in one? There are several ways to respond to this. Perhaps the most thought provoking is simply to ask, "Do you think if Jehovah wanted to manifest himself in a human body he would be able to do so?" If they even admit that this is possible, you have made significant progress.

Another way is to make a simple analogy. Acknowledge at the outset that all analogies to God are inadequate because God is unique. However, one comparison is that space consists of length, width, and height. They are different from each other and yet together the three comprise space. Another comparison is that time consists of past, present, and future. They are different from each other and yet together the three comprise time.[2]

Acknowledge that you haven't proved your beliefs yet or even attempted to prove them. All you are doing so far is making sure they understand what you believe.

Now invite them to give you a basic statement of what they believe. If they try to show you proof texts, say, "I would appreciate it if you would hold off on the proof texts for a little bit. First, I want to make sure I understand what it is you believe." Then restate in your own words what they have told you. If necessary, ask questions to clarify what they believe but don't get into arguments as to why they believe it.

Summarizing the importance of the differences

Once you have clarified what the Witnesses believe, say, "We haven't tried to prove our respective positions to each other yet, but already I can see how important this issue is to our relationship with God. If the Watchtower is right, then Jehovah never came to earth but sent someone else to become a man and die for our sins. But if I am right, then God himself, in the person of Jesus Christ, personally came and bore the consequences of his own righteous wrath against sin in order to save us. The Good Shepherd of Psalm 23 himself came to earth and gave his life for the sheep. That's a big difference, isn't it?"

If the Witnesses have previously told you about their worldview of life being a sovereignty struggle between God and the devil, you can add, "Another important difference occurs to me. If the Watchtower's view is correct, Jehovah required Jesus to prove his loyalty as part of a cosmic struggle for sovereignty between God and Satan. In order to pass this test, Jesus had to endure suffering and death in order to prove worthy to be our Savior. But if my understanding is correct, then Jesus always was worthy and he came—not to resolve a sovereignty battle between God and Satan—but to save us from our sins because of his great love for us."

At this point, ask the Witnesses if it would be all right for you to show them from the Bible why you believe Jesus—as well as the Father—is God and get their take on those passages. After that, you'll be glad to have them show you from the Bible why they believe Jesus is a created being.

THE DEITY OF CHRIST

You will use four lines of Bible evidence to show the Witnesses that Jesus is God.

1. Jesus is explicitly called God

Most Christians would cite John 1:1 first as proof of the deity of Christ: "In the beginning was the Word, and the Word was with God, and the Word was God." The problem with using this verse with Jehovah's Witnesses is that the Watchtower's New World Translation renders it "...and the Word was *a god*" (RNWT, emphasis added). Even though this is a mistranslation of the passage, you will make little headway with them because they consider the Watchtower's translation to be the most trustworthy. For this reason, I recommend that you do the unexpected and bypass John 1:1 altogether.

Instead, ask one of the Witnesses to read aloud John 20:27-29: "Then he [Jesus] said to Thomas, 'Put your finger here; see my hands. Reach out your hand and put it into my side. Stop doubting and believe.' Thomas said to him, 'My Lord and my God!' Then Jesus told him, 'Because you have seen me, you have believed; blessed are those who have not seen and yet have believed.'"

This passage gives Jehovah's Witnesses real problems. Most likely they will give you one of three explanations.

- Sometimes they will say that Jesus is "a god" and that only the Father is Almighty God.[3] If that's what they tell you, say, "This passage says Jesus is Thomas' God. Is Jesus your God as well?" They will have to say no. Their God is Jehovah. Ask, "Then you have a different God than Thomas did?"
- Sometimes they will say that Thomas directed the "My Lord" portion of his comment to Jesus and the "my God" portion to Jehovah. If this is what they say, point out that John 20:28 says: "Thomas said *to him*..." (emphasis added).
- Sometimes Witnesses will tell you that Thomas does not really call Jesus his Lord and God. After all, they will say, Thomas had heard Jesus call his Father "the only true God" (John 17:3). What happened was that Thomas was so awe-struck by the appearance of the resurrected Christ that he burst forth with the exclamation, "My Lord and my God!!!" But if Thomas had uttered such an expletive referring to God, wouldn't Jesus have immediately

rebuked him? What would an elder do if they blurted out "My Lord and my God!" at a Kingdom Hall? Point out that not only didn't Jesus rebuke Thomas—he acknowledged his faith.

2. The Old Testament prophesied that Jehovah himself would come to Israel

Zechariah 2:10-12: Jehovah sends Jehovah

Have one of the Witnesses read aloud Zechariah 2:10-12: "'Shout for joy, O daughter of Zion; for I am coming, and I will reside in your midst,' declares Jehovah. 'Many nations will join themselves to Jehovah in that day, and they will become my people; and I will reside in your midst.' And you will have to know that Jehovah of armies has sent me to you. Jehovah will take possession of Judah as his portion on the holy ground, and he will again choose Jerusalem" (RNWT).

The two points you want to get across from this passage are:

- Jehovah himself will reside with the Israelites.
- Jehovah will send Jehovah to the Israelites.

Give them time to ponder this before moving on.

Isaiah 40:3 and Matthew 3:3: Preparing the way for Jehovah

Ask one the Witnesses to read aloud Isaiah 40:3: "A voice of one calling out in the wilderness: 'Clear up the way of Jehovah! Make a straight highway through the desert for our God'" (RNWT).

Ask, "Who does the voice clear the way for?" If they try to argue with you, point out that the passage in their own translation says it is Jehovah.

Ask the other Witness to read aloud Matthew 3:3 regarding John the Baptist: "This, in fact, is the one spoken of through Isaiah the prophet in these words: 'A voice of one calling out in the wilderness: "Prepare the way of Jehovah! Make his roads straight"'" (RNWT).

Ask, "Who was this talking about?" Jesus, of course, but the prophecy was that John would prepare the way for *Jehovah* to come.

They will attempt to explain this by saying that Jesus came as the representative of Jehovah, his Father.[4] To that argument, respond, "Think of how you would react if someone told you that the President of the United States was coming to town and you went to see him. When the time comes, a Secret Service agent pushes through the crowd and announces in a loud voice, 'Ladies and gentlemen, make way for the President of the United States!' Out of the crowd steps—not the President, but his son. The President is still back at the White House. You'd say, 'Hey, this isn't what we were promised!' Would you be satisfied if the Secret Service agent said, 'Sure it is. The son is his father's representative'?"

3. Old Testament "Jehovah alone" passages are applied to Jesus

The only creator

Ask one Jehovah's Witness to read aloud Isaiah 44:24: "This is what Jehovah says, your Repurchaser, who formed you since you were in the womb; 'I am Jehovah, who made everything. I stretched out the heavens by myself, and I spread out the earth. Who was with me?" (RNWT).

Ask, "According to this passage, who assisted Jehovah in stretching out the heavens and spreading out the earth?"

Next ask the other Jehovah's Witness to read aloud John 1:3, which says of Jesus: "Through him all things were made; without him nothing was made that has been made." Make sure they understand the point you are making—the Old Testament says that Jehovah stretched out the heavens and earth *by himself,* but the New Testament says that Jesus did it. Ask, "Based on that, do you see why I believe that Jesus—as well as the Father—is Jehovah?"

Most likely, they will tell you that a rich man might say, "I built that hotel over there." You would understand that he means he paid for it but that workers did the actual construction.

To that, reply, "That's true, but would the rich man ever say, 'I put up the girders and laid all the bricks *by myself*?' Everyone would know that wasn't true. And if he asked, 'Who was with me?' hundreds of construction workers would raise their hands and yell, 'We were!' So the comparison isn't valid, is it?"

Reiterate your point: Either Jehovah did it by himself or he did it through Jesus but not both—unless Jesus as well as the Father is Jehovah. Then there would be no contradiction.

You can also ask one of the Witnesses to read aloud Psalm 102:24-27: "So I said: 'Do not take me away, O my God, in the midst of my days; your years go on through all generations. In the beginning you laid the foundations of the earth, and the heavens are the work of your hands. They will perish, but you remain; they will all wear out like a garment. Like clothing you will change them and they will be discarded. But you remain the same, and your years will never end.'"

Ask the other Witness to read aloud Hebrews 1:10-12, which Hebrews 1:8 says was the Father speaking of the Son, "He also says, 'In the beginning, O Lord, you laid the foundations of the earth, and the heavens are the work of your hands. They will perish, but you remain; they will all wear out like a garment. You will roll them up like a robe; like a garment they will be changed. But you remain the same, and your years will never end.'"

They will tell you once again that Jehovah created through Jesus. Say, "In Psalm 102, it is *God* who laid the foundations of the earth and the heavens are the work of *his* hands. *He* is the one who is the same forever and whose years never end. But in Hebrews 1, this identical passage is quoted as being the Father's statement about *Jesus*. So it seems to me that the only way these can both be correct is if Jesus as well as the Father is the creator, Jehovah God."

The only one worthy of God's glory

Ask one Jehovah's Witness to read aloud Isaiah 42:8: "I am Jehovah. That is my name; I give my glory to no one else, nor my praise to graven images" (RNWT).

Ask the other Witness to read aloud John 17:5, where Jesus says, "And now, Father, glorify me in your presence with the glory I had with you before the world began." Make sure they understand your point. Jehovah does not give his glory to anyone else, yet Jesus shares his Father's heavenly glory.

Ask, "Do you see why this leads me to conclude that Jesus—as well as the Father—is Jehovah?"

I once posed that question to a Jehovah's Witness and he answered yes! He told me later that after they left our house his partner upbraided him because of his answer. He said, "I told him, 'Dave didn't ask me if I agreed with him. He asked if I could see why he drew that conclusion from that passage, and I do understand.'" That moment was an important step in that man's journey out of the Watchtower to Christ.

The ultimate judge

Ask one Jehovah's Witness to read aloud Psalm 50:6: "And the heavens proclaim his righteousness, for God himself is judge."

Ask the other Witness to read aloud John 5:22-23: "Moreover, the Father judges no one, but has entrusted all judgment to the Son, that all may honor the Son just as they honor the Father. He who does not honor the Son does not honor the Father, who sent him."

Often, Witnesses will tell you that Jehovah is the ultimate judge but that he has delegated to Jesus the authority to pronounce the judgments. If that is what they tell you, make sure they understand your point. Psalm 50 says specifically that God *himself* is Judge. Yet John 5 states that the Father judges no one. He has entrusted all judging to the Son so that all may honor the Son just as they honor the Father.

Ask, "Do you see why from this I believe that Jesus as well as the Father is God and should be given the same honor?"

You can also ask, "If you prayed John 5:23 aloud at the Kingdom Hall and said, `Jehovah, we honor you and we honor your son, Jesus Christ, just as we honor you,' how would your fellow Witnesses react?"

The only one who knows men's hearts

Ask one of the Witnesses to read aloud the part of Solomon's prayer to Jehovah contained in 1 Kings 8:39: "...then hear from heaven, your dwelling place. Forgive and act; deal with each man according to all he does, since you know his heart (for you alone know the hearts of all men)."

Ask the other Witness to read aloud Jesus' warning in Revelation 2:23: "I will strike her children dead. Then all the churches will know that I am he who searches hearts and minds, and I will repay each of you according to your deeds." Point out that in Revelation 2:23, Jesus reveals that he is the one who knows what 1 Kings 8:39 says Jehovah alone knows.

The only spiritual rock

Ask one Jehovah's Witness to read aloud Isaiah 44:8, where Jehovah says: "Do not tremble, do not be afraid. Did I not proclaim this and foretell it long ago? You are my witnesses. Is there any God besides me? No, there is no other Rock; I know not one."

Ask the other Witness to read aloud 1 Corinthians 10:4: "...for they drank from the spiritual rock that accompanied them, and that rock was Christ." Your point is that in Isaiah 44:8, Jehovah knows of no other spiritual rock but himself. Yet, 1 Corinthians 10:4 says the spiritual rock was Christ.

4. Revelation identifies both Jehovah and Jesus as the Alpha and Omega, the first and the last, and the one who is coming

Have one Jehovah's Witness read aloud Revelation 22:12-13: "'Look! I am coming quickly, and the reward I give is with me, to repay each one according to his work. I am the Alpha and the Omega, the first and the last, the beginning and the end" (RNWT).

Say, "The Alpha and the Omega, the first and the last, the beginning and the end says that he is coming quickly. Who is this?" Because Revelation 1:8 identifies the Alpha and Omega as Almighty God, Jehovah's Witnesses will tell you that this is Jehovah.[5]

Now have them read aloud Revelation 22:20 to see who the speaker is. "The one who bears witness of these things says, 'Yes, I am coming quickly.' Amen! Come, Lord Jesus" (RNWT).

Ask, "Doesn't this show that *Jesus* is the Alpha and Omega, the first and the last, the beginning and the end?"

The Witnesses will tell you that the speakers change in Revelation 22. The first speaker is Jehovah, but in verse 16 the speaker switches to Jesus. Point out that the speaker in Revelation 22:12-13 says he is coming quickly. Yet in their own translation, John says in verse 20 that there is *one* who is speaking and coming quickly, and that is Jesus.

Ask, "Is the Father coming or is Jesus?" If they say that both are coming, ask them when the Father is coming to the earth.

Next draw their attention to the phrase "the first and the last." That is an Old Testament title of Jehovah God. Have one of the Witnesses read aloud Isaiah 44:6: "This is what Jehovah has said, the King of Israel and his Repurchaser, Jehovah of armies, 'I am the first and I am the last. There is no God but me" (RNWT).

But who bears the title "the first and the last" in Revelation? Have one of the Witnesses read aloud Revelation 1:17-18: "When I saw him, I fell as dead at his feet. And he laid his right hand on me and said: "Do not be afraid. I am the First and the Last, and the living one, and I became dead, but look! I am living forever and ever, and I have the keys of death and of the Grave" (RNWT). Clearly, this is Jesus. So Jesus is the first and the last. But Jehovah is the first and the last.

Ask, "Do you see from this why I believe that Jesus as well as the Father is Jehovah God?"

Witnesses may try to get around this in two ways. First, they may tell you that Jesus is "the first and the last" in a different sense. If so, point out that Revelation uses the same title for both and makes no such distinction. Second, in order to try to argue that both the Father and Jesus can be "the first and the last," they may point out that Jesus is called an "apostle" in Hebrews 3:1 but that doesn't mean he was the only apostle or that the other apostles were equal in rank to him.[6] If they give you that answer, say, "Many people can be apostles, but how can you have two firsts and two lasts?"

If you get this far in your presentation, you will have done very well! You can summarize your points for the Witnesses, or, even better, see if you can get *them* to summarize the points. Then you can offer them the opportunity to present their case.

ANSWERING WATCHTOWER PROOF TEXTS

One advantage you have in dealing with Jehovah's Witnesses is that they will tell you what the Watchtower has trained them to say. Because of this, the points they will make and the proof texts they will use to support them are quite predictable, so you will be able to prepare yourself to meet them. In my opinion, what appears below are the Watchtower's best arguments and proof texts against the deity of Christ as well as the most effective ways to respond to them.

Jehovah is one Jehovah

Jehovah's Witnesses often quote both Deuteronomy 6:4 and Mark 12:29 to the effect that "Jehovah our God is one Jehovah" (RNWT). Based on this, they argue that God cannot be a Trinity.

In reply to this argument, point out that Trinitarians do not claim that there are three Gods. We agree that there is only one God. However, just as length, width, and height comprise one space—not three—so the Father, Son, and Holy Spirit constitute one God, not three.

The Father is the only true God

Jehovah's Witnesses are quick to point out that in John 17:3 Jesus called his Father "the only true God." The claim they are making is that Jesus himself stated that only the Father is the Almighty God, Jehovah. There are several good responses you can make to that argument:

- Have one of the Witnesses read aloud Jude 4: "My reason is that certain men have slipped in among you who were long ago appointed to this judgment by the Scriptures; they are ungodly men who turn the undeserved kindness of our God into an excuse for brazen conduct and who prove false to our only owner and Lord, Jesus Christ" (RNWT). Ask, "By calling Jesus 'our only owner and Lord' is the scripture saying that the Father is *not* our owner and Lord? That's the same reasoning you are using to say that Jesus' calling the Father 'the only true God' proves that Jesus can't be the true God as well.
- You can also ask, "If Jesus meant to exclude himself when he called the Father 'the only true God,' then wouldn't that make Jesus a false god?"
- If they try to convince you that—as the Watchtower translation renders John 1:1—Jesus is "a god," (RNWT) the best reply is simply to ask, "Is Jesus a true god or a false god?"[7]

- In John 20:28, Thomas called Jesus, "My Lord and my God." Literally, "the Lord of me and the God of me." If Jesus meant to exclude himself as being "the true God," why didn't he rebuke Thomas for his statement?

Jesus has a God

John 20:17 reads as follows: "Jesus said [to Mary Magdalene], "Do not hold on to me, for I have not yet returned to the Father. Go instead to my brothers and tell them, 'I am returning to my Father and your Father, to my God and your God.'"

Their argument is that Jesus cannot be God because he has a God—Jehovah. The answer you can give them is that, of course, as a man Jesus did have his Father as his God. There is no contradiction.

Jehovah's Witnesses will sometimes ask, "If Jesus is God, did he pray to himself?" The answer is no, that as a man, he prayed to his Father in heaven. Make clear that the Trinity doctrine does *not* claim that Jesus and the Father are the same *person*.

Christ is subordinate to the Father

It's likely the Witnesses will cite you many of the subordination passages I covered when discussing the humanity of Christ. Remind them that you cited those very passages to them. You agree that Jesus is fully human. Being a man, Jesus humbles himself and subordinates himself to his Father. Even in the resurrection, Christ is still a man and always will be. The Watchtower denies this, claiming that he is now Michael the archangel. However, you can point out the Bible says that as the mediator of the new covenant, he is a man (1 Timothy 2:5), and he will judge the world as a man (Acts 17:31).

Philippians 2:6: "No consideration to a seizure"

In line with its teachings about Christ, the Watchtower has a strange rendering of Philippians 2:6: "who, although he was existing in God's form, gave no consideration to a *seizure*, namely, that he should be equal to God" (RNWT, emphasis added). By using the word "seizure," the Watchtower makes it seem as if Christ would be a sinful rebel if he, like Satan, claimed equality with God.

To counter this you can say, "You don't have to seize something you already have. Christ already existed in God's form. He could have chosen to remain in heaven where he was positionally equal to his Father. Although he never gave up his divine identity, he chose additionally to become a man, come to earth, and as a man subject himself to the will of the Father. In other words, he voluntarily lowered his position without changing his identity."

Christ had a beginning

Revelation 3:14: Beginning of the creation by God

The Watchtower argues that Christ had a beginning and therefore cannot be God. They cite Revelation 3:14: "...These are the things that the Amen says, the faithful and true witness, the beginning of the creation by God..." (RNWT).

The Christian answer is that Christ is the "beginning" of the creation by God in that he is the one who began the creation. You can point out that this meaning of "beginning" completely accords with Revelation 21:6, where God calls himself "the beginning and the end" (RNWT). It doesn't mean that he had a beginning. It means that he is the one who began the creation by bringing it into existence.

Colossians 1:15: Firstborn of all creation

Jehovah's Witnesses often cite Colossians 1:15, which calls Christ "the firstborn of all creation" (RNWT). Their argument is that he was the first thing Jehovah created.

Point out that in the Bible the word "firstborn" often refers to preeminence, not order of creation. Show them that King David was the youngest of Jesse's eight sons, so he was the last son born to his father, not the first (1 Samuel 17:12-14). Nevertheless, in Psalm 89:27, Jehovah says that he "will also appoint him [David] my firstborn, the most exalted of the kings of the earth." Here, "firstborn" obviously means "preeminent," not "first one created." Likewise, point out that Ephraim was Joseph's second son (Genesis 41:52), yet in Jeremiah 31:9, Jehovah says, "I am Israel's father, and Ephraim is my firstborn son."

If we substitute for "firstborn" the word "preeminent" in Colossians 1:15-17, we find that it fits the context perfectly: "He is the image of the invisible God, [preeminent] over (of: RNWT) all creation; For by him all things were created in heaven and on earth, visible and invisible, whether thrones or powers or rulers or authorities; all things were created by him and for him. He is before all things, and in him all things hold together."

You need to be aware that in the New World Translation (RNWT), the Watchtower has inserted "other" four times in this passage before the word "things" in order to make it appear that Christ was one of the things created. However, the word "other" appears nowhere in the original Greek text. You can point this out to Jehovah's Witnesses using their own *Kingdom Interlinear Translation*, which gives the Greek interlined with the English translation.

Proverbs 8:22-24: Jehovah produced me

The Watchtower notes that Christ is called "the power of God and the wisdom of God" (1 Corinthians 1:24). They try to show that this proves that Christ was a created being by connecting this passage with Proverbs 8:22-24 in which "wisdom" says: "Jehovah produced me as the beginning of his way, the earliest of his achievements of long ago. From ancient times I was installed, from the start, from times earlier than the earth. When there were no deep waters, I was brought forth, when there were no springs overflowing with water" (RNWT).

The best response to this is to ask, "Doesn't 1 Corinthians 1:24 actually show that Jesus is God? How can a mere creature be the power and wisdom of God? Besides, is wisdom something God created or is it a part of him? Was there ever a time when God was without his power and wisdom?"

No man has seen God

When you are discussing John 1, Jehovah's Witnesses will often cite John 1:18: "No man has seen God at any time; the only-begotten god who is at the Father's side is the one who has explained Him" (RNWT).

With regard to the term "only-begotten," you can note that the Greek word *monogenes* means "unique one," not "created."[8]

Jehovah's Witnesses often cite the part of John 1:18 that says, "No man has seen God at any time" (RNWT) in order to make the following argument:

1. No man has seen God at any time.
2. Many men have seen Jesus Christ.
3. Therefore, Jesus Christ cannot be God.

If they make this argument to you, show them three Old Testament passages where people did see God—Exodus 24:9-10, Exodus 33:20-23, and Isaiah 6:1. Have them read those passages aloud and ask for their explanation. The common factor of these passages is that although they saw some manifestation of God, they did not see him in his entirety, that is, the entire essence of his being. It is true that no human has seen God's entire essence, but they have seen Jesus Christ, and he reveals to us what the Father is like (John 14:9). So in no way does John 1:18 disprove the deity of Christ.

The Bible says there are many gods

In support of its contention that John 1:1 should be translated "and the Word was a god" (RNWT), the Watchtower cites a number of Bible passages that refer to gods. Some of those include the following:

Isaiah 9:6

Isaiah 9:6: "For to us a child is born, to us a son is given, and the government will be on his shoulders. And he will be called Wonderful Counselor, Mighty God, Everlasting Father, Prince of Peace." Their point is that here Jesus is called "mighty," not "Almighty."

However, point out that in Isaiah 10:20-21, Jehovah is also identified as "the Mighty God." As we saw earlier in our examination of Revelation, the Alpha and Omega is the Almighty, and the Alpha and Omega is identified as Jesus.

Psalm 82:1 and John 10:35-36

Psalm 82:1 says, "God presides in the great assembly; he gives judgment among the 'gods'..." Referring to this passage, Jesus said in John 10:35-36, "If he called them 'gods,' to whom the word of God came—and the Scripture cannot be broken—what about the one whom the Father set apart as his very own and sent into the world? Why then do you accuse me of blasphemy because I said, 'I am God's Son'?"

The Watchtower uses these verses to argue that there are many "gods," so it is proper to call Jesus "a god." However, you should point out that these "gods" were false gods against whom God brought judgment. In other words, those Israelite judges were called "gods" as a term of derision. Jesus' point was that during their history the Israelites were quick to embrace false gods but then called him a blasphemer because he rightly called himself the Son of God.

In response to the Watchtower's contention that the Bible recognizes the existence of many gods, point out that 1 Corinthians 8:5-6 distinguishes God the Father and Christ from all these false gods and false lords: "For even though there are so-called gods, whether in heaven or on earth, just as there are many 'gods' and many 'lords,' there is actually to us one God, the Father, from whom all things are and we for him; and there is one Lord, Jesus Christ, through whom all things are and we through him" (RNWT).

By saying "there is actually to us one God, the Father..." this passage is not excluding Christ from being God any more than it is excluding the Father from being Lord when it says "there is one Lord, Jesus Christ..." The passage isn't contrasting the Father and Christ. It is putting the Father and Christ together and distinguishing them from all the other so-called gods and so-called lords.

You can also point out that in Isaiah 43:10, the verse from which Jehovah's Witnesses take their name, Jehovah specifically indicates that neither Jesus nor anyone else is a secondary "god": "...I am he. Before me no god was formed, nor will there be one after me."

Likewise, Isaiah 45:5-6 says: "I am Jehovah, and there is no one else. There is no God except me. I will strengthen you, although you did not know me, In order that people may know from the rising of the sun to its setting that there is none besides me. I am Jehovah, and there is no one else" (RNWT).

Your main point in this part of the discussion is that these verses make clear that Jehovah is the only true God, and that there are a multitude of false gods (idols and other things that men serve instead of Jehovah). There is no other choice. If Jesus is in any sense God, which the Scriptures are clear that he is, then he is either Jehovah God or he is a false god.

CONCLUSION

Although you will try to persuade Jehovah's Witnesses that the Watchtower is wrong on this important subject, it often takes a great deal of time for them to get past the Watchtower indoctrination. You will have accomplished a lot if you have even caused them to give serious consideration to what you have presented.

If you have done a good job, you may well have shaken the Witnesses' confidence in their position, whether they acknowledge it or not. Keep praying for them and keep the door open for further conversations.

Chapter 14:
The Holy Spirit Is God
Approach

"Then Peter said, 'Ananias, how is it that Satan has so filled your heart that you have lied to the Holy Spirit and have kept for yourself some of the money you received for the land? Didn't it belong to you before it was sold? And after it was sold, wasn't the money at your disposal? What made you think of doing such a thing? You have not lied to men but to God'" (Acts 5:3-4).

The objective of this approach is to show Jehovah's Witnesses that the Holy Spirit is both a person and God himself, not an impersonal, "active force" that emanates from God.

The Holy Spirit points people to Christ rather than to himself. However, the nature and identity of the Holy Spirit often comes up when you are discussing who Jesus is, and you need to be prepared to deal with it. If you are defending the doctrine of the Trinity, you will need to be able to present a positive case that the Holy Spirit is a person—one who speaks, thinks, decides, and has emotions. You will also need to be able to show the biblical evidence that the Holy Spirit is truly God, and to be able to answer Watchtower proof texts and objections.

A word of caution. Don't get sidetracked into discussing issues of tongues or miracles or healing with Jehovah's Witnesses. Focus instead on the basics of the identity of the Holy Spirit.

THE HOLY SPIRIT IS A PERSON

The Witnesses will expect you to begin by proclaiming your belief that the Holy Spirit is the third person of the Trinity. Instead, you will come at the subject a different way—by asking them first to explain and defend what the Watchtower teaches about the nature of Satan. You will then use their own arguments to show them that the Holy Spirit is a person, not an impersonal force.

Begin by saying, "Before we talk about the Holy Spirit, I'd like you to clarify what you believe about Satan. Do you believe that Satan is an angelic spirit person or is 'Satan' just the Bible's way of referring to an evil force in the universe, sort of like 'the dark side of the Force' in Star Wars?"

They will tell you that Satan is a real spirit person, a created angel who rebelled against Jehovah. Ask them how they know that. Keep drawing them out on this until they show you that Satan did what persons do—he carried on a conversation with Jesus, he planned and carried out supernatural attacks on Job and his family, and the like. The more details they give you, the better.

Then say, "That's very similar to my reasons for believing that the Holy Spirit is a person rather than a force. I would like to show you some Bible verses about the Holy Spirit and get your take on them." Because the Watchtower tells Jehovah's Witnesses so often that the Holy Spirit is an impersonal force, I have found that it is often difficult to get them to focus on what the Bible really says about this important subject. Make sure they actually read the Scripture passages you cite. You may at times want to ask them to summarize the point you are trying to make. Anything you can do to get them to think—instead of merely parroting the Watchtower responses—will be helpful.

The Holy Spirit speaks directly

Acts 13:2-4: To the disciples at Antioch

Once you get agreement to proceed, ask one of the Witnesses to read aloud Acts 13:2-4: "While they were worshiping the Lord and fasting, the Holy Spirit said, 'Set apart for me Barnabas and Saul for the work to which I have called them.' So after they had fasted and prayed, they placed their hands on them and sent them off. The two of them, sent on their way by the Holy Spirit, went down to Seleucia and sailed from there to Cyprus."

Draw the Witnesses' attention to the fact that the Holy Spirit addressed them using first person singular pronouns: "set apart for *me*... *I* have called them." Make sure they understand why you consider that significant.

Acts 10:19-20: To Peter in Joppa

In Acts 10:19-20, the Holy Spirit spoke to Peter and gave him specific instructions. Ask one of the Witnesses to read those verses aloud: "While Peter was still thinking about the vision, the Spirit said to him, "Simon, three men are looking for you. So get up and go downstairs. Do not hesitate to go with them, for I have sent them.""

Once again, emphasize to the Witnesses that the Holy Spirit spoke using the first person pronoun: "*I* have sent them..."

Acts 8:29: To Philip

Ask one of the Witnesses to read aloud Acts 8:29: "The Spirit told Philip, 'Go to that chariot and stay near it.'" Point out that although no first person pronouns are used, this is another example of the Holy Spirit directly addressing and giving instruction to a Christian.

Ask, "Can you see why this leads me to conclude that the Holy Spirit is a person, not just a force?"

Acts 21:11: To Paul through Agabus

Ask one of the Witnesses to read aloud Acts 21:11, which refers to the prophet Agabus: "Coming over to us, he took Paul's belt, tied his own hands and feet with it and said, 'The Holy Spirit says, "In this way the Jews of Jerusalem will bind the owner of this belt and will hand him over to the Gentiles."'"

Say, "Agabus quotes directly specific prophetic words spoken to him by the Holy Spirit. Do you see why I believe this shows the Holy Spirit is a person?"

The Watchtower explanation

The Watchtower's explanation for instances in which the Holy Spirit is quoted directly is that it was really Jehovah speaking through human beings, using "holy spirit" like we might use radio waves:

While some texts refer to the spirit as 'witnessing,' 'speaking,' or 'saying' things, other texts make clear that it spoke through persons, having no personal voice of its own. [Citations omitted] It may thus be compared to radio waves that can transmit a message from a person speaking into a microphone and cause his voice to be heard by persons a distance away, in effect, 'speaking' the message by a radio loudspeaker. God, by his spirit, transmits his messages and communicates his will to the minds and hearts of his servants on earth, who, in turn, may convey that message to yet others.[1]

There are two ways to refute this explanation.

First, you can point out that in the Acts 13 statement to the disciples at Antioch, there is no indication that there was a human prophet through whom the Holy Spirit spoke. In the Acts 8 and Acts 10 passages, there was no other person present through whom the Holy Spirit could have spoken. In Acts 21, although Agabus relayed the message, he quoted the Holy Spirit directly as being the one who gave him the words to speak.

Second, emphasize that no one would say, "The radio transmitter said to me..." We would attribute the statements to the person at the other end. Similarly, point out that in narrative Bible passages the speaker is quoted directly. For example, Genesis 4:6 says, "Then Jehovah said to Cain, 'Why are you so angry and dejected?'" (RNWT). So when a passage says, "The Holy Spirit said..." shouldn't we assume that the Holy Spirit is a person and that he is the one who is being quoted?

To show Jehovah's Witnesses the absurdity of the Watchtower argument, put it in modern terms. Imagine that the captain of a ship uses the intercom system to give the navigator an order. Would the navigator tell his aides, "The ship's intercom-transmitter-and-receiver-system just said to me, 'Head for Cyprus immediately and await further instructions'?" Of course not! He would simply say, "The captain just ordered me to..." Similarly, if the Holy Spirit were like an impersonal radio wave, no prophet would say, "The Holy Spirit said..." He would simply say, "Jehovah said..."

To drive home this point, ask the Witnesses to read aloud Acts 16:6-7: "Moreover, they traveled through Phrygia and the country of Galatia, because they were forbidden by the holy spirit to speak the word in the province of Asia. Further, when getting down to Mysia they made efforts to go into Bithynia, but the spirit of Jesus did not permit them" (RNWT).

Ask, "Would anyone ever say, 'They were forbidden by the transmitter-and-receiver system to go to Asia. Further, when getting down to Mysia they made efforts to go into Bithynia, but the transmitter-and-receiver system did not permit them'?"

The Holy Spirit displays many other attributes of personality

The Holy Spirit is a helper who will hear, speak, prophesy, and glorify Christ

Ask one of the Witnesses to read aloud John 16:7-14:

Nevertheless, I am telling you the truth, it is for your benefit that I am going away. For if I do not go away, the helper will not come to you; but if I do go I will send *him* to you. And when that one comes, *he* will give the world convincing evidence concerning sin and concerning righteousness and concerning judgment: first concerning sin, because they are not exercising faith in me; then concerning righteousness, because I am going to the Father and you will see me no longer; then concerning judgment, because the ruler of this world has been judged. I still have many things to say to you, but you are not able to bear them now. However, when that one comes, the spirit of the truth, *he* will guide you into all the truth, for *he* will not speak of *his* own initiative, but what *he* hears *he* will speak, and *he* will declare to you the things to come. That one will glorify me, because *he* will receive from what is mine and will declare it to you (RNWT, emphasis added).

Notice that here, even in the Watchtower translation, the Holy Spirit is referred to nine times with masculine pronouns. The Watchtower tries to explain this away through a footnote which says, "Jesus used 'the helper' (which has the masculine gender in Greek) as a personification of the holy spirit, an impersonal force, which has the neuter gender in Greek."

But does this make sense? Jesus said that the Holy Spirit gives evidence, guides people into truth, hears, speaks, declares things to come, glorifies Christ, and both receives from what is Christ's and declares it to his followers. These are all acts that only a person can do.

The Holy Spirit has a mind

Ask one of the Witnesses to read aloud 1 Corinthians 2:10-11: "For it is to us God has revealed them through his spirit, for the spirit searches into all things, even the deep things of God. For who among men knows the things of a man except the man's spirit within him? So, too, no one has come to know the things of God except the spirit of God" (RNWT).

Ask, "How can an impersonal force search into anything? How can an impersonal force know the things of God? In fact, how can an impersonal force know anything at all?"

The Holy Spirit has a will

Choosing spiritual gifts. In discussing spiritual gifts, 1 Corinthians 12:11 states: "But all these operations are performed by the very same spirit, distributing to each one respectively *just as it wills*" (RNWT, emphasis added).

Despite the fact that the Watchtower's version refers to the Holy Spirit as "it," ask, "How can an impersonal force choose who gets what spiritual gifts? How can an impersonal force have a will? If the Watchtower view of the Holy Spirit is right, shouldn't that verse say that the spirit distributes to each one respectively just as Jehovah wills?"

Establishing requirements. In Acts 15:28-29, the apostles wrote to the believers at Antioch, "It seemed good to the Holy Spirit and to us not to burden you with anything beyond the following requirements: You are to abstain from food sacrificed to idols, from blood, from the meat of strangled animals and from sexual immorality. You will do well to avoid these things. Farewell."

Ask, "How can a course of action seem good to an impersonal force?"

Interceding with the Father. Ask one of the Witnesses to read aloud Romans 8:26: "In like manner, the spirit also joins in with help for our weakness; for the problem is that we do not know what we should pray for as we need to, but the spirit itself pleads for us with unuttered groanings" (RNWT).

Once again, the Watchtower version calls the Holy Spirit "it." Rather than arguing with them over this, say: "This is not the situation of the Father using a force to communicate with us. Here, the Holy Spirit is pleading with the Father for us. How can an impersonal force plead and groan?"

If the Witnesses ask why the Holy Spirit would have to plead with the Father if the Holy Spirit is God, point out that you do not believe that the Holy Spirit is the same person as the Father. They communicate and act in concert.

The Holy Spirit experiences emotions

Grief. Ask one of the Witnesses to read aloud Ephesians 4:30: "And do not grieve the Holy Spirit of God, with whom you were sealed for the day of redemption."

Ask, "How can an impersonal force experience grief?" If the Witnesses counter by asking how you can been sealed with a person, point out that the Holy Spirit can indwell a person. After all, Satan is a spirit person, not a force, and he is said to have entered Judas Iscariot (John 13:27).

Outrage. Ask one of the Witnesses to read aloud Hebrews 10:29: "How much greater punishment do you think a person will deserve who has trampled on the Son of God and who has esteemed as of ordinary value the blood of the covenant by which he was sanctified, and who has outraged the spirit of undeserved kindness with contempt?" (RNWT).

Ask, "How can an impersonal force be outraged?"

Love. Ask one of the Witnesses to read aloud Romans 15:30: "I urge you, brothers, by our Lord Jesus Christ and by the love of the Spirit, to join me in my struggle by praying to God for me."

Ask, "How can an impersonal force love someone?"

ANSWERING WATCHTOWER ARGUMENTS AGAINST THE PERSONALITY OF THE HOLY SPIRIT

Argument #1: "Spirit" means "active force"

The Watchtower refers to the Holy Spirit as "Jehovah's active force" so often that Jehovah's Witnesses simply accept it as true. Point out that angels are called "spirits" (Hebrews 1:14) but they have personality. The mere use of the term "spirit," therefore, does not disprove personality.

Argument #2: The Holy Spirit's supposed personality is only personification

The Watchtower's explanation of the Holy Spirit being called a "helper," issuing commands, and exhibiting other attributes of mind, will, and emotions, is that the Bible is merely using a literary device called personification.[2] The Witnesses may use Proverbs 8 as an example. There, "wisdom" is directly quoted at length as making statements and using first person pronouns.

You can come back to the topic of Satan to further expand on this point. Ask the Witnesses, "What would you say to someone who made the personification argument about Satan, claiming that he isn't really a person, that when Bible verses describe his thoughts and actions, that's just a literary device personifying an evil, impersonal force?"

In demonstrating that Satan is a person, not a mere personification of evil, the Watchtower has said, "Can an unintelligent 'force' carry on a conversation with a person? Also, the Bible calls Satan a manslayer, a liar, a father (in a spiritual sense) and a ruler... Only an intelligent person could fit all those descriptions... Every quality, every action, which can indicate personality, is attributed to him in language which cannot be explained away."[3]

Whether they quote that article or merely give you the basic reasoning behind it, you can compare what the Bible says about Satan with what it says about the Holy Spirit.

- Satan is a murderer (John 8:44); the Holy Spirit gives life (Romans 8:2, 11).
- Satan is a liar (John 8:44); the Holy Spirit is the Spirit of truth (John 14:17; 15:26; 16:13).

- Satan is a spiritual father of the wicked (John 8:44); Christians are born of the Holy Spirit (John 3:5-8; Galatians 4:29).
- Satan is a ruler (Ephesians 6:12); the Holy Spirit issues commands to Christians (Acts 8:29).

Point out that personification is a common literary device in poetry or in wisdom literature such as the book of Proverbs. In contrast, the book of Acts is written as historical narrative. There, an isolated occurrence of a phrase like "the Holy Spirit said" might be taken as personification, but multiple instances of the Holy Spirit not just "speaking," but being quoted verbatim in extended conversation, cannot be explained away in such a fashion.

We agree with the Witnesses that Satan is a person. Using the identical criteria and reasoning, the Holy Spirit must also be a person.

Argument #3: The Holy Spirit's actions are inconsistent with personality

Filling, baptizing, anointing

The Watchtower states: "A comparison of Bible texts that refer to the holy spirit shows that it is spoken of as 'filling' people; they can be 'baptized' with it; and they can be 'anointed' with it. (Luke 1:41; Matt. 3:11; Acts 10:38) None of these expressions would be appropriate if the holy spirit were a person."[4]

In response, ask them to read aloud Ephesians 1:23, which says that Christ, who is clearly a person, "fills everything in every way." Show them also Luke 22:3, which tells us, "Then Satan entered Judas, called Iscariot, one of the Twelve." Yet Satan is a person.

Being poured out

Referring to Acts 2:4, the Watchtower asks in a study question, "How does the pouring out of holy spirit on Jesus' followers prove that it is not a person?"[5]

In response, show them Philippians 2:17 and 2 Timothy 4:6, where Paul says that he is "being poured out like a drink offering." Since Paul was a person who could be said to be poured out, the fact that the Holy Spirit is poured out does not disprove his personality. Similarly, the Messianic Psalm 22:14 says, "I am poured out like water," but this does not make the Messiah an impersonal force.[6]

Argument #4: The Holy Spirit doesn't have a personal name

The Watchtower says, "The Holy Scriptures tell us the personal name of the Father—Jehovah. They inform us that the Son is Jesus Christ. But nowhere in the Scriptures is a *personal* name applied to the holy spirit"[7] (emphasis original).

In response, ask them to read aloud 2 Corinthians 3:17-18 in the Watchtower's own translation: "Now Jehovah is the Spirit, and where the spirit of Jehovah is, there is freedom. And all of us, while we with unveiled faces reflect like mirrors the glory of Jehovah, are transformed into the same image from one degree of glory into another, exactly as it is done by Jehovah the Spirit" (RNWT).

Ask, "Since Jehovah is the Spirit and since Jehovah is the most holy Spirit in existence, do you see why I believe that the Holy Spirit—as well as the Father—is Jehovah?"

Even if the Witnesses don't concede that this passage calls the Holy Spirit "Jehovah," absence of a specific name in the Bible wouldn't disprove personality. Demons are persons—not impersonal forces—yet they are not usually named in the Bible. Instead, they are identified by their natures, such as unclean or evil spirits (Matthew 10:1). Likewise, the designation "Holy Spirit" is descriptive of his character.[8]

Also, direct them to Matthew 28:19, where Jesus commands us to baptize "in the name of the Father and of the Son and of the Holy Spirit." Ask, "What name would all three share but 'Jehovah'?"

The Witnesses may counter with the following Watchtower response: "A 'name' can mean something other than a personal name. When, in English, we say, 'in the name of the law,' or 'in the name of common sense,' we have no reference to a person as such. By 'name' in these expressions we mean 'what the law stands for or its authority' and 'what common sense represents or calls for.'"[9]

In reply, point out that Matthew 28:19 has a parallel structure. The Father and Son are clearly persons. Does it make sense to say "in the name of the Father and of the Son and of an impersonal, active force"?

Argument #5: The Holy Spirit is mentioned alongside impersonal things

The Watchtower states, "Further evidence against the idea of personality as regards the holy spirit is the way it is used in association with other impersonal things, such as water and fire (Mt 3:11; Mr 1:8)... So, too, persons are spoken of as being 'filled' with it along with such qualities as wisdom and faith (Ac 6:3, 5; 11:24) or joy (Ac 13:52); and holy spirit is inserted, or sandwiched in, with a number of such qualities at 2 Corinthians 6:6. It is most unlikely that such expressions would be made if the holy spirit were a divine person."[10]

What the Watchtower is referring to is that in 2 Corinthians 6:6-7 Paul says that he shows himself a minister of God "in purity, understanding, patience and kindness; in the Holy Spirit and in sincere love; in truthful speech and in the power of God; with weapons of righteousness in the right hand and in the left."

In response, note that Jesus metaphorically called himself "bread" (John 6:48, RNWT) and a "door" (John 10:9, RNWT). This does not prove that Jesus was an impersonal object.[11] With regard to each of the qualities referred to in 2 Corinthians 6:6, Homer Duncan notes that "the Holy Spirit is included in this list to show that it is the virtue of His influence which produces these graces and other gifts."[12]

Argument #6: The Greek definite article is not used with regard to the Holy Spirit

The Watchtower says, "...in a large number of cases the expression 'holy spirit' appears in the original Greek without the [definite] article, thus indicating its lack of personality."[13]

I don't recommend that you delve into Greek articles unless you know the language, but if the Witnesses insist on discussing it, be aware that Duncan notes that there are at least 73 times in the Greek New Testament where the definite article *is* used with reference to the Holy Spirit.[14] One of those places is in Acts 13:2-4 where the Holy Spirit speaks using first person pronouns.

He goes on to note that the Greek word for "Jesus" occurs 909 times in the New Testament, 359 times without the definite article. He remarks, "Thus, if we follow the arguments presented by the [Watchtower] writers concerning the use of the article with the Holy Spirit, we could also prove that Jesus is not a person!"[15]

Argument #7: The Greek word and pronoun for "spirit" are neuter in gender

The Watchtower sometimes argues that the Holy Spirit must be an "it" because the Greek word for "spirit" and the related pronouns are neuter in gender.

However, in Greek, the gender of a noun or pronoun is a matter of grammar; it has nothing to do with personhood or actual gender. For example, the word translated "girl" in Mark 5:41-42 is a neuter Greek word, *korasion*. Likewise, the fact that the Greek word for "spirit" is neuter does not make a spirit an "it." The Watchtower agrees, for example, that demonic spirits are persons, and the Bible even says that "God is a Spirit" (John 4:24, RNWT).

Argument #8: The Holy Spirit is not seen in visions of heaven

The Watchtower says, "Acts 7:55, 56 reports that Stephen was given a vision of heaven in which he saw 'Jesus standing at God's right hand.' But he made no mention of seeing the holy spirit. (See also Revelation 7:10; 22:1, 3.)"[16]

You can reply that Stephen didn't say he saw angels either. Does that mean that there are no angels in heaven or that angels are impersonal forces? Of course not. Given that the point he was emphasizing was Jesus' exalted position in heaven, Stephen's failure to make specific mention of the Holy Spirit is hardly proof that the Holy Spirit is only an impersonal force.

THE HOLY SPIRIT IS GOD

Contrary to the Watchtower's teaching, the Bible clearly says that the Holy Spirit is God himself.

The Holy Spirit is called God

Ask one of the Witnesses to read aloud Acts 5:3-4: "Then Peter said, 'Ananias, how is it that Satan has so filled your heart that you have lied to the Holy Spirit and have kept for yourself some of the money you received for the land? Didn't it belong to you before it was sold? And after it was sold, wasn't the money at your disposal? What made you think of doing such a thing? You have not lied to men but to God.'"

Ask, "According to verse 3, to whom did Ananias lie?" (The Holy Spirit) "According to verse 4, to whom did Ananias lie?" (God)

You cannot lie to an impersonal force like electricity or radio waves. You can only lie to a person. And that person is identified here as God.

The Holy Spirit is called Jehovah

As I noted in response to Watchtower Argument #4 above ("The Holy Spirit doesn't have a personal name"), the Watchtower's own rendering of 2 Corinthians 3:17-18 (RNWT) actually calls the Holy Spirit "Jehovah."

If you haven't already discussed that passage, this would be a good time to do so. Make sure they understand your point, that the Holy Spirit—not just the Father—is Jehovah.

The Holy Spirit is included in Trinitarian Passages

All three persons of the Trinity are mentioned together in parallel fashion in a number of scriptures. In addition to the baptismal verse cited earlier (Matthew 28:19), you can refer the Witnesses to the following passages:

- 1 Corinthians 12:4-6: "There are different kinds of gifts, but the same Spirit. There are different kinds of service, but the same Lord. There are different kinds of working, but the same God works all of them in all men."
- 2 Corinthians 13:14: "May the grace of the Lord Jesus Christ, and the love of God, and the fellowship of the Holy Spirit be with you all."
- Jude 20-21: "But you, dear friends, build yourselves up in your most holy faith and pray in the Holy Spirit. Keep yourselves in God's love as you wait for the mercy of our Lord Jesus Christ to bring you to eternal life."

ANSWERING WATCHTOWER OBJECTIONS TO THE DEITY OF THE HOLY SPIRIT

Most of the Watchtower's objections to the deity of the Holy Spirit relate to its arguments that the Holy Spirit is not a person. In addition, it makes two further arguments.

Argument #1: The Trinity doctrine wasn't formulated until the 4th century

One of its specific arguments against the deity of the Holy Spirit is historical. The Watchtower says, "Not until the fourth century C.E. did the teaching that the holy spirit was a person and part of the 'Godhead' become official church dogma. Early church 'fathers' did not so teach; Justin Martyr of the second century C.E. taught that the holy spirit was an 'influence or mode of operation of the Deity'; Hippolytus likewise ascribed no personality to the holy spirit."[17]

These claims regarding the teachings of the early church fathers are false. If the Witnesses make such claims, ask them to find you the actual quotations on the internet. You can research this issue yourself and show them what you find. Justin Martyr taught that the Father, Son, and Holy Spirit were all worshipped by early Christians. Hippolytus taught that God exists in a plurality, Father, Son, and Holy Spirit. Other church fathers had similar teachings.[18]

What the Watchtower also fails to state is that it wasn't until the fourth century that the creeds of the church began to be formed at all, and when they were, they did not agree with the Watchtower's position either with regard to the Holy Spirit or to the deity of Christ.

Argument #2: The doctrine of the Trinity is unreasonable

The Watchtower argues that the doctrine of the Trinity is difficult to understand and is therefore unreasonable.

But surely, the fact that something is difficult to understand does not prove that it is false. The laws of genetics, chemistry, and physics are often difficult to understand. Must we therefore reject them as being unreasonable?

Is it in fact unreasonable to believe that God is at least as complex as various aspects of the universe he created? We human beings do not fully understand ourselves. How much less should we expect the nature of God to be fully comprehensible?

The question is not what view of God is easiest for us to understand but rather what the Scriptures reveal about him.

CONCLUSION

Nowhere does the Bible tell us that having the right understanding of the Holy Spirit is essential to our salvation. The Holy Spirit points people to Jesus rather than to himself. However, a well-prepared defense of the personality and deity of the Holy Spirit can go a long way toward leading Jehovah's Witnesses to think independently of the Watchtower. It may make them more likely to give serious consideration to what you have to say about the identity of Jesus and God's real plan of salvation.

SECTION 4:
DISCUSSING
WATCHTOWER
SIGNATURE
ISSUES

Chapter 15:
Watchtower Signature Issues

This section of the book addresses nine doctrinal issues: (1) the name of God, (2) war, (3) birthdays and holidays, (4) paid clergy, (5) collections, (6) the cross, (7) hell, (8) blood transfusions, and (9) 1914 and Armageddon. I call them "Watchtower signature issues" for the following reasons:

- The Watchtower Society considers them all to be important salvation matters.
- By introducing them into the conversation, Jehovah's Witnesses usually catch Christians off guard and unprepared. This renders the Christian passive and fosters the illusion that Jehovah's Witnesses are Bible experts.
- Jehovah's Witnesses usually put Christians on the defensive on each of these topics, making it difficult for us to give an effective witness for Christ.
- Jehovah's Witnesses often shake the faith of Christians by using these issues to portray the churches of Christendom as pagan.

I recommend that you avoid introducing these topics into your discussions with Jehovah's Witnesses. It is difficult to bring them up without appearing to be attacking or persecuting Witnesses for their beliefs. Moreover, they do not involve doctrines Christians consider essential to salvation. That is, a person can be wrong about all of these matters and still come to saving faith in Christ.

However, to Jehovah's Witnesses there are no minor doctrines. They consider their positions on these issues to be distinctives that separate "the truth" (the Watchtower religion) from pagan and worldly teachings and practices of Christendom. Consequently, Witnesses frequently inject these subjects into the conversation and insist on discussing them, so it is important that you be prepared to deal with them.

In this chapter, I will simply set out the Watchtower and Christian positions on these issues. In the chapters that follow, I will give you approaches for discussing them effectively with Jehovah's Witnesses.

1. THE NAME OF GOD

The Old Testament Scriptures contain many names for God. In Hebrew, the Tetragrammaton, YHWH, is the covenant name God used most often in dealing with the Israelites. It appears more than 6,000 times in the Hebrew Scriptures. This is where we get the name that is rendered in English as "Jehovah" or "Yahweh."

Jehovah's Witnesses believe that "Jehovah" is God's personal name, that Jesus Christ placed great importance on making this name known, and that it is essential for Christians to use this divine name when referring to or praying to God.[1] They believe that Bible translators of Christendom have systematically removed this name from the Scriptures and that by so doing they have made God seem remote and impersonal.

The Watchtower claims that the name above all other names is "Jehovah." It states that God's followers "awoke to their obligation to exalt God's personal name, Jehovah, above all other names. They discerned their obligation to be witnesses to this God whose name had been overshadowed for centuries, and appropriately adopted the name 'Jehovah's witnesses' in the memorable year of 1931."[2]

In fact, the Watchtower's New World Translation rendering of Romans 10:13-14 appears to make familiarity with and use of this name of God a salvation issue: "For 'everyone who calls on the name of Jehovah will be saved.' However, how will they call on him if they have not put faith in him? How, in turn, will they put faith in him of whom they have not heard? How, in turn, will they hear without someone to preach?" (RNWT).

Christians note that the Bible contains many names for God, one of which is the anglicized name "Jehovah." However, we believe that both in prayer and in reference, Christians may also properly call him "God," "Father" or "Lord."[3] Moreover, we believe that we are saved by calling on the name of Jesus and that the New Testament exalts most highly the name of Jesus (Philippians 2:9-11), not the name "Jehovah."

2. WAR

In its current study book, the Watchtower claims that in order to please Jehovah, people must shun things that he hates, which includes "getting involved in wars or politics."[4]

The basic argument of the Watchtower is that Christians are supposed to be loyal to Jehovah and his kingdom, not to earthly governments. It makes sweeping statements such as the following: "It is a fact of ancient and modern-day history that in every nation and under all circumstances true Christians have endeavored to maintain complete neutrality as to conflicts between factions of the world. They do not interfere with what others do about sharing in patriotic ceremonies, serving in the armed forces, joining a political party, running for public office, or voting. But they themselves worship only Jehovah, the God of the Bible; they have dedicated their lives unreservedly to him and give their full support to his Kingdom."[5]

Christians believe that governments have been instituted by God (Romans 13:1-7) and respect the rights of individual Christians to follow the dictates of their own consciences with regard to military service. Accordingly, some Christians are pacifists or conscientious objectors. Others will serve in the military if drafted. Still others will enlist in the armed forces or even pursue a lifelong military career.

3. BIRTHDAYS AND HOLIDAYS

Jehovah's Witnesses believe that celebrating birthdays as well as holidays such as Christmas, Easter, New Year's, Halloween, Valentine's Day, Mother's Day, Father's Day, and political holidays is not biblical, either because these days are associated with pagan origins and practices or because they run counter to Jesus' statement that his followers are "no part of the world" (John 15:19, RNWT).[6]

The Watchtower cites an additional reason for prohibiting birthday celebrations. The only two birthdays referenced in the Bible are those of Pharaoh and Herod the tetrarch. Both of these events are mentioned in an unfavorable light.[7]

Christians believe that what days we do or do not choose to observe is a matter of individual conscience, so long as any celebrations are carried out in a righteous manner. Christians should not pass judgment on one another with regard to such issues (Romans 14:5-6; Colossians 2:16-17).

4. PAID CLERGY

Jehovah's Witnesses believe that a separate clergy class is unbiblical. Christian workers in local congregations should be volunteers.[8]

Christians believe that clergy should be paid because the worker is entitled to his wages (1 Corinthians 9:13-14; 2 Corinthians 11:8; 1 Timothy 5:17-18).

5. COLLECTIONS

Jehovah's Witnesses believe that passing collection plates and making appeals for money impose worldly pressure on people to make public donations. An anonymous contribution box is the preferred biblical method for collecting contributions.[9]

Christians believe that there are many acceptable ways to raise funds for the church, including taking public collections and requesting donations.[10]

6. THE CROSS

Jehovah's Witnesses believe that Christians should not display or wear crosses. Specifically, the Watchtower teaches: (1) Jesus died on an upright, one-piece "torture stake," not a cross, (2) the cross is a pagan sex symbol that was used in pagan worship, (3) veneration of the cross is idolatrous, and (4) the instrument on which Jesus was unjustly tortured and killed should not be cherished by Christians, but rather shunned.[11]

Christians believe that Jesus died on a cross. The cross is a symbol of Jesus' atonement and victory over death.[12] For this reason, it is perfectly acceptable for Christians to display and wear crosses if they choose to do so.

7. HELL

Jehovah's Witnesses do not believe that human beings have separate souls or spirits that survive physical death. They believe that at death, a person goes out of existence until the resurrection in the end times.[13] They believe that hell is nothing more than the common grave of humankind and that no one—not even Satan—will suffer conscious everlasting torment. Rather, they believe the fate of the unrepentant wicked is everlasting nonexistence.[14]

Christians believe that all human beings have a conscious soul or spirit that survives physical death.[15] Although some Christians believe in annihilation of those who are not saved, the traditional position—and the one which this book defends as biblical—is that the unrepentant dead will be judged and undergo punishment in proportion to their sins. This will be an everlasting, conscious punishment in hell.[16] Satan and demons will also suffer everlasting, conscious punishment in the lake of fire.[17]

8. BLOOD TRANSFUSIONS

Jehovah's Witnesses believe that the Bible prohibits the taking of blood transfusions for any reason.[18]

Christians believe that biblical commands regarding blood have no application to blood transfusions.

9. 1914 AND ARMAGEDDON

Jehovah's Witnesses believe that Christ began ruling as King of Jehovah's government in 1914 and claim that God's judgment at Armageddon and Christ's millennial reign are coming soon.[19] Christians attach no special importance to 1914.

FOR FURTHER STUDY

- Chapter 16, "The Divine Name Approach," explains how to deal with the Watchtower's emphasis on the name "Jehovah" and show Witnesses the surpassing importance the New Testament gives to the name "Jesus."
- Chapter 17, "The Christian Freedom Approach," explains how to challenge the Watchtower's doctrines regarding war, birthdays and holidays, paid clergy, collections, and the cross.
- Chapter 18, "The Justice for the Wicked Approach," explains how to show Jehovah's Witnesses that the Watchtower's annihilation-of-the-wicked doctrine is neither just nor biblical.
- Chapter 19, "The Life and Death Issues Approach," explains how to show Jehovah's Witnesses that the Watchtower is not the reliable source it claims to be in that it has made radical changes in its teachings regarding life and death health care issues.
- Chapter 20, "The False Prophecies Approach," explains how to show Jehovah's Witnesses that the Watchtower organization is not a reliable guide regarding the end times in that it has made numerous false prophecies.

Chapter 16:
The Divine Name Approach

"Therefore God exalted him to the highest place and gave him the name that is above every name, that at the name of Jesus every knee should bow, in heaven and on earth and under the earth, and every tongue confess that Jesus Christ is Lord, to the glory of God the Father" (Philippians 2:9-11).

The objective of this approach is to show Jehovah's Witnesses that, while it is fine to refer to God as "Jehovah," it is not necessary. In fact, in the New Testament the name that is above every other name is "Jesus."

Given the fact that the Watchtower calls its followers "Jehovah's Witnesses," it's obvious that the name "Jehovah" is an important part of the Watchtower religion. It claims that no one can have a close personal relationship with God unless they know and use this name. Prayer is to be directed to Jehovah by name. One of the Witnesses' primary missions in life is to make Jehovah's name known.

They believe that instead of exalting the divine name, superstitious Jews before the Christian era stopped using the name altogether in order to be certain that they would not be guilty of taking the name in vain in violation of Exodus 20:7. Christian scribes followed suit by systematically and wrongfully removing the name from Greek New Testament manuscripts in over 200 places. They believe this is why most English Bibles today use the term "the LORD" as a replacement. The Watchtower has "restored" the name "Jehovah" in its Bible versions, the New World Translation (NWT) and the Revised New World Translation (RNWT).

Witnesses believe that use of and reverence for the name "Jehovah" is a major difference between their true Christian religion and the counterfeit Christianity that comprises Christendom. They will present you with around half a dozen Watchtower arguments to try to persuade you that true worshippers of God must use and exalt the divine name. Of course, if they could convince you that they are right, you would be well on your way to becoming a Jehovah's Witness.

Most likely, they will expect you to be uncomfortable with referring to God as "Jehovah." To the contrary, you will neither show discomfort nor in any way try to discourage them from using that name. Rather, your approach will be to show them many scriptures that call into question the claim that the divine name *must* be used.

In addition, you will show them scriptures which demonstrate that the Father and Son are not in competition for honor, and that the Father has designated "Jesus" as the name that is above all other names. You will stress that giving this exalted status to the name of Jesus does not dishonor the Father. In fact, it honors the Father and the Son equally, and this is exactly what the Father desires.

USING THE NAME "JEHOVAH"

When the Witnesses start talking about the importance of knowing and using the divine name, tell them that you have no problem with them using the covenant name God disclosed to the Israelites. Encourage them to give you reasons why they think knowing and using the name is so important. It's fine to let them quote you one or two verses, but don't let them take you on an extended Bible hopscotching expedition. Say, "I'll be glad to look at specific verses a little later. For now, I'd just like to have you tell me what you think is important for me to know about the name 'Jehovah' and why."

Most likely, they will present you with one or more of the following claims.

Watchtower Claim #1: Jesus mentioned God's name repeatedly in his own prayers

The Witnesses will tell you that Jesus believed the name "Jehovah" was of critical importance, and therefore we should also. The Watchtower asks, "How important is God's name? Consider the model prayer that Jesus Christ gave. It begins this way: 'Our Father in the heavens, let your name be sanctified.' (Matthew 6:9) Later, Jesus prayed to God: 'Father, glorify your name.' In response, God spoke from heaven, saying: 'I both glorified it and will glorify it again.' (John 12:28) Clearly, God's name is of the utmost importance."[1] Witnesses may also tell you that God's name "was clearly of crucial importance to him [Jesus] since he mentioned it repeatedly in his own prayers."[2]

Ask the Witnesses to show you one passage where Jesus begins one of his prayers by addressing God as "Jehovah." They won't be able to find one. Instead, he addressed God as "Father"

(Matthew 11:25; 26:39,42; Luke 10:21; 22:42; 23:34,46; John 11:41; 12:27-28; 17:1,5,11,21,24-25) or, when he was dying, as, "My God, my God" (Matthew 27:46; Mark 15:34)—never as "Jehovah," not even in the Watchtower's own New World Translation.

Also ask them to show you any verse where Jesus taught his disciples to begin their prayers by saying, "Jehovah..." In the Lord's Prayer (model prayer), Jesus said to address him as "Father" (Luke 11:2, RNWT). Apparently, "sanctifying God's name" did not require them to address him by the divine name.

Make it clear that you don't believe Jesus was saying that they could address God only as "Father." Ask them to read aloud Luke 2:29, where godly Simeon addressed God as "Sovereign Lord" (RNWT). Ask them to read aloud Acts 4:24 and Revelation 6:10, where the disciples and tribulation martyrs call him that as well. Nowhere are they rebuked for failing to address God either as "Jehovah" or as "Father."

Say, "I certainly don't criticize you for beginning your prayers with, 'Jehovah...' but do you see why from the verses we just looked at I don't think that is required or more spiritual than other respectful forms of address? We can be respectful or flippant, intimate or detached, engaged or ritualistic, regardless of what form of address we use. It seems to me that God is interested in our hearts, not in formalities."

Watchtower Claim #2: We must use the name "Jehovah" in order to have intimacy with God

The Watchtower says that we must use the name "Jehovah" in order to have an intimate relationship with God: "In replacing God's name with titles, Bible translators make a serious mistake. They make God seem remote and impersonal, whereas the Bible urges humans to cultivate 'intimacy with Jehovah.' (Psalm 25:14) Think of an intimate friend of yours. How close would you really be if you never learned your friend's name? Similarly, when people are kept in ignorance about God's name, Jehovah, how can they become truly close to God?"[3]

You can respond by saying, "Is use of someone's personal name the most intimate way to address them? My children don't call me [insert your name]. They call me 'Dad/Mom.' In a similar way, isn't it more intimate to address God as 'Father' than as 'Jehovah'?"

How did Jesus' closest friends refer to him? Have one of them read John 13:13 aloud. There Jesus said that it was proper for his disciples to address him as "Teacher" and "Lord." Even his inner circle of disciples—Peter, James, and John—addressed and referred to him in this way (Matthew 14:28-30; Luke 9:54). If Jesus' closest friends properly called him by titles of respect like "Teacher" and "Lord" instead of by his name—Jesus—why would it be wrong to refer to his Father as "God" or "Lord" instead of using the name "Jehovah"?

Watchtower Claim #3: Jesus used the name "Jehovah" when referring to God

Jehovah's Witnesses will claim that Jesus personally used the name "Jehovah" when referring to God in conversation. In fact, their New World Translation quotes him as using the name "Jehovah" 25 times. Twenty-two of these occur when he was directly quoting Old Testament passages where YHWH appears in the Hebrew.[4] The Watchtower assumes that Jesus must have spoken the divine name when doing so. The other three instances occur in verses where the Watchtower thinks Jesus was referring to his Father and not to himself.[5]

The New Testament was originally written in Greek. Ask the Witnesses if they have a Greek interlinear Bible with them. Ask them to show you one instance where the name "Jehovah" or the Hebrew Tetragrammaton (YHWH) from which it is derived appears in the Greek New Testament. It isn't there.

Although none of the original writings is still in existence, there are still thousands of copies available to us. Although the Tetragrammaton (YHWH) appears over 6,000 times in the Old Testament Hebrew, it does not appear in any of the Greek New Testament manuscripts, not even in passages that quote Old Testament verses where it was located. The Watchtower's own *Kingdom Interlinear Translation of the Greek Scriptures* verifies the total absence of the Tetragrammaton. In the introduction to this interlinear translation, it states: "One of the remarkable facts, not only about the extant manuscripts of the original Greek text, but of many versions, ancient and modern, is the absence of the divine name."[6]

Ask, "Given that neither the Tetragrammaton nor the name 'Jehovah' or 'Yahweh' appears in any Greek New Testament manuscript, is it unreasonable to conclude that its use cannot be of critical significance to the Christian faith?"

Watchtower Claim #4: Scribes who copied the Scriptures tampered with God's Word by removing the divine name

Referring to Acts 15:4, the Watchtower asks, "If Christians are to be a people for God's name, why should his name, represented by the Tetragrammaton, be abolished from the Christian Greek Scriptures?"[7]

Their conclusion is "that the original text of the Christian

Greek Scriptures has been tampered with... at least from th century A.D. onward, the divine name in Tetragrammaton furm has been eliminated from the text by copyists who did not understand or appreciate the divine name or who developed an aversion to it, possibly under the influence of anti-Semitism. In place of it they substituted words derived from the Greek words *kyrios* (usually translated 'the Lord') and *theos*, meaning 'God.'"[8]

Your first response to this claim should be, "Don't you believe that God has preserved his Word over the centuries? How is it that we can trust in the complete reliability of the New Testament except for this one issue? If the New Testament copyists removed the name 'Jehovah' in hundreds of places from all the Greek manuscripts, wouldn't we have to ask what other alterations they have made to the Bible text out of fear, superstition, bias, or prejudice? The reliability of the entire New Testament text would be called into question."

The irony is that in every other respect, the Watchtower vigorously defends the reliability of the Scriptures. They quote with approval this statement of Greek scholar Sir Frederick Kenyon:

> The first and most important conclusion derived from the examination of them [the papyri] is the satisfactory one that they confirm the essential soundness of the existing texts. No striking or fundamental variation is shown either in the Old or the New Testament. *There are no important omissions or additions of passages, and no variations which affect vital facts or doctrines. The variations of the text affect minor matters, such as the order of words or the precise words used...* But their essential importance is their confirmation, by evidence of an earlier date than was hitherto available, of the integrity of our existing texts.—(London, 1933), p. 15.[9] (emphasis added)

If you sense that it is appropriate to be more confrontational, you can ask, "If all of the existing manuscripts contain a particular Greek word (such as *kyrios*), then in order to provide a faithful and accurate translation, don't you need to use the English equivalent of that word ("Lord") in your translation rather than giving the impression that the manuscript actually says something else ("Jehovah")?

The Witnesses may note that some Greek manuscripts contain words that others do not. That is true, and scholars have criteria for determining which copies are accurate and which are not. One of those criteria involves comparing copies made by scribes from different parts of the world. However, there are no Greek New Testament manuscripts from anywhere in the world that contain the Tetragrammaton. Witnesses will sometimes point out that the Septuagint contains it. However, the Septuagint is a Greek version of the Old Testament, not of the New.

Watchtower Claim #5: We must make Jehovah's name known because Jesus did so

The Watchtower argues as follows:

Jesus declared in prayer to his Father: "I have made your name known... and will make it known." (John 17:26) Jesus would undoubtedly have pronounced God's name on numerous occasions when he read, quoted, or explained portions of the Hebrew Scriptures containing that important name. Jesus would thus have used God's name just as freely as all the prophets did before him. If any Jews were already avoiding the use of God's name during the time of Jesus' ministry, Jesus would certainly not have followed their tradition. He strongly criticized the religious leaders when he said to them: "You have made the word of God invalid because of your tradition.—Matthew 15:6."[10]

Reply, "Does making God's name known mean using the word 'Jehovah' or does it mean proclaiming and reverently showing what God is like—the greatness of his person and character?"

You can use a personal illustration by saying, "If you ask me what my father's name is, and I tell you, 'His name is [give your father's name]', have I told you much of consequence about him? Would I be 'honoring his name' by using his name frequently and encouraging other people to do so? Wouldn't it be far more important for me to tell you what he is like and to exhibit all his good qualities and teachings in my own life? Likewise, it seems to me that this is what Jesus was talking about—extolling and demonstrating the great qualities of his Father. If so, it is God's character—not the verbalizing of the name 'Jehovah'—that is important."

Witnesses will insist that "making God's name known" involves actually using the name "Jehovah." But wouldn't we expect that if Jesus used the divine name frequently in public, the scribes and Pharisees would have accused him of blasphemy for violating their interpretation of the Third Commandment? After all, they accused him of everything else they could think of, including trivial things like allowing his disciples to eat with unwashed hands in violation of their tradition.

Ask the Witnesses to show you anywhere in the Scriptures where any such confrontation occurred. Point out that the religious leaders did accuse Jesus of blasphemy but they never accused him of doing so because he uttered the divine name.

You can also point out that if Jesus used the divine name in public and emphasized its use as of crucial importance, we would expect to see him rebuking the scribes and Pharisees for giving in to fear and superstition by their refusal to use it. Ask them to show you any such confrontation in the Scriptures. He rebuked the religious leaders for many things, but never for failing to speak the divine name.

They may show you verses in the Watchtower translation where Jesus used the name "Jehovah," but that begs the question. Is the Watchtower translation supported by the evidence?

You can summarize your point by saying, "Given the facts that no Greek New Testament manuscript uses the Tetragrammaton and that the Bible contains no confrontation between the religious leaders and Jesus over his using the name in public, what is the more reasonable conclusion—that Jesus used the divine name frequently in public or that he didn't?"

Watchtower Claim #6: We must call on the name of Jehovah in order to be saved

The Watchtower claims that using the name "Jehovah" is a salvation issue. Their Bible renders Romans 10:13 as follows: "For 'everyone who calls on the name of Jehovah will be saved'" (RNWT).

Have the Witnesses look up that verse in their Greek interlinear Bible. Although Romans 10:13 quotes an Old Testament verse where the Tetragrammaton appears (Joel 2:32), neither the Tetragrammaton nor the name "Jehovah" or "Yahweh" appear in the Greek. Instead, the Greek word *kyrios* (which means "Lord") is used. Show the Witnesses that the context of the passage emphasizes the importance of *Jesus*. For example, Romans 10:9 says that "if you confess with your mouth, 'Jesus is Lord,' and believe in your heart that God raised him from the dead, you will be saved."

Point out to the Witnesses Acts 4:12, which says of the name of Jesus, "Salvation is found in no one else, for there is no other

name under heaven given to men by which we must be saved."
Likewise, Acts 22:16 says that we get our sins washed away by
"calling on his name" (RNWT).

THE NAME THE NEW TESTAMENT
EXALTS MOST HIGHLY IS "JESUS"

Having responded to each of the Watchtower's claims about
the importance of the name "Jehovah," you can now build a
positive case for the fact that the name the New Testament exalts
most highly is "Jesus."

Point #1: The name above all other names is "Jesus"

Ask the Witnesses, "According to the New Testament, what
name is above every other name?" Most likely they will tell you,
"Jehovah."

Then have one of them read aloud Philippians 2:9-11:
"Therefore God exalted him [Jesus] to the highest place and gave
him the name that is above every name, that at the name of Jesus
every knee should bow, in heaven and on earth and under the
earth, and every tongue confess that Jesus Christ is Lord, to the
glory of God the Father."

Follow up with, "According to this passage, what name does
God want us to exalt above every other name?"

Point #2: God chose for his followers to be called
"Christians," not "Jehovah's Witnesses"

Have one of the Witnesses read aloud Acts 11:26 in their
Bibles: "It was first in Antioch that the disciples were by divine
providence called Christians" (RNWT).

Ask, "According to this verse, what does God want his followers to be called? If God wanted the name 'Jehovah' exalted most highly, why did he, in his divine providence, have the early believers called 'Christians' instead of 'Jehovah's Witnesses'?"

They may argue that God no longer feels that way because the title "Christian" has been tarnished over the centuries. However, the point is in Acts 11:26 God was emphasizing the disciples' relationship to Christ rather than to the name "Jehovah."

Point #3: Jesus emphasized his own name

Point out that Jesus emphasized his own name far more often than his Father's. Have the Witnesses read aloud the following passages (all quotations below are from the RNWT). Point out that he could have said "on account of Jehovah's name" or "for the sake of Jehovah's name," but he didn't. Instead, he said "my name."

- Matthew 10:22: "And you will be hated by all people on account of my name, but the one who has endured to the end will be saved."
- Matthew 19:29: "And everyone who has left houses or brothers or sisters or father or mother or children or lands for the sake of my name will receive a hundred times as much and will inherit everlasting life."
- Matthew 24:9: "Then people will hand you over to tribulation and will kill you, and you will be hated by all the nations on account of my name."
- Luke 21:12, 17: "But before all these things happen, people will lay their hands on you and persecute you, handing you over to the synagogues and prisons. You will

be brought before kings and governors for the sake of my name... 17 and you will be hated by all people because of my name."

- Acts 9:15-16: "But the Lord said to him: 'Go! because this man is a chosen vessel to me to bear my name to the nations as well as to kings and the sons of Israel. For I will show him plainly how many things he must suffer for my name.'"

- Revelation 2:3: "You are also showing endurance, and you have persevered for the sake of my name and have not grown weary."

Point #4: The Father wants his Son to have equal honor with himself

Ask one of the Witnesses to read aloud John 5:22-23: "Moreover, the Father judges no one, but has entrusted all judgment to the Son, that all may honor the Son just as they honor the Father. He who does not honor the Son does not honor the Father, who sent him."

You can add, "If you learn that someone has been praising your son for his character and actions, are you offended or are you honored? Even if the speaker never mentions you in the conversation, you justly feel honored in that situation. Exalting the name of Jesus does not rob his Father of glory. Exalting the name of Jesus brings his Father glory."

The Witnesses will insist that they honor Jesus as God's Son and chosen king. To that, reply, "Yes, but can you honestly say that you honor the Son just as you honor the Father as verse 23 says the Father wants us to do?"

CONCLUSION

The Watchtower constantly stresses with the Witnesses the importance of the name "Jehovah." For this reason, don't be surprised or discouraged if there is no apparent change in their attitudes or beliefs. Consider it a success if you have been able to plant some seeds of doubt about the correctness of the Watchtower dogma with regard to this issue.

If, on the other hand, this turns into a fruitful discussion and you are able to present your case for exalting the name of Jesus, you may be able to follow up with a discussion concerning the importance of coming to Jesus for salvation.

Chapter 17:
The Christian Freedom Approach

"It is for freedom that Christ has set us free. Stand firm, then, and do not let yourselves be burdened again by a yoke of slavery" (Galatians 5:1).

The objective of this approach is to get Jehovah's Witnesses to think for themselves instead of simply accepting whatever the Watchtower says.

Jehovah's Witnesses are often known by what they *won't* do:

- They won't serve in the armed forces of any country.
- They won't celebrate birthdays or holidays.
- They won't hire "clergy" or pay wages to congregation elders.
- They won't pass a collection plate at their meetings.
- They won't display or wear a cross.

I personally don't care whether they do any of these things or not. As Christians, we know that none of these matters is a salvation issue. The problem is that to a Jehovah's Witness, all of these practices are salvation issues.

Witnesses consider their stance on each of these matters as proof that they are in the true Christian religion and that "Christians" who behave otherwise have made themselves a part of Babylon the Great by engaging in pagan, worldly, or immoral practices. They often bring these matters up to put us on the defensive and to try to persuade us that we must purify our relationship with God by becoming Jehovah's Witnesses and obeying all of their rules.

Elevating minor matters into major issues is a significant tool the Watchtower employs in controlling the minds and actions of Jehovah's Witnesses. They see themselves as the only ones who understand what God really requires.

It is usually best to wait for the Witnesses to bring up these issues. If you initiate the discussion, they are likely to view it as persecution, but once they introduce the topics as indictments of Christendom, it is only fair for you to respond.

Instead of becoming defensive, you will defend the Witnesses' freedom to follow their convictions in these matters without being judged or condemned by people who disagree with them. You will show them that the Bible allows Christians freedom to follow their own consciences in these areas. In other words, these are not matters on which all Christians must agree.

ISSUE #1: WAR

Jehovah's Witnesses see military service as unchristian: "If true Christians in one nation were to go to war against another nation, they would be fighting against fellow believers, against people who prayed for help to the same God that they did. Appropriately, Christ directed his followers to lay down the sword."[1]

Some Christians agree with this position. If this describes your own conviction, I recommend that you simply tell the Witnesses, "I agree with your position on the issue of war and the military."

If you have no objections to Christians serving in the armed forces, your objective should not be to try to persuade the Witnesses to replace their convictions with your own. Rather, you should try to show them that your position is perfectly defensible from the Scriptures. That is, military service is a matter on which Christians are free to follow the dictates of their individual consciences, not an issue on which all Christians are required to agree.

Say, "Because you believe it is wrong to serve in the military, I believe you should have the right to be conscientious objectors. However, I personally don't think that position is required by the Bible."

God and war in the Old Testament

Point out that in the Old Testament God required male Israelites to serve in the military and directed them to fight in order to take possession of the Promised Land. In addition, have the Witnesses read aloud what God says in Jeremiah 25:8-9 regarding his use of the Babylonian army to discipline Israel: "Therefore this is what Jehovah of armies says, 'Because you would not obey my words, I am sending for all the families of the north,' declares Jehovah, 'sending for King Nebuchadnezzar of Babylon, *my servant*, and I will bring them against this land and against its inhabitants and against all these surrounding nations. I will devote them to destruction and make them an object of horror and something to whistle at and a perpetual ruin'" (RNWT, emphasis added).

Make your point clear: Given that we still live in a fallen world, God still has purposes for the armies of this world to fulfill. It will remain so until Christ returns with the armies of heaven.

God and war in the New Testament

Jehovah's Witnesses will acknowledge that Jehovah directed Israel to engage in numerous wars in the Old Testament, but they will tell you that God's arrangement has changed in the Christian era. In support of this contention, they will cite a number of scriptures. Tell them that while you understand their point, none of the passages directly addresses the issue of whether it is acceptable for Christians to serve in the armed forces. Instead, the contexts show that they deal with the following issues:

1. Personal relationships between individuals rather than dealings between nations (Luke 6:27-31; 2 Corinthians 10:3-4; James 4:4)
2. God's specific plans for Jesus and his disciples at his first coming (Matthew 26:52-54; John 6:15)
3. How things will be different when Jesus returns (Isaiah 2:4; 2 Thessalonians 1:6-8; Revelation 19:11-21). Point out that while these things will happen someday, that day has not yet arrived. We are living in a fallen world where police and armies are still needed.

Then you can say, "I would like to get your take on several New Testament scriptures that do address the subject of whether it is possible to follow Christ and still serve in the armed forces."

John the Baptist

Ask them to read aloud what John the Baptist said to soldiers who came to him to be baptized. Luke 3:14: "Then some soldiers asked him, 'And what should we do?' He replied, 'Don't extort money and don't accuse people falsely—be content with your pay.'"

Ask:

- If it was wrong for followers of Jehovah to serve in the army, why didn't John the Baptist tell them that?
- Why did he just tell them to serve in an honorable manner?

Jesus and a Roman centurion

Moving to the views of Jesus himself, ask one of the Witnesses to read aloud the encounter between Jesus and a Roman centurion recorded in Matthew 8:5-10 in which Jesus stated, "I tell you the truth, I have not found anyone in Israel with such great faith."

Ask:

- Roman centurions commanded a hundred soldiers. If serving in the Roman army was detestable to Jehovah, why would Jesus commend this man for his level of faith and also heal his servant?
- Why didn't Jesus tell this man that in order to demonstrate genuine faith in Jehovah he and his servant needed to leave the Roman army?

Cornelius

Have one of the Witnesses read aloud Acts 10:1-2: "At Caesarea there was a man named Cornelius, a centurion in what was known as the Italian Regiment. He and all his family were devout and God-fearing; he gave generously to those in need and prayed to God regularly" (Footnotes in the Revised New World Translation indicate that Cornelius was a centurion who was in command of 100 soldiers and that the Italian unit was a cohort or a Roman army unit of 600 soldiers).

Have them also read aloud Peter's comment about this man in Acts 10:34-35: "I now realize how true it is that God does not show favoritism but accepts men from every nation who fear him and do what is right."

Ask the Witnesses:

- How is it that this man could be both a Roman military commander and "a devout and God-fearing man"?
- How could Peter describe Cornelius as a man who "fears God and does what is right" when this man was an active commander of 100 Roman soldiers?
- Invite them to show you anywhere in the Scriptures where Cornelius was told by God or Peter to give up his military career. It isn't there.

Governments as God's servants

Have one of the Witnesses read aloud Romans 13:1-4 regarding the proper role of earthly governments in the Christian era.

Romans 13:1-2: "Everyone must submit himself to the governing authorities, for there is no authority except that which God has established. The authorities that exist have been established by God. Consequently, he who rebels against the authority is rebelling against what God has instituted, and those who do so will bring judgment on themselves."

Ask the Witnesses:

- According to these verses, where do the governments of this world get their authority—God or Satan?
- Who has placed these governments in their relative positions? God or Satan?

Romans 13:3-4: "For rulers hold no terror for those who do right, but for those who do wrong. Do you want to be free from fear of the one in authority? Then do what is right and he will commend you. For he is God's servant to do you good. But if you do wrong, be afraid, for he does not bear the sword for nothing. He is God's servant, an agent of wrath to bring punishment on the wrongdoer."

Ask the Witnesses:

- According to these verses, governments are whose servants? God's or Satan's?
- Who authorized these governments to bear the sword? God or Satan?
- The governments are agents of whose wrath? God's or Satan's?
- Do you understand from these scriptures why I believe military service can be an honorable calling for Christians?

Whom did God use to stop Hitler?

Say something like this: "In this fallen system, when nations use violence for evil purposes, what agency does God use to stop them? Whom did God use as his instruments to stop Hitler's genocidal rampage? It wasn't diplomats. Diplomacy was tried but it failed. It wasn't Jehovah's Witnesses. Hitler did not repent because someone knocked on his door at Berchtesgaden. Instead, God used the military forces of the Allies. As Romans 13:4 says, they were his servants to carry out God's wrath against the evildoer."

You can conclude by saying, "If your conscience tells you not to take up arms, I certainly respect that decision. But in this fallen world, someone has to serve as police officers and as soldiers in order to restrain evil, and I personally believe that it's better for righteous men and women to serve in those roles. So I also respect the decisions of Christians who serve in those capacities, and I think you should as well."

ISSUE #2: BIRTHDAYS AND HOLIDAYS

When the Witnesses tell you that genuine Christians do not celebrate birthdays or holidays, ask one of them to read aloud Romans 14:5, 10: "One man judges one day as above another; another judges one day the same as all others; let each one be fully convinced in his own mind... But why do you judge your brother? Or why do you also look down on your brother? For we will all stand before the judgment seat of God" (RNWT).

Say, "These verses say that we shouldn't judge each other based on what days we do or don't celebrate. But it seems to me that the Watchtower does pass judgment on such things and leads you to believe that your behavior is more acceptable to God than mine. Given that the Bible says this is a conscience matter, why does the Watchtower require all Jehovah's Witnesses to think and act alike?"

The Witnesses will give you several Watchtower arguments. Here is what you can expect them to say, along with my recommendations about how to respond.

Watchtower Argument #1: Birthdays are occasions for sin in the Bible

In support of its prohibition against celebrating birthdays, the Watchtower states: "Jehovah's Witnesses take note that God's Word reports unfavorably about birthday celebrations and so shun these."[2] It is referring to two passages of Scripture. Genesis 40:20-22 says that it was on his birthday that Pharaoh hanged his chief baker. Matthew 14:6-10 says that Herod's birthday was the occasion for his beheading John the Baptist.

In response, ask, "If Pharaoh's putting his chief baker to death on his birthday means that birthday celebrations are bad, then by the same logic why doesn't the fact that Pharaoh graciously released his chief cupbearer from prison on the same day mean that birthday celebrations are good?" You can add, "Pharaoh and Herod were evil men who murdered people on many occasions, not just birthdays. If they had done these evil deeds on their wedding anniversaries instead of on their birthdays, would that prove that it is wrong for Christians to celebrate wedding anniversaries?"

Watchtower Argument #2: Birthdays and holidays have pagan origins

Witnesses will tell you that birthday celebrations were held in honor of pagan deities[3] and that pagans used birthday candles in order to bring good fortune, similar to their practice of offering sacrificial fires to their gods.[4]

Jehovah's Witnesses are trained to make similar arguments regarding specific holidays.[5] In response, say, "I'm sure that pagans engaged in many practices common today such as exchanging wedding rings and celebrating wedding anniversaries. Does that mean it displeases God when we exchange rings and celebrate our wedding anniversaries? Of course not. It seems to me that the same principle applies to celebrating holidays. But if such celebrations trouble your conscience, then don't celebrate them. My own conscience doesn't bother me with regard to these matters because I know I am not worshipping pagan deities in my celebrations."

You can add, "It would be hard for me to imagine a stronger pagan connection than eating meat that has just been offered in sacrifice on a pagan god's altar. But in 1 Corinthians 8, Paul says it's the person with a *weak* conscience who is troubled by such things. Help me understand why it's okay to eat meat I know a pagan offered on his idol's altar three hours ago but wrong to celebrate Jesus' resurrection because pagans worshipped a false goddess at Easter 3,000 years ago."

If they point out that Paul says we should not cause others to stumble, ask, "If I take part in birthday or holiday celebrations, am I causing you to stumble? Am I leading you to participate in violation of your own conscience? As Paul said, why should my freedom be judged by another's conscience? If I take part in birthday or holiday activities with thankfulness to God, why am I denounced because of something I thank God for?" (1 Corinthians 10:28-30)

Witnesses sometimes focus on the evils of Halloween because of its association with the occult. I deal with that by saying something like this: "I know Christians who don't participate in Halloween at all because of its connections to the occult. Others do participate with costumes and parties so long as there is no glorification of witches or witchcraft involved. I believe that different Christians can legitimately draw the line at different places as their individual consciences dictate."

Watchtower Argument #3: Birthdays and holidays promote commercialism, greed, and immorality

The Watchtower decries the commercialism and greed associated with Christmas.[6] Not surprisingly, it also condemns the overeating, drunkenness, and loose conduct often associated with New Year's celebrations.[7]

Respond by saying, "Of course, Christians need to celebrate in a righteous manner. But why am I being condemned for someone else's excesses? Although there is often commercialism and greed associated with Christmas, I have found that there can also be great generosity as well as gratitude for the gift of Jesus Christ. And while people who cannot control their drinking would be wise to forego Christmas and New Year's parties where alcohol is served, mature Christians can celebrate these and other events without engaging in debauchery. Those who can't shouldn't participate."

Watchtower Argument #4: Celebrating holidays constitutes excessive involvement with the world

With regard to celebrating holidays commemorating a nation's political history, the Watchtower cites scriptures which say that Jesus' followers are to be no part of this world.[8]

In response, you can say, "I really don't understand that. Is celebration of a holiday evil because the government promotes it? Doesn't Romans 13:1 say that governments have been instituted by God? What about Thanksgiving, for example? Doesn't the Bible tell us in many places to give thanks to God? Help me understand why it is wrong to set aside a special day for thanking him for blessing our country."

To sum up your position regarding birthdays and holidays, have one of the Witnesses read aloud Colossians 2:16-17: "Therefore do not let anyone judge you by what you eat or drink, or with regard to a religious festival, a New Moon celebration or a Sabbath day. These are a shadow of the things that were to come; the reality, however, is found in Christ."

ISSUE #3: PAID CLERGY

The Watchtower boasts, "What group is noted for having no paid clergy, all of its members being preachers?"[9] It teaches Jehovah's Witnesses to be proud of how different they are: "Some religious leaders do preach for money... In contrast, the Witnesses have no paid clergy, and often their Bible literature is offered without price to sincere seekers of truth..."[10]

Your objective is to show the Witnesses from the Scriptures that those who preach the gospel have a right to be paid for their work, although if they wish to decline such financial support, they are free to do so.

Have one of the Witnesses read aloud 1 Corinthians 9:13-14: "Don't you know that those who work in the temple get their food from the temple, and those who serve at the altar share in what is offered on the altar? In the same way, the Lord has commanded that those who preach the gospel should receive their living from the gospel."

Ask, "What does verse 14 say Lord commanded?" Sometimes they will reply, "But 1 Corinthians 9:12 says that Paul didn't take money from the Corinthians. He didn't accept any money, and neither do we!"

In response, say, "Read all of 1 Corinthians 9. The Corinthians were accusing Paul of improper motives. It was for this reason that he decided not to take any money from them to pay for his own expenses. However, he told them that the Lord commands that those who proclaim the good news should make their living by means of doing so. That means, does it not, that the congregation is required to make a good faith offer to pay their preachers a suitable wage and that it's purely up to the preachers whether to accept money or not? There is absolutely nothing wrong with preachers making a living by preaching. You just read that in verse 14."

Ask the Witnesses to read aloud 2 Corinthians 11:7-8, where Paul says, "...did I commit a sin by humbling myself that you might be exalted, because I gladly declared the good news of God to you without cost? Other congregations I deprived by accepting provisions in order to minister to you" (RNWT). Ask, "Doesn't this show that Paul did take money to support his ministry, just not from the Corinthians?"

You can also refer them to Philippians 4:15-17: "Moreover, as you Philippians know, in the early days of your acquaintance with the gospel, when I set out from Macedonia, not one church shared with me in the matter of giving and receiving, except you only; for even when I was in Thessalonica, you sent me aid again and again when I was in need. Not that I am looking for a gift, but I am looking for what may be credited to your account."

Ask, "There is nothing wrong with Christian workers accepting financial support for their ministry, is there? Paul did so again and again."

You can sum up this issue by having one of the Witnesses read aloud 1 Timothy 5:17-18: "The elders who direct the affairs of the church well are worthy of double honor, especially those whose work is preaching and teaching. For the Scripture says, 'Do not muzzle the ox while it is treading out the grain,' and 'The worker deserves his wages.'" Ask, "What does this passage say about whether or not elders deserve to be paid?"

I recommend that you finish this topic by adding something like this: "I'm sure that Jehovah's Witness elders have administrative, teaching, counselling, and disciplinary duties. In addition, I would suppose that they are expected to be good examples in the door-to-door witnessing. If they are not paid for any of this work, they must have secular jobs as well in order to earn a living. This must put a lot of stress on them and on their families. That seems to me to be the reason why the Bible says that the worker is entitled to his wages. Given what the Scripture says, help me understand why the Watchtower doesn't make a bona fide offer to pay them."

ISSUE #4: COLLECTIONS

The Watchtower knows that many churchgoers are put off by collections and frequent requests for money. They use this to recruit members and to tout the superiority of their religion over that of Christendom.

Typical is the following account from a 1996 issue of *Awake!*: "We started going to different churches on Sundays... They would often pass the money plate three times at one meeting, which resulted in many leaving with their pockets turned inside out. We went to many churches, but we found only more collection plates being passed and social gatherings."[11]

Through a steady diet of such stories, the Watchtower leads Jehovah's Witnesses to believe that these practices are commonplace in churches. By way of contrast, the Watchtower places contribution boxes in its Kingdom Halls so people can give anonymously.

Your objective is to show the Witnesses from the Scriptures that there are many acceptable ways to raise money for the church, including passing collection plates and making public requests for funds.

Essentially, the Watchtower's disdain for collection plates comes down to two issues: (1) that other people can see what you are or aren't giving, and (2) that churches are forever making public appeals for more money. If Witnesses raise this issue with you, you can assure them that your church donations are private.

With regard to appeals for funds, ask, "If I went to Watchtower meetings with you, wouldn't I hear speakers from time to time making public appeals for money for various projects? Don't the elders remind Jehovah's Witnesses that God loves a cheerful giver? How is that any different from public appeals made by churches?"

Have one of the Witnesses read aloud 1 Corinthians 16:1-4: "Now about the collection for God's people: Do what I told the Galatian churches to do. On the first day of every week, each one of you should set aside a sum of money in keeping with his income, saving it up, so that when I come no collections will have to be made. Then, when I arrive, I will give letters of introduction to the men you approve and send them with your gift to Jerusalem. If it seems advisable for me to go also, they will accompany me."

Ask, "Since Paul directed congregations in two large regions to take weekly collections in advance and have their offerings ready for him, there is nothing wrong with making a public appeal for money or with instructing Christians to donate weekly based on their ability to pay, is there?"

You can add, "All of 2 Corinthians 8-9 is devoted to an offering." Ask one of the Witnesses to read aloud 2 Corinthians 9:1-5. Ask, "Didn't Paul press the Corinthians about their offering so neither he nor they would be embarrassed when the Macedonians came to receive the money? Based on this example, there is nothing wrong with making open appeals for money and publicly urging generous offerings in order to support the work, is there?"

In summarizing this issue, make clear that you aren't criticizing the Watchtower's methods of obtaining donations. In fact, you are saying that there are many acceptable ways of raising funds, including public appeals and public collections.

ISSUE #5: THE CROSS

As late as the 1920s, the Watchtower used a cross-and-crown symbol. However, now it says that this practice was impure, pagan and idolatrous and that the organization was progressively cleansed of such things.[12]

In and of itself, the issue seems rather frivolous. I don't think most Christians care about the shape of the instrument on which Christ died—whether it was shaped like a traditional cross, whether it was an upright pole with no crossbeam, whether it was shaped like a plus sign, or whether it was shaped like a letter X. Whatever its shape, the important thing is that Christ died a sacrificial death on it to pay for our sins in accordance with the Scriptures.

However, the Watchtower attacks Christians over this issue and has convinced Jehovah's Witnesses that it is one of the marks that distinguishes the authentic Christian faith from the false Christianity of Christendom. Therefore, the Holy Spirit may lead you to address the issue head-on in order to defend your faith, shake the Jehovah's Witnesses' confidence in their organization, and redirect their thinking toward Jesus and what he did on the cross.

Your objective will be to show Witnesses from the Scriptures that Jesus died on a cross and that it is acceptable for Christians to display and wear crosses if they choose to do so. In fact, the practice honors Christ and his sacrifice.

In order to achieve this goal, let's look at four Watchtower arguments and how to respond to each of them.

Watchtower Argument #1: Jesus died on an upright stake, not a cross

The Watchtower often quotes secular books and Greek lexicons to try to prove its claim that Jesus died on a single upright stake. I recommend that rather than trying to counter these materials with similar sources, you simply cite the internal evidence from the Bible itself.

Ask them to show you how they believe Jesus was executed. Watchtower illustrations show Jesus impaled on a single upright pole without any crossbeam. His hands are shown as being together above his head, with a single nail pinning both hands to the stake.

Have one of the Witnesses read aloud Thomas' comments in John 20:25: "So the other disciples were telling him: 'We have seen the Lord!' But he said to them: 'Unless I see in his hands the print of the *nails* and stick my finger into the print of the *nails* and stick my hand into his side, I will never believe it'" (RNWT, emphasis added). So the Watchtower shows there being only one nail that held Jesus' hands, but its own Bible translation says there was more than one nail, indicating that Jesus was not held in the manner the Watchtower illustrations indicate. He was crucified on a cross, not a single upright stake.[13]

Ask, "According to this passage, was there one nail or more than one nail in Jesus' hands?"

Next, have one of the Witnesses read aloud Matthew 27:37: "They also posted above his head the charge against him, in writing: 'This is Jesus the King of the Jews'" (RNWT). This verse refers to Pontius Pilate posting the message above Jesus' *head*. It doesn't say that the message was posted above his *hands*, as would be the case if the Watchtower illustrations were correct.

Also have one of them read aloud John 21:18-19, where Jesus says to Peter, "'I tell you the truth, when you were younger you dressed yourself and went where you wanted; but when you are old you will stretch out your hands, and someone else will dress you and lead you where you do not want to go.' Jesus said this to indicate the kind of death by which Peter would glorify God. Then he said to him, 'Follow me!'"

Granted, this refers to Peter's death rather than Jesus'. However, this reference to the stretching out of hands does show that the traditional cross was in use at this time. Demonstrate the two different arm positions as you ask, "Doesn't this indicate that crucifixion involved the stretching out of a person's hands at his sides rather than a stretching out of his arms with his hands being nailed together above his head?"

Watchtower Argument #2: The cross is a pagan sex symbol used in pagan worship

The Watchtower states, "According to history, Tammuz was a Babylonian god, and the cross was used as his symbol. From its beginning in the days of Nimrod, Babylon was against Jehovah and an enemy of true worship. (Gen. 10:8-10; Jer. 50:29) So by cherishing the cross, a person is honoring a symbol of worship that is opposed to the true God."[14]

In rebuttal, you can say something like this: "To me, the cross is the instrument on which Christ paid for my sins and purchased my salvation. My conscience isn't troubled at all because of what it might have represented to some pagans thousands of years ago."

Watchtower Argument #3: Veneration of the cross is idolatrous

You can agree with the Witnesses that it would be wrong to actually worship the cross itself or to use it as some sort of good luck charm. You can add, "Any object can become an idol if a person places faith in that object rather than in Christ. However, I believe that to brand a person an idolater merely because he or she displays or wears a cross violates the Romans 14:1-4 command against passing judgment on another person regarding matters of individual conscience. I don't worship the cross. I don't think it has some sort of magical powers. To me, it symbolizes Christ's suffering and death that purchased my salvation. It testifies to what he did. That is not idolatrous."

Watchtower Argument #4: The instrument on which Jesus died should be shunned, not cherished

Jehovah's Witnesses cannot understand why you or I would "cherish the old rugged cross." The Watchtower is actually repulsed by it. Witnesses often render unsuspecting Christians speechless by making the following argument:

"How would you feel if one of your dearest friends was executed on the basis of false charges? Would you make a replica of the instrument of execution? Would you cherish it, or would you rather shun it?"15

I recommend that you answer this argument by saying, "Let's use your translation's term 'torture stake.' Let's see what Paul has to say about the torture stake."

Have one of the Witnesses read aloud Philippians 3:18-19: "For there are many—I used to mention them often but now I mention them also with weeping—who are walking as enemies of the torture stake of the Christ. Their end is destruction, and their god is their belly, and their glory is really their shame, and they have their minds on earthly things" (RNWT).

Ask:

- According to Paul, is being an enemy of the torture stake a good thing or a bad thing?
- Why does Paul consider it wrong to be an enemy of the torture stake?

Next, have one of them read aloud 1 Corinthians 1:17-18: "For Christ sent me, not to baptize, but to declare the good news, and not with wisdom of speech, so that the torture stake of the Christ should not be made useless. For the speech about the torture stake is foolishness to those who are perishing, but to us who are being saved, it is God's power" (RNWT).

Ask:

- Why do those who are perishing consider speech about the torture stake to be foolishness?
- What does Paul say the torture stake represents to those who are being saved?
- In what way does the torture stake represent God's power?

Then have one of the Witnesses read aloud Galatians 6:14: "But may I never boast, except in the torture stake of our Lord Jesus Christ, through whom the world has been put to death with regard to me and I with regard to the world" (RNWT).

Ask:

- Why did Paul boast in the torture stake of Christ?
- Do you boast in the torture stake of Christ? Why or why not?

Then ask:

- How would you summarize what the torture stake meant to Paul?
- Based on all the passages we've looked at, would you say Paul considered the torture stake to be a symbol of evil, defeat, and shame or a symbol of victory and triumph?
- What does the torture stake mean to you?

You can sum up this issue on a positive note of witness by saying, "Do you see from these scriptures why, to me, the cross is not a symbol of evil and defeat but of victory? Satan tried to use it to destroy the Messiah, but God turned it into the instrument on which Christ defeated Satan's plan and purchased salvation. It is Christ's victory and his sacrifice that Christians are testifying to when we identify ourselves using the symbol of the cross."

CONCLUSION

The topics covered in this chapter are not issues on which I would recommend that you initiate discussion unless you sense that the Holy Spirit is definitely leading you to do so. However, Jehovah's Witnesses often bring up one or more of them in order to try to prove that the Watchtower religion is the only true Christianity.

The suggestions in this chapter will enable you to be prepared to answer them. Remember that you are not asking the Witnesses to agree with you regarding these issues. Instead, your focus is on the freedom of conscience the Bible allows in these matters. If you can get them to think for themselves on these issues, you will have taken important strides in helping to break the hold the Watchtower organization has on them.

Chapter 18:
The Justice for the Wicked Approach

"Anyone who rejected the law of Moses died without mercy on the testimony of two or three witnesses. How much more severely do you think a man deserves to be punished who has trampled the Son of God under foot, who has treated as an unholy thing the blood of the covenant that sanctified him, and who has insulted the Spirit of grace?" (Hebrews 10:28-29).

The objective of this approach is to show Jehovah's Witnesses that the Watchtower's everlasting-nonexistence-of-the-wicked doctrine is neither just nor biblical.

"What would you think of a parent who held his child's hand over a fire to punish the child for wrongdoing? 'God is love.' (1 John 4:8). Would he do what no right-minded human parent would do? Certainly not!"[1]

This emotional Watchtower challenge often flusters Christians. If you defend the doctrine of hell, you seem to be portraying God as a sadistic monster. On the other hand, if you accept the illustration and argument, you are conceding that the Watchtower is right and that Christian teaching is wrong.

The Watchtower calls the concept of conscious everlasting punishment of unrepentant human beings a "God-dishonoring doctrine" originated by Satan as a slander on God.[2] It states, "Hellfire is not a Bible teaching. The very idea of eternal torment is repugnant to God. His maximum punishment for the wicked is to revoke the gift of life."[3]

It teaches that human beings do not have conscious souls or spirits which survive death. When people die, they simply go out of existence. That is the end of them unless God chooses to resurrect them.

This one-size-fits-all punishment raises moral and biblical issues Jehovah's Witnesses never consider. Your approach will be to question the justice of the Watchtower's everlasting-nonexistence-of-the-wicked doctrine in light of biblical revelation.

JUSTICE REQUIRES
GRADATIONS OF PUNISHMENT

Begin this way: "The Watchtower teaching that the wicked will all receive the identical punishment of everlasting nonexistence troubles me. Doesn't justice require different levels of punishment? Otherwise wouldn't an unrepentant petty thief receive the identical punishment for his sins as Hitler receives for his? That doesn't seem right to me. What am I missing?"

If the Watchtower were right, then after torturing and exterminating six million people—including many Jehovah's Witnesses—Hitler experienced a quick and relatively painless death by committing suicide and simply going out of existence.

Would Jehovah really consider that outcome to be justice?

Don't let them put you on the defensive. If they ask you if you think everlasting fiery torment is justice, point out that all you have said so far is that it seems to you that justice requires gradations of punishment, not a one-punishment-fits-all system. Ask them to explain why that is wrong.

Add, "Jesus said that some people would be punished more severely than others. All I am saying is that that seems to me to be much more just than a system in which everyone gets the identical punishment no matter how great the disparity in the sins they have committed. How do you view it?"

Most likely, this will surprise them because they have been taught to believe that the doctrine of hell is a one-size-fits-all torture of the wicked. However, that is not what the Bible teaches. Although it describes hell in terms of fire, it is clear from the Scriptures that the punishment of the unrepentant is individualized in accordance with the extent of their sins and the amount of spiritual light they had available to them.

Ask them to read aloud Matthew 11:20-24:

Then Jesus began to denounce the cities in which most of his miracles had been performed, because they did not repent. "Woe to you, Korazin! Woe to you, Bethsaida! If the miracles that were performed in you had been performed in Tyre and Sidon, they would have repented long ago in sackcloth and ashes. But I tell you, it will be more bearable for Tyre and Sidon on the day of judgment than for you. And you, Capernaum, will you be lifted up to the skies? No, you will go down to the depths. If the miracles that were performed in you had been performed in Sodom, it would have remained to this day. But I tell you that it will be more bearable for Sodom on the day of judgment than for you."

Ask, "If the punishment of the unrepentant of Tyre, Sidon, and Sodom is everlasting nonexistence and if the punishment of the unrepentant of Korazin, Bethsaida, and Capernaum is identical, then how is it more bearable in the end for the former than for the latter?"

Have one of them read aloud Luke 12:47-48: "That servant who knows his master's will and does not get ready or does not do what his master wants will be beaten with many blows. But the one who does not know and does things deserving punishment will be beaten with few blows. From everyone who has been given much, much will be demanded; and from the one who has been entrusted with much, much more will be asked."

Ask, "Doesn't this teach different levels of punishment of the wicked?"

Ask one of them to read aloud Hebrews 10:28-29: "Anyone who rejected the law of Moses died without mercy on the testimony of two or three witnesses. How much more severely do you think a man deserves to be punished who has trampled the Son of God under foot, who has treated as an unholy thing the blood of the covenant that sanctified him, and who has insulted the Spirit of grace?"

Ask them what greater punishment the writer of Hebrews is referring to. If they tell you that the former will be resurrected and have another chance in the millennium and the latter will not, ask them to explain how people who rejected the law of Moses and were justly put to death under Jehovah's law could possibly have proved worthy of a resurrection and a second chance.

WHAT ABOUT SATAN?

The Watchtower teaches that Satan himself will not undergo conscious everlasting punishment. Instead, God will annihilate him.[4] Ask them to explain how that is justice. Surely, Satan deserves far worse punishment than Adolf Hitler and all the other tyrants of human history combined.

Ask one of the Witnesses to read aloud Revelation 19:20: "But the beast was captured, and with him the false prophet who had performed the miraculous signs on his behalf. With these signs he had deluded those who had received the mark of the beast and worshiped his image. The two of them were thrown alive into the fiery lake of burning sulfur."

In Revelation 20:2-3, Satan is then bound and sealed into the abyss for 1,000 years. Revelation 20:10 indicates that at the end of the 1,000 years, "...the devil, who deceived them, was thrown into the lake of burning sulfur, where the beast and the false prophet had been thrown. They will be tormented day and night for ever and ever."

Ask them to explain how is it that if the beast and false prophet went out of existence in the lake of fire, they are still there 1,000 years later and capable of being tormented? When even the Watchtower translation says that "they will be tormented day and night forever and ever," is it truly unreasonable and "God-dishonoring" for you to conclude that they will be tormented day and night forever and ever?

A footnote in the Watchtower Bible claims that "tormented" means being "restrained" or "imprisoned." That is a unique definition of torment, but even assuming that it were accurate, if a person is completely gone, in what sense is he being restrained or imprisoned? How can even God restrain or imprison someone who no longer exists?

DEALING WITH WATCHTOWER PROOF TEXTS

Ecclesiastes 9:5

At some point the Witnesses will refer you to Ecclesiastes 9:5: "the dead know nothing at all…" (RNWT). Some Witnesses have memorized an earlier version: "the dead… are conscious of nothing at all…" (NWT). Jehovah's Witnesses repeat those words like a mantra. They consider this verse to be the definitive declaration of the state of the dead—all other Bible passages are required to be interpreted to conform to it.

In order to focus on the context, ask one of the Witnesses to read Ecclesiastes 9:5-6 aloud: "For the living know that they will die, but the dead know nothing at all, nor do they have any more reward, because all memory of them is forgotten. Also, their love and their hate and their jealousy have already perished, and they no longer have any share in what is done under the sun" (RNWT).

Say, "Just because a statement is made in the Bible doesn't mean that it expresses God's viewpoint. Does no one have any further reward beyond the grave? Is all memory of them forgotten? Is there no further hope of life on earth? Doesn't that contradict the Watchtower's teaching that we can live forever in paradise on earth?" Let them struggle with the contradiction and try to explain it to you. Keep them focused on these verses and avoid letting them jump to other scriptures.

Then ask them to look at the larger context of passage. Much of the book of Ecclesiastes is expressed—not from God's eternal perspective—but from the perspective of a man who sees this present life as all there is, the only possible source of satisfaction. Have one of the Witnesses read aloud Ecclesiastes 1:2, where the preacher laments that everything is meaningless. Is this God's view of life? If so, there would be no point reading on to the next verse, let alone all the way to Ecclesiastes 9!

So the context of Ecclesiastes 9:5—the entire verse, the verses around it, and the book as a whole—refutes the idea that this is God's revelation concerning the state of the dead to which our interpretation of all other Bible passages must conform.

Ezekiel 18:4

Jehovah's Witnesses usually only quote the last part of Ezekiel 18:4: "The soul who sins is the one who will die" (RNWT). Often they will use an earlier translation, which reads, "The soul that is sinning—it itself will die" (NWT). Encourage them to read the rest of Ezekiel 18. Point out that the topic under discussion is not the condition of the dead. It is whether God judges a person for his own sins or for the sins of others. Here, the word "soul" is simply being used as a synonym for "person," which is one of that word's meanings.

Psalm 146:4

In the Watchtower Bible version, Psalm 146:4 reads: "His spirit goes out, he returns to the ground; on that very day his thoughts perish" (RNWT). The Watchtower quotes this verse in isolation as if it were speaking about the condition of the dead. However, the context is verse 3: "Do not put your trust in princes, nor in a son of man, who cannot bring salvation" (RNWT). The passage isn't talking about whether people have souls or spirits which are still conscious after death. It is simply explaining why we shouldn't place our trust in powerful men. They die and are buried, and all their plans and promises die with them.

THE RICH MAN AND LAZARUS

One of the primary passages that refutes the Watchtower's everlasting-nonexistence-of-the-wicked doctrine is Jesus' account of the rich man and Lazarus in Luke 16:19-31. Have one of the Witnesses read the entire passage aloud.

Ask, "If conscious suffering after death is contrary to Scripture and a God-dishonoring teaching, why would Jesus use such concepts as the basis for his story?"

What the Watchtower says Jesus meant

Because Ecclesiastes 9:5 says that "the dead know nothing," the Watchtower concludes that Jesus' account of the rich man and Lazarus can't really be about two men who actually died, remained conscious after death, and experienced either paradise or torment.

It attempts to escape the plain meaning of Jesus' words by ridiculing a straw man interpretation of the passage. "If taken literally," the Watchtower says, "Jesus' story would mean that those enjoying divine favor could all fit into the bosom of one man, Abraham; that the water on one's fingertip would not be evaporated by the fire of Hades; that a mere drop of water would bring relief to one suffering there. Does that sound reasonable to you? If it were literal, it would contradict other parts of the Bible. If the Bible were thus contradictory, would a lover of truth use it as the basis for his faith? But the Bible does not contradict itself."[5]

Having thus debunked a completely literal meaning for every word and phrase—an interpretation that no responsible scholar espouses—it then goes to the opposite extreme and insists that Jesus' story is nothing more than an allegory about a reversal of fortunes in this life. It inserts its own meanings for all the people and events in Jesus' account and then proclaims itself defender of reasonableness and biblical consistency. What it ends up with is a fanciful and self-contradictory interpretation of its own creation.

According to the Watchtower, virtually everything in this story is symbolic. Ask the Witnesses to go back through the entire passage with you and explain to you what everything means. Don't argue with them. If necessary, ask specific questions to draw out their entire explanation. Here is what the Watchtower teaches:

The "rich man" represents a class—the religious leaders who had been favored with special privileges and opportunities before John the Baptist and Jesus began preaching. "Lazarus" represents another class—the common people who hungered for spiritual nourishment but received next to nothing from those religious leaders. "Abraham" represents Jehovah God, and the bosom position with Abraham represents having God's favor.

"Death" represents both classes "dying" to their previous condition as a result of their response to the preaching of the kingdom message by John the Baptist and Jesus. The common people accepted Jesus' message and so "died" to their previous condition of spiritual hunger. They now receive abundant spiritual food from Jesus. The religious leaders rejected Jesus' kingdom message and so "died" to their previous condition of supposed favor with God. When the new covenant replaced the law covenant at Pentecost, it became clear that Jesus' disciples, rather than the Pharisees and other religious leaders, were favored by God.

The rich man's "torment" is what the religious leaders are experiencing because of the "fiery judgment messages proclaimed by Jesus' disciples." When the rich man requests that Abraham send Lazarus to "dip his finger in water" and "cool my tongue," that means that these religious leaders are asking Jehovah to have Jesus' disciples let up from preaching the fiery messages that are causing them this torment.

The "great chasm" that prevents people crossing from Jesus' disciples' side to the religious leaders' side (and the reverse) is God's unchangeable, righteous judgment.

The "five brothers" represent the religious leaders' allies. The spiritual "father" of the religious leaders and their allies is Satan. When the rich man asks Abraham to send Lazarus to his five brothers, it's not because he wants his brothers to hear the gospel message and repent. Instead, he is asking Jehovah to have Jesus' disciples *water down* their judgment messages so that his religious allies will not also be tormented by them.

Abraham's response is that if the brothers want to avoid torment, they need to read Moses and the prophets, recognize Jesus as the Messiah, and become his disciples. The religious leaders tell Abraham that "if someone from the dead goes to them, they will repent." However, they are told that God will not provide special signs or miracles in order to convince them. Instead, they must read and obey the Scriptures.[6]

Discussing the passage

Make sure the Witnesses give you this entire explanation. If necessary, keep asking questions about what they believe each element of the story stands for. Tell them that you find this interpretation confusing because it is so different from what you have been taught.

Go through the key verses covered below, asking questions similar to the ones I have set out. These questions highlight the flaws in the Watchtower's explanation of the passage. If they don't give you satisfactory answers, you may have to clarify or rephrase your questions.

In verse 26, Abraham says, *"A great chasm has been fixed between us and you, so that those who want to go over from here to you cannot, neither may people cross over from there to us"* (RNWT).

Ask:

- Why would those who are in Jehovah's favor want to go over to the disfavored side except to help people who are there?
- If all these events take place in this life, why can't Christians go over to the disfavored side to help those people?
- If all these events take place in this life, why can't people who realize that they are not in God's favor repent and cross over to God's side?
- Isn't the way open for anyone to repent as long as they are still alive?

In verse 28, the rich man asks Abraham to send Lazarus to his five brothers *"in order that he may give them a thorough witness so that they will not also come into this place of torment"* (RNWT).

Ask:

- Aren't the brothers already in the same place of torment as the rich man? Haven't they experienced the same reversal of circumstances? Haven't they also been hearing Christians' tormenting messages?
- If the rich man doesn't want his brothers tormented by Lazarus' message, why does he ask Abraham to send Lazarus *to* them? Wouldn't he rather ask Abraham to keep Lazarus *away from* them?
- Isn't asking that Lazarus give the brothers "a thorough witness" the opposite of asking Abraham to have Jesus' disciples back off or water down the message?
- How would Lazarus' giving the brothers a thorough witness help them avoid torment? According to the Watchtower interpretation, wasn't it a thorough Christian witness that was causing their torment?
- Why does Abraham refuse to send Lazarus to give the brothers a thorough witness? Aren't Christians supposed to try to give everyone a thorough witness?

In verse 30, the rich man talks about his five brothers and says, *"If someone from the dead goes to them, they will repent"* (RNWT).

Ask:

- What does the rich man mean when he says, "If someone from the dead goes to them"? If "death" in this story is only symbolic of a change in circumstances, why doesn't the rich man just "go from the dead" to his brothers himself? Why does he ask Abraham to send Lazarus to them?

- Why does he claim that if Abraham will send Lazarus to them they will repent? Does this mean that he wants his brothers to repent? (The Watchtower teaching denies this, although the individual Witness may not be aware of that.)

- If he does want his brothers to repent in order to avoid this place of torment, what prevents him from repenting himself and ending his own torment? Why doesn't Abraham even suggest that he do so?

In verse 31, Abraham answers, *"If they do not listen to Moses and the Prophets, neither will they be persuaded if someone rises from the dead"* (RNWT).

Ask:

- If, in Jesus' story, "death" is only symbolic of a change of circumstances in this life, what does "rising from the dead" symbolize?

- Was the rich man asking Abraham for a special sign or miracle in which someone would literally rise from the dead and go to his brothers?

- Since the only person they were discussing sending to the brothers was Lazarus, wouldn't that mean that Lazarus was literally dead?

- Why would "death" be figurative throughout the story but literal at the very end?

Giving the Christian interpretation

Sometimes Witnesses will ask you for your interpretation of the passage. If they give you this opportunity, I suggest making the following points:

- In view of what Jesus says here, Ecclesiastes 9:5-6 should be interpreted as the mistaken worldview of the human narrator rather than as being God's viewpoint. After all, in Ecclesiastes 9:5 the narrator says the dead "have no further reward," and that certainly isn't consistent with God's revelation elsewhere in the Bible.

- If the rich man and Lazarus really are dead, as Jesus said, that would explain his references to "being buried" and "rising from the dead." It would also explain why neither Lazarus nor the rich man can go give a warning to the five brothers.

- The rich man seems to want his five brothers to avoid coming to the place of torment. Yet he doesn't repent and join Abraham and Lazarus in order to end his own torment, and they never try to persuade him to do so. That leads me to believe that after a person dies, it is too late for him to repent. He can't get to God's side, nor can anyone from God's side get to him to help him.

- Although the rich man describes his torment in terms of agony in flame, he is not screaming in pain as he would if he were actually on fire. He describes his agony in terms of extreme thirst. That leads me to believe that his punishment is like a longing that never gets satisfied.

- This interpretation accords with Jesus' teaching in Matthew 11 and the statement in Hebrews 10 which show that there are different levels of punishment depending on the nature and depth of the person's sins and the amount of light he had.

OTHER SCRIPTURES THAT SHOW CONSCIOUS EXISTENCE AFTER DEATH

Draw the Witnesses' attention to the following passages. Have the Witnesses read them aloud one at a time.

John 11:25-26

"I am the resurrection and the life. He who believes in me will live, even though he dies; and whoever lives and believes in me will never die. Do you believe this?"

Ask, "Because Jesus says that whoever lives and believes in him will never die, do you see why I believe that there is a part of us that never ceases to exist?"

2 Corinthians 5:1

"Now we know that if the earthly tent we live in is destroyed, we have a building from God, an eternal house in heaven, not built by human hands."

Ask, "Doesn't this say that our physical bodies are merely earthly tents in which we live?"

2 Corinthians 5:8-9

"We are confident, I say, and would prefer to be away from the body and at home with the Lord. So we make it our goal to please him, whether we are at home in the body or away from it."

Ask, "Doesn't this passage show that Christians exist either at home inside their bodies or with the Lord outside of their bodies and that this part of them survives physical death?"

Philippians 1:21-24

"For to me, to live is Christ and to die is gain. If I am to go on living in the body, this will mean fruitful labor for me. Yet what shall I choose? I do not know! I am torn between the two: I desire to depart and be with Christ, which is better by far; but it is more necessary for you that I remain in the body."

Ask, "According to this passage, did Paul expect to go out of existence for thousands of years until the resurrection or did he expect to leave his body and be with Christ immediately as soon as he died?"

CONCLUSION

Because of the emotional barriers, the subject of conscious everlasting punishment of the unrepentant is a very difficult topic to discuss with anyone, especially Jehovah's Witnesses.

This approach appeals to their sense of justice by pointing out that in order for the Judge of all the earth to do right (Genesis 18:25), a man like Adolf Hitler would have to be punished more severely than an ordinary unrepentant sinner. You will have made substantial progress if you are able to lead Witnesses to question the reasonableness and the righteousness of the Watchtower's one-size-fits-all annihilationist position.

Chapter 19:
The Life and Death Issues Approach

"Nothing outside a man can make him 'unclean' by going into him. Rather, it is what comes out of a man that makes him 'unclean'" (Mark 7:15).

The objective of this approach is to show Jehovah's Witnesses that the Watchtower is not Jehovah's channel of communication (as it claims to be) as shown by the fact that it has made radical changes in its teachings regarding life and death health issues.

Jehovah's Witnesses will die and will let their children die rather than consent to a life-saving blood transfusion. Why? Because they believe God's law requires it of them.[1]

Because they expect to be persecuted for obeying "Jehovah's law" to "abstain from blood," you will do the opposite. That is, you will go out of your way not to impugn the character of Jehovah's Witnesses or the sincerity of Watchtower authorities responsible for the blood transfusion ban.

Rather, you will show them evidence that the Watchtower has radically changed its teachings on life and death health issues. Of course, this raises the questions, "If the Watchtower speaks for

Jehovah God, then why the changes? What about Witnesses who died needlessly before the changes were made?"

JUSTIFYING THE INVESTIGATION

Coming up with a non-threatening reason for examining the Watchtower's record on life and death health issues is not difficult. Many people ask Jehovah's Witnesses about the blood transfusion issue. They understand why non-Witnesses are concerned about this doctrine. If they ask you exactly what you want to look up, just tell them it's the Watchtower's past and current teachings on life and death health issues like blood transfusions.

I recommend that you say something like this: "It's well known that Jehovah's Witnesses refuse to take blood transfusions. If I were to become a Witness, I would have to do that as well. Before I would make a commitment like that, I would want to do research about what your organization has taught about these sorts of life and death health issues to see if it has been consistent and reliable. I hope you won't see that as a personal attack. I just want to be cautious. I would want to do the same sort of research if you were representatives of any other religion that claims to speak for God regarding such important matters."

What many Jehovah's Witnesses don't know is that not long ago the Watchtower also taught that Bible principles required Witnesses to refuse vaccinations and organ transplants. The organization has since abandoned those teachings. Of course, the Watchtower can't undo the harm those teachings caused to the Witness families who faithfully followed them because they thought God was demanding it of them.

Although this approach deals with these health care issues, your concern needs to be focused on the Watchtower organization itself, on its claims to speak for Jehovah God and with his authority. That is, the problem is not with the substance of old Watchtower doctrines that the organization has abandoned. The real issue is the fact that the Watchtower taught what it said came from Jehovah and then changed its teachings. Those teachings were just the misguided doctrines of fallible men. Moreover, it took decades before they realized their errors and changed those teachings.

All but one of the Watchtower documents I refer to in the sections on vaccinations and organ transplants are available for printing for your own personal use at David Reed's website, www.AnswerJW.com/rescue/medical.htm. This is part of an online version of his book, *How to Rescue Your Loved One from the Watchtower* (Baker Book House, Grand Rapids, Michigan, 1989).

HOW TO PRESENT THE EVIDENCE

1. Print only the Watchtower reprints themselves to show the Witnesses. Omit any additional comments, headings, or numbering provided by Reed.
2. Print out a separate copy for each Witness.
3. Present the documents one at a time and complete your discussion of each item before going on to the next one. Otherwise, the Witnesses will just thumb through without reading them.
4. When presenting any item, ask one of the Witnesses to read it out loud before inviting their comments. That is the best way I know to ensure that they will actually examine the Watchtower's errors and changes.

SPECIFIC CHANGES AND
SUPPORTING DOCUMENTATION

Vaccinations

1931: Vaccinations banned

"Vaccination is a direct violation of the everlasting covenant that God made with Noah after the flood" (Source: *The Golden Age*, 2/4/31, p. 293).

This means that faithful Jehovah's Witnesses could not receive vaccinations or allow their children to be vaccinated for any reason. In addition to the serious medical consequences of obeying this directive, Jehovah's Witnesses faced serious legal problems due to compulsory vaccination laws.

Remember that the refusal to be vaccinated wasn't a choice Witnesses made for medical reasons. It was required because the Watchtower told them God had so decreed. It is one thing to hear that the Watchtower used to teach this. It is far more powerful to see it in print.

1952: Vaccination ban dropped

Ask the Witnesses to help you find out when this ban was dropped and why. The answer is that it stood for 21 years. Unfortunately, Reed's website doesn't include a copy of the publication where the change was made. If the Witnesses have trouble finding it, you can tell them that you read that the change came in the 12/1/52 edition of *The Watchtower* and ask them to locate and provide you a copy.

Each individual has to take the consequences for whatever position and action he takes toward a case of compulsory vaccination, doing so according to his own conscience and his appreciation of what is for good health and the interests of advancing God's work. And our Society cannot afford to be drawn into the affair legally or take the responsibility for the way the case turns out. After consideration of the matter, it does not appear to us to be in violation of the everlasting covenant made with Noah, as set down in Genesis 9:4, nor contrary to God's related commandment at Leviticus 17:10-14... Hence all objection to vaccination on Scriptural grounds appears to be lacking (Source: *The Watchtower*, "Questions from Readers", 12/15/52, p. 764).

If Witnesses look up this article, they will discover that no explanation was given for the complete reversal in Bible interpretation. The only reason the article gives for the change is that the Watchtower cannot afford to take legal responsibility for such decisions. No reference was made at all to the opposite "truth" that Jehovah's Witnesses had been required to follow for more than two decades.

How to follow up regarding vaccinations

Once you have shown the Witnesses the change in doctrine, ask questions similar to the following, as many as are needed to make your point:

- At the time the Watchtower writers published the doctrine that vaccinations were forbidden by the Scriptures, do you think they honestly believed that this teaching came from Jehovah? (Of course, they have to say yes.)

- Looking back on it now, would you say that that doctrine really came from Jehovah? (If they say yes, then ask, "Then why did the Watchtower abandon it?" If they say the organization got new light, ask, "Are you saying that it was Jehovah who changed his mind on a life and death matter like this?")
- In their role as Jehovah's channel of communication, how do the Watchtower writers know that such a teaching truly comes from Jehovah and isn't just their fallible human understanding? (This is a question most Witnesses have never considered.)
- Do you see why I'm concerned about making a commitment that would require me to make life and death decisions regarding myself and my family based on Watchtower teachings that might be discarded later?

If the Witnesses complain that you are dredging up doctrines the Watchtower no longer teaches, you can say, "That's just the point! I realize this happened many years ago. But it had a major impact on Jehovah's Witnesses' lives. I think, 'How would I have felt if I were a Jehovah's Witness parent and my child died during those 21 years because I refused to allow them to be vaccinated, and then the Watchtower later acknowledged that this tragedy was not really required by Jehovah after all?' I personally think I would be burdened with guilt and filled with anger. How would you feel if that happened to you?"

Stop and let them wrestle with the issue. The more you can get them thinking about these kinds of questions in regards to the older issues of vaccinations and organ transplants, the more they are likely to consider them in the setting of blood transfusions.

Organ transplants

1967: Organ transplants banned as cannibalism

"Those who submit to such operations are thus living off the flesh of another human. That is cannibalistic. However, in allowing man to eat animal flesh Jehovah God did not grant permission for humans to try to perpetuate their lives by cannibalistically taking into their bodies human flesh, whether chewed or in the form of whole organs or body parts taken from others" (Source: *The Watchtower*, "Questions from Readers", 11/15/67, p. 702).

1968: Organ transplant ban repeated

"Not to be overlooked are the religious, the Scriptural issues involved. There are those, such as the Christian witnesses of Jehovah, who consider *all* transplants between humans to be cannibalism; and is not the utilizing of the flesh of another human for one's own life cannibalistic?" (Source: *Awake!* 6/8/68, p. 21, emphasis original).

1980: Organ transplant ban dropped

"While the Bible specifically forbids consuming blood, there is no biblical command pointedly forbidding the taking of other human tissue... It is a matter for personal decision. (Gal. 6:5) The congregation judicial committee would not take disciplinary action if someone accepted an organ transplant" (Source: *The Watchtower*, "Questions from Readers", 3/15/80, p. 31).

How to follow up regarding organ transplants

After the Witnesses have seen the evidence, you can make comments such as these:

- I think of Jehovah's Witnesses who out of obedience allowed parents or spouses or children to die rather than have an organ transplant. When the Watchtower changed its teaching and it became evident that they died for a mistake, what did the Watchtower authorities do to take responsibility for the consequences of that erroneous teaching?

- Do you see why this troubles me so much? I think of Jehovah's Witnesses during the period from 1967 to 1980 who might have gone blind because they faithfully refused a cornea transplant or who might even have allowed a child to die by refusing a life-saving kidney transplant. Given these major shifts in what the Watchtower has taught that God's law requires, help me understand why you feel you would have to let a loved one die in reliance on what they say God requires regarding various medical procedures. Aren't they just fallible men?

Blood transfusions

Witnesses are unlikely to dispute that the Watchtower used to forbid all blood products. If they do, refer them to the 1963 article below. There is no photocopy available online, so ask them to look it up for you. Your goal will be to get them to examine the Watchtower literature to see these changes for themselves.

1963: Anything derived from blood is forbidden

"As to blood transfusions, he knows from his study of the Bible and the publications of the Watch Tower Society that this is an unscriptural practice... He need only ask the doctor... 'Where did you get this substance?' If the answer is 'Blood,' he knows what course to take, for it is not just whole blood but anything that is derived from blood and used to sustain life or strengthen one that comes under this principle" (Source: *The Watchtower*, "Carry Your Own Load of Responsibility", 2/15/63, p. 124).

An obedient Jehovah's Witness, accepting this as truth from God's organization, would have died or let a spouse or child die rather than allowing a doctor to treat them with *anything* that is derived from blood.

2000: Blood fractions are a matter of conscience

This article regarding blood fractions is available in the Watchtower online library at JW.org.

Should Christians accept these fractions in medical treatment? We cannot say. The Bible does not give details, so a Christian must make his own conscientious decision before God.

Some would refuse anything derived from blood (even fractions intended to provide temporary passive immunity). That is how they understand God's command to "abstain from blood." They reason that his law to Israel required that blood removed from a creature be "poured out on the ground." (Deuteronomy 12:22-24) Why is that relevant? Well, to prepare gamma globulin, blood-based clotting factors, and so on, requires that blood be collected and processed. Hence, some Christians reject such products, just as they reject transfusions of whole blood or of its four primary components. Their sincere, conscientious stand should be respected. Other Christians decide differently. They too refuse transfusions of whole blood, red cells, white cells, platelets, or plasma. Yet, they might allow a physician to treat them with a fraction extracted from the primary components. Even here there may be differences. One Christian may accept a gamma globulin injection, but he may or may not agree to an injection containing something extracted from red or white cells (Source: *The Watchtower*, "Questions from Readers", 6/15/00, p. 30).[2]

How to follow up regarding blood transfusions

After Witnesses acknowledge that the Watchtower has changed its teachings regarding the use of blood fractions, you can make comments such as these:

- Isn't the light supposed to get brighter and brighter as time goes by? So why is there less certainty and less unity on this matter now than there was before?
- What changed in the year 2000? The Bible didn't change, so why did the Watchtower teaching change?
- What troubles me is that either the Watchtower is Jehovah's channel of communication or it isn't. I can't help thinking about how I would feel if I let my child die without needed blood fractions because the Watchtower said it was required by Jehovah, only to have them come out a few months later and say that taking those life-saving fractions was not forbidden by Jehovah after all. Please help me understand why you or I or anyone should allow people whose doctrines change that kind of life-and-death control over our children's lives.

WATCHTOWER ARGUMENTS REGARDING BLOOD

I recommend that you try to keep the focus of the discussion on the changeability of Watchtower "truth" rather than on the substance of the teachings themselves.

Because the Watchtower has abandoned its prohibitions on vaccinations and organ transplants, Jehovah's Witnesses will not try to justify those requirements from the Bible. However, they may insist on making scriptural arguments in support of the current Watchtower ban on blood transfusions, so you need to be prepared to respond.

In order to challenge the Watchtower's teachings about blood transfusions on scriptural grounds, first ask one of the Witnesses to read aloud and explain how Jesus' own statement at Mark 7:15 applies to the issue: "Nothing outside a man can make him 'unclean' by going into him. Rather, it is what comes out of a man that makes him 'unclean.'"

They will not have a good answer to that question. What you are likely to get instead are standard Watchtower arguments justifying its blood transfusion ban. Here is what Witnesses will tell you and how I recommend you respond.

Eating blood forbidden

The Watchtower cites four proof texts in support of its blood transfusion ban:

Genesis 9:3-4: "Everything that lives and moves will be food for you. Just as I gave you the green plants, I now give you everything. But you must not eat meat that has its lifeblood still in it."

Leviticus 7:26-27: "And wherever you live, you must not eat the blood of any bird or animal. If anyone eats blood, that person must be cut off from his people."

Leviticus 17:10-12: "Any Israelite or any alien living among them who eats any blood—I will set my face against that person who eats blood and will cut him off from his people. For the life of a creature is in the blood, and I have given it to you to make atonement for yourselves on the altar; it is the blood that makes atonement for one's life. Therefore I say to the Israelites, 'None of you may eat blood, nor may an alien living among you eat blood.'"

Acts 15:28-29: "It seemed good to the Holy Spirit and to us not to burden you with anything beyond the following requirements: You are to abstain from food sacrificed to idols, from blood, from the meat of strangled animals and from sexual immorality. You will do well to avoid these things. Farewell."

Tell the Witnesses you understand that the Old Testament prohibited the eating of animal blood, and that the New Testament advised believers to continue that prohibition in order not to offend Jews. Then tell them you are confused as to why they think that that prohibition applies to the use of human blood for *medical* purposes.

The Watchtower's argument is as follows: "Is a transfusion really the same as eating blood? In a hospital, when a patient cannot eat through his mouth, he is fed intravenously. Now, would a person who never put blood into his mouth but who accepted blood by transfusion really be obeying the command to 'keep abstaining from... blood'? (Acts 15:29) To use a comparison, consider a man who is told by the doctor that he must abstain from alcohol. Would he be obedient if he quit drinking alcohol but had it put directly into his veins?"[3]

If the Witnesses give you this argument, you can ask them, "Isn't there a big difference between drinking blood for nourishment and taking donated blood to replace blood you have lost? Whether you take alcohol or a medication orally or intravenously, it serves exactly the same purpose. But while blood taken by mouth is broken down and used for nourishment just like any other food, blood taken intravenously acts completely differently. It is not food but rather a transport medium, moving oxygen, nutrients, and chemicals and cells to fight infection and heal wounds. That's just fulfilling blood's designed purpose, isn't it?"

You can follow this up by asking, "How could the Bible have been referring to this lifesaving medical procedure of blood transfusion, given that it didn't even become possible until thousands of years after the Bible was written?"

Sanctity of life

The Watchtower says, "Out of respect for the sanctity of life, godly people do not accept blood transfusions, even if others insist that such a procedure would be lifesaving."[4]

If the Witnesses make this argument, ask, "How is the sanctity of life respected by letting a person die for lack of a transfusion? Is the symbol of life more important than life itself?"

Disrespect for the ransom

The Watchtower has said, "...only sacrificial use of blood has ever been approved by God, and... since the animal sacrifices offered under the Mosaic Law foreshadowed the sacrifice of Christ, disregard for the requirement that Christians 'abstain from blood' would be an evidence of gross disrespect for the

ransom   sacrifice   of   Jesus   Christ.   (Lev.   17:11, 12;
Heb. 9:11-14, 22)"[5]

If the Witnesses make that argument, ask them to show you
in the Scriptures where it says that saving a life by means of a
blood transfusion is grossly disrespectful of Christ's sacrifice. It
isn't there. In fact, it was Jesus himself who was distraught by the
Pharisees' legalistic view of Bible commandments. In Mark 3:4,
he rhetorically asked them, "Which is lawful on the Sabbath: to
do good or to do evil, to save life or to kill?"

Ask, "Given Jesus' question to the Pharisees concerning
breaking the Sabbath, what would his attitude be toward religious
authorities who require people to die to uphold the sanctity of life
rather than allowing them to have a life-saving blood
transfusion?"

Disease transmission

If they try to sidetrack you with discussions of diseases that
can be transmitted through blood transfusions, say, "Refusing a
blood transfusion because of medical risk is one thing. Refusing
a blood transfusion because a religious authority figure tells you
that God requires you to do it even if it will cause death to yourself
or your child is quite another matter altogether, wouldn't you
agree?"

CONCLUSION

Whenever the Watchtower makes doctrinal changes,
Jehovah's Witnesses are trained to focus on the "new light" and
to ignore completely the previous teachings, much the same way
as you or I might toss out yesterday's newspaper.

When you show them evidence that the Watchtower once taught the opposite of what it teaches today, Witnesses genuinely fail to see the relevance. They will often say, "Why do you want to talk about that? That's old light. The Watchtower doesn't teach that any longer." You need to explain to them why these changes trouble you. It boils down to this:

1. The Watchtower used to forbid Jehovah's Witnesses to accept any blood fractions, vaccinations, or organ transplants.

2. The Watchtower taught that those prohibitions came from Jehovah. Jehovah's Witnesses were required to obey them even if it cost them or loved ones their lives.

3. The fact that the Watchtower has abandoned those teachings shows that the prohibitions really came from men, not from God.

4. Many loyal Jehovah's Witnesses died needlessly because those teachings of men were mistakenly presented for decades as being requirements from God.

5. There is no guarantee that what is taught as truth from Jehovah today won't be similarly discarded tomorrow.

6. Given this track record, you are genuinely puzzled and concerned as to why anyone should give admittedly fallible men that degree of control over their lives and over the lives of their children.

Chapter 20:
The False Prophecies Approach

"When the prophet speaks in the name of Jehovah and the word is not fulfilled or does not come true, then Jehovah did not speak that word. The prophet spoke it presumptuously. You should not fear him'" (Deuteronomy 18:22, RNWT).

The objective of this approach is to show Jehovah's Witnesses that the Watchtower organization is not the reliable guide it claims to be in that it has made numerous false prophecies.

Throughout its history, claiming to be God's chosen channel of communication, the Watchtower has repeatedly predicted specific years or time frames during which end times events including the resurrection of the dead will occur. When the events failed to take place as predicted, the Watchtower simply set new dates or emphasized that Armageddon is surely now closer than ever.

The fervor thus created has repeatedly motivated Jehovah's Witnesses to increase their door-to-door preaching in "the short time remaining before Armageddon."[1] It has also helped keep

Witnesses obedient to the Watchtower in every particular, lest they disobey "the faithful and discreet slave" in the last days and be destroyed in the apocalypse along with the wicked.

Many Jehovah's Witnesses have been told that the Watchtower is a cult and that its leaders are false prophets. They have come to expect this type of verbal abuse. In contrast, you will go out of your way *not* to make such accusations. Instead, you will show them Christian love by presenting your documentation in a respectful way so as to avoid appearing to persecute them for their beliefs.

JUSTIFYING THE INVESTIGATION

You need to express a non-threatening reason for examining Watchtower prophetic history. The best way to do this is to begin unexpectedly by mentioning the late Harold Camping, a radio Bible teacher who had no connections with the Watchtower.

Say something like this: "When we start talking about the end times, I can't help thinking of a man named Harold Camping. He went on the radio and predicted that the rapture of the church and cataclysmic judgments would take place in the year 2011. Many people believed him and oriented their lives around his teaching. Later, I found out that he had made similar unfulfilled predictions for 1994. Because of that, I am wary of end-times predictions. If we are going to talk about that subject, I would want to do research about what your organization has taught about the end times over the years to see if it has been consistent and reliable. I hope you won't see that as a personal attack. I just want to be cautious. I would want to do the same sort of research if you were followers of Harold Camping or representatives of any other religion that claims to speak for God."

They may warn you against believing everything that you find on the internet or in non-Watchtower sources. Specifically, they may warn you that there are apostate Jehovah's Witnesses and other Watchtower opposers who have made slanderous attacks on Jehovah's organization. In response, you can enlist their assistance by telling them, "I certainly want to make sure the information I get is accurate. Would you be willing to help me check things out so I'm not being misled by people who may have a personal ax to grind?"

Don't ask the Witnesses to look at websites. Instead, tell them that you will do research online and show them copies of anything that might concern you. Assure them that you will allow them to give whatever explanations they may think are appropriate.

If they are opposed to this procedure and threaten to break off any further contact, then suggest that it would be best not to discuss the end times at all because you aren't trying to be offensive—only cautious. However, make your point by telling them that you are very concerned when representatives of any religion try to persuade you not to investigate the history of their organization's teachings. Ask them if they understand why.

The Watchtower documents I refer to in this chapter are all available for printing for your own personal use at David Reed's website, www.AnswerJW.com/rescue/prophet.htm. This is part of an online version of his book, *How to Rescue Your Loved One from the Watchtower* (Baker Book House, Grand Rapids, Michigan, 1989).

HOW TO PRESENT THE EVIDENCE

1. Print only the Watchtower reprints themselves to show the Witnesses. Omit any additional comments, headings, or numbering provided by Reed.
2. Print out a separate copy for each Witness.
3. Present the documents one at a time and complete your discussion of each item before going on to the next one. Otherwise, the Witnesses will just thumb through without reading them.
4. When presenting any item, ask one of the Witnesses to read it out loud before inviting their comments. That is the best way I know to ensure that they will actually examine the Watchtower's errors and changes.

THE WATCHTOWER STATEMENTS AND SUPPORTING DOCUMENTATION

Here is a summary of statements the Watchtower has made and the documentation Reed provides.

The Watchtower "prophet"

Jehovah's Witnesses act as a "prophet" of God. The only way to prove it "is to review the record." (Source: "They Shall Know that a Prophet Was Among Them," *The Watchtower*, 4/1/72, p. 197)

You can say, "This is one reason why I believe it's perfectly legitimate to investigate what the Watchtower has taught over the years. Several things that they have said trouble me, and I'd like to get your thoughts on them."

1914

"In view of this strong Bible evidence concerning the Times of the Gentiles, we consider it an established truth that the final end of the kingdoms of this world, and the full establishment of the Kingdom of God, will be accomplished at the end of A.D. 1914" (Source: *The Time is at Hand (Studies in the Scriptures,* Vol. II), Watch Tower Bible and Tract Society, 1889, 1908 edition, p. 99).

Ask:

- What exactly did the Watchtower say would happen in 1914?
- How certain were they that this was truth that came from Jehovah?

1918

"...in the year 1918, when God destroys the churches wholesale and the church members by millions, it shall be that any that escape shall come to the works of Pastor Russell to learn the meaning of the downfall of 'Christianity'" (Source: *The Finished Mystery (Studies in the Scriptures,* Vol. VII), Watch Tower Bible and Tract Society, 1917, p. 485).

Ask:

- What exactly did the Watchtower say would happen in 1918?
- Do you believe this came from Jehovah or from men?

1925

"...we may confidently expect that 1925 will mark the return of Abraham, Isaac, Jacob and the faithful prophets of old, particularly those named by the Apostle in Hebrews chapter eleven, to the condition of human perfection" (Source: *Millions Now Living Will Never Die!* (Brooklyn: Watchtower Bible and Tract Society), 1920, pp. 89-90).

Ask:

- What did the Watchtower say we could confidently expect?
- What would have happened to a Jehovah's Witness who disagreed with this prediction and refused to teach it in the witnessing ministry?

1975

"According to this trustworthy Bible chronology six thousand years from man's creation will end in 1975, and the seventh period of a thousand years of human history will begin in the fall of 1975 C. E. ... It would not be by mere chance or accident but would be according to the loving purpose of Jehovah God for the reign of Jesus Christ, the 'Lord of the Sabbath,' to run parallel with the seventh millennium of man's existence" (Source: *Life Everlasting—In Freedom of the Sons of God* (Watchtower Bible and Tract Society, 1966), pp. 29-30).

Ask, "Do you think the Watchtower accurately understood what was about to happen?"

Nearness of Armageddon

"Are we to assume from this study that the battle of Armageddon will be all over by the autumn of 1975, and the long-looked-for thousand-year reign of Christ will begin by then? Possibly, but we wait to see how closely the seventh thousand-year period of man's existence coincides with the sabbathlike thousand-year reign of Christ... It may involve only a difference of weeks or months, not years" (Source: *The Watchtower*, "Why Are You Looking Forward to 1975?", 8/15/68, p. 499)

Ask:

- How many years have gone by since the autumn of 1975?
- How do you know that the Watchtower's current statements about the nearness of Armageddon truly come from Jehovah and aren't merely the mistaken expectations of fallible men?

Selling homes and property encouraged

"Reports are heard of brothers selling their homes and property and planning to finish out the rest of their days in this old system in the pioneer service. Certainly this is a fine way to spend the short time remaining before the wicked world's end" (Source: *Our Kingdom Ministry*, 5/1974, p. 3).

Ask:

- Do you think the Watchtower expected the old system to still be in operation today?
- What was the Watchtower encouraging Jehovah's Witnesses to do in 1974?
- If they had done this, where would they be financially today?
- Do you see why this troubles me?

RESPONDING TO
WATCHTOWER DEFENSES

The Watchtower has given Jehovah's Witnesses several defenses with which to deflect such criticisms. Let's look at what they are and see how to respond.

Defense #1: The Watchtower doesn't claim to be inspired or infallible

A good response is, "The Watchtower does claim to be Jehovah's channel of communication. Do its prophecies come from God or from men?"

Defense #2: Proverbs 4:18 says that the light is getting brighter and brighter

You can respond, "The problem I have with using that verse is that anybody who teaches something that is wrong can claim that it applies to them. They just don't have enough light yet. But was something that was untrue ever 'light' at all? If any person or organization uses that, my thought would be, 'If you don't have enough light so that you are frequently having to change your teachings, why are you saying that I have to believe and obey everything you tell me? Why are you claiming to be acting as God's spokesman? Is God responsible for your errors or are you?'"

If necessary, take them through some of the specific prophecies and ask if those statements were true or false. Once they admit that they were false, ask them if those teachings were ever light from Jehovah at all or whether they were merely the mistaken precepts of men.

Clearly, these are confrontational questions, but make clear that you would apply this same standard to *any* person or organization that claims to be God's exclusive spokesman.

Defense #3: The Watchtower humbly admits its mistakes

Ask them to show you specific examples where the Watchtower has said, "We were wrong." They will have a hard time finding such a statement.

Add, "If I had been a Jehovah's Witness and really had faith that the Watchtower writers weren't just speaking their own opinions but were communicating truth from God, then I would have oriented my entire life around their predictions. I wouldn't have set aside any money for my retirement because I would never be growing old in the present system. I wouldn't have gone to college because there would be no point preparing for a career that I would never have. I would have oriented my entire life around someone else's mistake. I think of all the sincere Jehovah's Witnesses who must have done that. Do you see why this issue troubles me so greatly?"

Defense #4: Jesus' apostles had wrong expectations also

They will cite you examples, such as the apostles asking Jesus if he was about to restore the kingdom to Israel (Acts 1:6).

I recommend that you reply by asking, "Can you show me an example in the Bible where the apostles taught their misunderstandings as truths from Jehovah?"

Defense #5: God's prophet Jonah told the Ninevites their city would be destroyed in 40 days, but it didn't happen

Point out that no one was misled. Jonah and the Ninevites understood that if the Ninevites repented of their sins, God might not bring that judgment (Jonah 3:1-4:2).

Defense #6: Jehovah corrects his prophets

They will cite you the example of the prophet Nathan telling King David he should build the temple, only to have God correct him (2 Samuel 7:1-13).

You can emphasize the difference this way: "The very night Nathan made the statement, God corrected him and sent him to David so that David wouldn't act on a false message that supposedly came from Jehovah. However, many of the Watchtower's errors seem to have gone uncorrected for years. Do you see why this troubles me?"

CONCLUSION

You can tell the Witnesses that you are concerned that claiming to speak for God while erroneously predicting a specific date or time frame for Armageddon or the resurrection brings discredit on God and on his Word. That certainly happened when Harold Camping's highly publicized prophecies came to nothing.

You can point out that if you had lived in the late nineteenth or early twentieth century and trusted the Watchtower as Jehovah's chosen channel of communication, you would have been required to preach as truth that God was about to overthrow all earthly governments in 1914. In addition, you might well have decided to forego a career, marriage, or children in view of that expected tribulation.

When that prediction failed, if you remained loyal to the organization, you would have had to embrace the "new light" and to preach that God would destroy all the churches of Christendom in 1918.

When that didn't happen, if you remained loyal to the organization, you would have had to embrace even more "new light" and to preach that the resurrection of Abraham, Isaac, and Jacob would take place in 1925.

If you had been a faithful Jehovah's Witness in the late 1960s and early 1970s, you might well have heeded the Watchtower's encouragement to sell your home and your property in order to devote yourself to the door-to-door ministry in the short time remaining before the end of this wicked world system. Where would that have left you?

Given this track record, you can ask the Witnesses to help you understand how the Watchtower has demonstrated any greater claim to speak for God regarding the chronology of the end times than the late Harold Camping, whose predictions also failed.

SECTION 5:
NOW TAKE
ACTION!

Chapter 21:
Where Will You Go
from Here?

The next time Jehovah's Witnesses come to your door will you hide behind the curtain and pretend you're not home? Will you open the door but tell them, "No thank you. I have my own religion" and send them on their way? Or will you see them as people for whom Christ died, invite them in, and share the gospel with them using the approaches you have learned from this book?

What would Jesus have you do? I trust that he will give you compassion for these people and confidence that if you step out in faith the Holy Spirit will empower you to share the gospel with them effectively. Granted, they won't all come to saving faith in the Lord Jesus Christ, but some of them will.

Don't count on someone else to do it. Remember that because Jehovah's Witnesses won't attend a church or listen to messages or read literature of "Christendom," you may represent their only opportunity to hear the real gospel and see their need to come to Jesus instead of relying on their works of obedience to the Watchtower organization for their salvation.

Let's take things a step further. When you think about encountering Jehovah's Witnesses, you naturally tend to think almost exclusively in terms of the usual scenario in which two of them come to your front door while they happen to be canvassing your neighborhood as part of their door-to-door field service ministry. This is a very convenient witnessing opportunity. They seek you out and ask to talk to you about God!

But what if they don't come by very often? What if you become proficient in sharing the gospel with them only to find that the local elders have warned the congregation to bypass your home? Does this end your opportunities to put into practice what you have learned from this book? Not at all. Consider expanding your opportunities to witness to Jehovah's Witnesses and others with Watchtower backgrounds.

TALK TO PEOPLE YOU ALREADY KNOW

Active Witnesses

Do you have any family members, friends, co-workers, or neighbors who are Jehovah's Witnesses? There's no reason why you can't take the initiative in talking to them. If they are active Witnesses, they should be happy to talk with you. It will probably be refreshing to them to get into a Bible conversation without having to experience a lot of rejection going door-to-door trying to find someone who is interested in talking with them. There's another incentive for them to meet with you—they can count the time they spend with you on their monthly field service report.

The primary word of advice I would give you is not to appear overeager. Tell them you would like to understand what Jehovah's Witnesses believe and why, and how it agrees with or differs from your own understanding. Then follow the principles set out in this book.

One of the advantages to talking with people you already know is that you have already built relational bridges with them. They may be willing to talk with you one-on-one rather than insisting on having another Witness sit in on your discussions. There is nothing wrong with your suggesting such an arrangement. Tell them you'd be much more comfortable talking with them friend-to-friend than going into some formal witnessing setting with people you've never met.

Witness children

If you have contact with Jehovah's Witness children, be aware that they are not allowed to participate in birthday or holiday activities, patriotic observances, competitive sports, and many other normal childhood activities. They are not even allowed to develop close friendships with "worldly" people (non-Witnesses).

Because of these restrictions, many Witness children feel ostracized or humiliated. In addition, the Watchtower trains them to expect persecution from you ("the world") because of their religion. Since they are minors and under the authority of their parents, you are limited in what you can do. The most important thing is to make sure that neither you nor your children feed this negativity by your words, attitudes, or actions.

In fact, I recommend that you go out of your way to let Witness children know you understand that their family's religion has restrictions they have to abide by and that you realize this can be hard to deal with at times. Ask them to alert you to any acceptable alternative activities in which they would like to participate. Let them know that you will always consider yourself their friend and that you are more than willing to listen if at any time they would find it helpful to talk any of this over with you.

Inactive Witnesses

Reaching out to people you already know can expand your witnessing opportunities in another way. If you wait for

Jehovah's Witnesses to knock on your door, the only ones you will encounter are the ones who are active in the field service ministry. But some Witnesses are relatively inactive, attending meetings sporadically and rarely, if ever, going door-to-door.

Because these people are Jehovah's Witnesses, they have been trained in Watchtower doctrines and understand the Watchtower mindset. Try to find out why they are inactive. Don't grill them as if you were a cross-examining attorney. Listen more than you talk. Did they have bad experiences in the door-to-door work? Do they have doubts about specific Watchtower teachings? Do they still believe the doctrines but resent the constant pressures the organization puts on them? Have they been mistreated in some way by the elders or by other Witnesses? Are they burned out?

You may be the only person in their life who really cares about them and understands what they are going through. Because you have studied this book, you are in a unique position to minister to them.

Studies

Keep your eyes and ears open. You may already know people who are not baptized Jehovah's Witnesses but who are studying with them. Perhaps they are members of your family or close personal friends. Maybe you have a friend who is deeply concerned because a loved one is involved in a Watchtower study.

What can you do to help?

It is almost always counterproductive to tell a person who is studying with the Witnesses point blank that the Watchtower is a cult and that they should stop their study. The Witnesses will have told them to expect this sort of opposition to their "learning the truth." You will only be enhancing the credibility of the Watchtower.

Instead, listen to find out the degree to which they have already bought into the Watchtower mindset. If they are just starting out, commend them for their interest in the Bible, tell them that you have seen some things that concern you about the Watchtower and its teachings, and ask them to look at both sides of things before making any commitment.

Once you have studied the doctrinal information and approaches set out in this book, you might even volunteer to come with them to their "home Bible study" to present a balanced view. Most likely, the Witnesses won't agree to such an arrangement. In that event, ask the person to discuss these matters with you separately and give you equal time in order to get your response to what the Witnesses are saying.

Usually, the Watchtower indoctrination will not be as strong with studies as it is with people who have been Witnesses for years. Their interest in religious topics may be a great opportunity for you to lead them to Christ.

On the other hand, sometimes you may find that a person who is studying with the Witnesses has already developed such a level of trust in the Watchtower that they consider any "other side" to be satanic. In fact, because they have been welcomed at the Kingdom Hall and have never seen or experienced the downside of life as a Jehovah's Witness, they may have a starry-eyed view of the Watchtower organization. In that situation, the best thing to do is to tell them that you respect their right to make their own religious commitments. Then engage them in discussion as if they were already a fully committed Jehovah's Witness.

Ex-Jehovah's Witnesses

You may know someone who used to be a Witness but who has completely drifted away, has formally disassociated, or who has been disfellowshipped by the elders. Based on statistics published by the Watchtower organization itself, it has been estimated that as many as 950,000 Jehovah's Witnesses have left the organization in a 10-year period.[1]

Listen to them to find out why they left. Don't assume just because they have left the organization that they disagree with its theology or look favorably on Christianity. Some leave the Watchtower because they are exhausted or because of a moral lapse but still believe the Watchtower system is "the truth." Still others leave because they see or experience mistreatment by Watchtower leaders or other Jehovah's Witnesses. Some people leave the Watchtower because they are burned out on religion altogether. Many have become agnostics or atheists.

Adjust your approach depending on what they reveal to you. If they aren't interested in discussing religious issues with you, respect their decision. However, if they are open to the gospel, your commitment and the knowledge you have gained from studying this book can be invaluable.

REACH OUT TO STRANGERS

Street work

Sometimes you will encounter Jehovah's Witnesses who are handing out magazines on street corners in urban areas. They may have literature carts set up in various locations. If you want to expand your witnessing opportunities, go over and talk with them.

If you strike up a conversation with them, you may be able to set up a series of meetings with them—if not in your home, then perhaps in a public place such as a nearby coffee shop or restaurant. Even if arranging for such meetings isn't possible, you don't have to bypass them. You can plant some gospel seeds in the course of one brief dialogue.

If you know you will be encountering Witnesses who are involved in street ministry, you can prepare one of the approaches in this book—perhaps "The Come to Jesus Approach" or "The Faith and Works Approach." Select one aspect of the approach to concentrate on and focus on planting a seed.

You could also prepare a small card to give them with the addresses of two websites—www.4witness.org and www.jwfacts.com—along with your own contact information. The first site was created by Christians who are former Jehovah's Witnesses or former Mormons who are trying to reach people in those faiths with the gospel. The second site is not Christian based, but it provides many citations to older Watchtower publications which contain the organization's false prophecies and doctrinal changes.

Jehovah's Witnesses who are obeying the Watchtower will not visit those sites and will probably just throw your card away, but you may be able to interest others who are harboring doubts or are at least willing to investigate. Although recommending either of these websites to a Witness in your living room would most likely produce antagonism that might end their willingness to meet with you, there is little downside to doing so with a Jehovah's Witness whom you will only encounter once in the course of their street ministry.

Internet outreach

Another fruitful area for expanding your witnessing opportunities is internet outreach. Social media such as Facebook have online discussion groups involving Witnesses and ex-Witnesses. In addition, there are now support groups online for ex-Jehovah's Witnesses and for current Jehovah's Witnesses who suspect something is wrong with the Watchtower and are looking for answers. These are good places to learn about how Jehovah's Witnesses think and feel and to read about people's struggles within the Watchtower organization.

The largest of these sites is called JWN, located at www.jehovahs-witness.com/forum. In many of these forums, posting is done by username rather than actual names in order to preserve anonymity. Forum members may or may not still believe in God. Many of them have been turned off by religion and don't welcome people trying to witness to them. Of course, this is their right.

Some sites have rules against evangelizing in your postings. However, there are people on such forums who *are* looking for a Christian alternative to the Watchtower. Perhaps they have never heard a good explanation or good defense of Christian teachings. You can usually stay within the rules by using the private messaging capability of such forums. If you see postings from a person who indicates faith in God or from a person who admits that they are struggling with what to believe, you can send them a private message, tell them you believe in God and Christ, and offer to dialogue with them if they are interested. If they say they aren't interested, stop.

Let those who are willing to talk set the agenda. Maybe all they want is to find a listening ear. That's fine. Be that listening ear. Show them genuine Christian love. It often helps to assure them that you are not trying to get them to join some other religious organization.

Before you initiate private online discussion of a topic you know is likely to be controversial with Watchtower-trained correspondents—issues like the Trinity or hell, for example—first ask them if they really want to get into that particular subject with you. Let them know that if they don't want to discuss a particular issue, you will honor their wishes.

Some of my online correspondents have expressed interest in visiting churches in their area and have asked me for my thoughts on where to look. Since you won't be able to attend alongside them, I recommend that you tell them that before they try out churches they should study the Bible and decide what they are going to believe or at least what ideas they are willing to consider. Also explain to them the negative triggers they are likely to encounter at a church because of Watchtower indoctrination about all the "pagan" doctrines and practices of "Christendom"— calling Jesus "God," praying to him, displaying crosses, passing collection plates, and the like. Offer to help them work through those issues.

Make sure they understand that the key to salvation is not finding the "right" organization but coming to Jesus himself. I recommend that you have them read John 5:39-40 and John 6:67-68. Tell them, "Jehovah's real arrangement for salvation is that we come to Jesus and rely on him, not that we place our trust in any organization run by fallible men."

If they decide to proceed to check out churches, explain to them how to obtain doctrinal statements in advance online from those institutions. Follow up with them after their visit to see what they thought and clear up any misconceptions.

Going to a Kingdom Hall

If you become proficient at witnessing to Jehovah's Witnesses, one way to find Witnesses to talk with is to attend a meeting at one of their Kingdom Halls. Men should wear business suits and neckties. Women are expected to wear dresses or blouses and skirts rather than slacks. If you are interested in trying this, let me offer you several suggestions.

First, remember what I said earlier in this book about the need to establish safeguards of accountability with trusted Christian friends to make sure you don't get sucked into the Watchtower. Almost everyone there will be a Jehovah's Witness, and the meetings will be centered on indoctrination in Watchtower theology.

Second, the best time to make your first appearance at a Kingdom Hall is at what Witnesses call the "Memorial." This annual meeting takes place near Easter. As the time approaches, the Watchtower will post the date on its website, jw.org. Witnesses pass bread and wine without partaking, and the public talk will explain the Watchtower's two-class salvation system. Because of this, you will know in advance what to study and which approaches to consider. The other advantage to attending this event is that the Watchtower always pushes Witnesses to invite as many non-Witnesses as possible to attend, so it will seem natural to them for strangers to be present. At this meeting, you can express interest in having Witnesses come to your home to explain their teachings further.

Third, recognize that you will only get to have extended discussions with a couple of Witnesses you meet at the Kingdom Hall. Word will travel quickly throughout that congregation that you raised tough questions instead of being a passive and compliant student. In all likelihood, you will not be able to set up meetings with other Witnesses from that same Kingdom Hall, except perhaps with elders whose primary interest will be in protecting their congregation from your influence.

CONCLUSION

I encourage you to expand your witnessing opportunities. Whether they are people you already know or total strangers, active Jehovah's Witnesses, inactive Witnesses, studies, or ex-Witnesses, they are all people for whom Christ died.

You may be the only Christian in their life who understands them and reaches out to them. Using what you have learned from this book, you may be able to lead them to saving faith in Christ. In any case, you can connect with them in some way and show them genuine, unconditional Christian love.

Don't assume that any Jehovah's Witness is unreachable. I personally start with the assumption that all Jehovah's Witnesses can be reached but that some are easier to get through to than others. Many are already secretly dissatisfied and looking for answers. Bill Cetnar, Joan Cetnar, Rob Sullivan, and Randall Watters, all former workers at Watchtower headquarters, left the organization and found salvation in Jesus Christ, as did Watchtower overseers and elders Peter Barnes, Leonard Chretien, Fred Gholson, and David Reed.

Former Jehovah's Witness elder Don Cameron states, "No matter how deeply captive they are to their organizational concept and no matter what pressures there are to keep them there, it is not so deep and the pressures are not so great that God cannot help them escape."[2]

Prepare well. Then step out in faith and see what God will do.

From the author

Thank you for reading this book. If you found it helpful, please leave a review on the website where you purchased it, giving your opinion and comments.

Please visit my website at **www.DAEnglund.com**.

There you can read my blog, leave comments on the book or blog, and contact me with any questions or comments. I would like to help you in any way that I can as you reach out to Jehovah's Witnesses.

David A. Englund

NOTES

Chapter 1: Here They Come—Now What?

1. F.F. Bruce, *The Epistles of John* (Grand Rapids: William B. Eerdmans Publishing Company, 1970), p. 142
2. This line of argument and accompanying proof texts are now set out for Jehovah's Witnesses in a 1985 Watchtower reference book entitled *Reasoning from the Scriptures* (Brooklyn: Watchtower Bible and Tract Society, 1985, 2009 printing), see pp. 162-166.
3. Ted Dencher, *Why I Left Jehovah's Witnesses* (Fort Washington, PA: Christian Literature Crusade, 1966, 1975 printing), pp. 10-11

Chapter 2: My Study with Jehovah's Witnesses

1. *The Truth That Leads to Eternal Life* (Brooklyn: Watchtower Bible and Tract Society, 1968), pp. 49-50
2. *The Truth That Leads to Eternal Life*, p. 50

Chapter 3: Encountering the Organizational Mindset

1. *The Truth That Leads to Eternal Life* (Brooklyn: Watchtower Bible and Tract Society, 1968), p. 16
2. *Reasoning from the Scriptures* (Brooklyn: Watchtower Bible and Tract Society, 1985, 2009 printing), p. 283
3. *Reasoning from the Scriptures*, pp. 283-284
4. *The Watchtower*, "What Does It Mean to Be Loyal?", 10/1/01, p. 22
5. *Reasoning from the Scriptures*, p. 204

Chapter 4: Witnessing Principles I Learned

1. Ted Dencher, *Why I Left Jehovah's Witnesses* (Fort Washington, PA: Christian Literature Crusade, 1966, 1975 printing), p. 73
2. *Reasoning from the Scriptures* (Brooklyn: Watchtower Bible and Tract Society, 1985, 2009 printing), p. 383
3. David Reed, *How to Rescue Your Loved One from the Watchtower* (Grand Rapids: Baker Book House Company, 1989), p. 44

Chapter 5: Irreconcilable Differences

1. *The Watchtower*, "Out of the Tombs to a 'Resurrection of Life'", 12/1/64, pp. 724-725
2. *Life Everlasting—In Freedom of the Sons of God* (Brooklyn: Watchtower Bible and Tract Society, 1966), p. 391
3. *The Watchtower*, "Have You Received 'the Spirit of the Truth'?", 2/1/02, p. 21
4. *Life Everlasting—In Freedom of the Sons of God*, p. 390
5. *The Watchtower*, "Questions from Readers", 10/1/74, pp. 607-608
6. *The Watchtower*, "Will You See Your Dead Loved Ones Again?", 9/1/67, pp. 521-526; *The Watchtower*, "Would You Want to Be There?", 5/15/74, p. 293; *The Watchtower*, "Make Jehovah's Everlasting Arms Your Support", 10/1/91, p. 14
7. *Insight on the Scriptures*, Volume 2 (Brooklyn: Watch Tower Bible and Tract Society & International Bible Students Association, 1988), p. 1169
8. *The Watchtower*, "Would You Want to Be There?", 5/15/74, p. 292
9. *The Watchtower*, "Benefiting Now from Christ's Ransom", 1/15/62, p. 39
10. *The Watchtower*, "Would You Want to Be There?", 5/15/74, p. 293
11. *Life Everlasting—In Freedom of the Sons of God*, p. 397
12. *The Watchtower*, "Holy Spirit's Role in the Outworking of Jehovah's Purpose", 4/15/10, p. 11
13. *The Watchtower*, "Would You Want to Be There?", 5/15/74, p. 292
14. *Life Everlasting—In Freedom of the Sons of God*, pp. 398-399
15. *Life Everlasting—In Freedom of the Sons of God*, p. 399

16. *Life Everlasting—In Freedom of the Sons of God*, p. 400
17. *Life Everlasting—In Freedom of the Sons of God*, p. 400
18. *The Watchtower*, "Questions from Readers", 8/15/06, p. 31

Chapter 7: The Come to Jesus Approach

1. *Reasoning from the Scriptures* (Brooklyn: Watchtower Bible and Tract Society, 1985, 2009 printing), p. 218
2. *What Does the Bible* Really *Teach?* (Brooklyn: Watchtower Bible and Tract Society, 2005, 2013 printing), p. 51
3. Arnold Hoffman, "A Few Effective Methods in Witnessing to Jehovah's Witnesses" at www.4jehovah.org/store/audio/effective-methods-in-witnessing-to-jehovahs-witnesses
4. Arnold Hoffman, "A Few Effective Methods in Witnessing to Jehovah's Witnesses"
5. The first three questions are quoted from Arnold Hoffman, "A Few Effective Methods in Witnessing to Jehovah's Witnesses"
6. *The Watchtower*, "Prayer: What About?", 10/1/10, p. 7

Chapter 8: The Faith and Works Approach

1. Keith Walker, "Jesus 2.0", video, www.evidenceminstries.org/jw-media/jesus-2-0

Chapter 9: The Bodily Resurrection Approach

1. *Reasoning from the Scriptures* (Brooklyn: Watchtower Bible and Tract Society, 1985, 2009 printing), pp. 423-424
2. *Reasoning from the Scriptures*, p. 217
3. *Reasoning from the Scriptures*, pp. 334-335
4. *Reasoning from the Scriptures*, p. 333
5. See Warren W. Wiersbe, *The Bible Exposition Commentary, New Testament*, Volume 2 (Colorado Springs: Victor, 1989, 2001 printing), p. 619

6. *Reasoning from the Scriptures*, p. 217
7. *Reasoning from the Scriptures*, p. 217
8. *Reasoning from the Scriptures*, p. 335
9. *Reasoning from the Scriptures*, p. 335
10. *Reasoning from the Scriptures*, p. 334
11. *Reasoning from the Scriptures*, pp. 217-218

Chapter 10: The New Birth Approach

1. *The Watchtower*, "Searching into 'the Deep Things of God'", 11/1/07, p. 29

Chapter 11: Who Exactly Is God?

1. <u>Father</u>: John 6:27; 1 Corinthians 8:6; 15:24; Galatians 1:1, 3; Ephesians 5:20; 6:23; Philippians 2:11; Colossians 1:3; 3:17; 1 Thessalonians 1:1; 2 Thessalonians 1:2; 1 Timothy 1:2; 2 Timothy 1:2; Titus 1:4; 1 Peter 1:2; 2 Peter 1:17; 2 John 3; Jude 1
2. <u>Son</u>: Matthew 28:19; Zechariah 11:13 and Matthew 26:14-15; Zechariah 2:8-11; 12:10; 2 Samuel 23:3 and 1 Corinthians 10:4; John 1:1-3, 14; 20:28; Hebrews 1:6, 8; Psalm 102:25-27 and Hebrews 1:10-12
3. <u>Holy Spirit</u>: Acts 5:3-4; Romans 8:27; 1 Corinthians 2:10-11; 3:16-17; 2 Corinthians 3:17-18
4. <u>One God</u>: Deuteronomy 6:4; Isaiah 45:5-6; Romans 3:30; 1 Corinthians 8:6; 1 Timothy 2:5
5. *Jehovah's Witnesses—Proclaimers of God's Kingdom* (Brooklyn: Watchtower Bible and Tract Society, 1993), p. 49
6. *Reasoning from the Scriptures* (Brooklyn: Watchtower Bible and Tract Society, 1985, 2009 printing), p. 411
7. *Reasoning from the Scriptures*, pp. 212-213
8. *Reasoning from the Scriptures*, pp. 406-407
9. *Reasoning from the Scriptures*, p. 51
10. *Man's Salvation Out of World Distress at Hand!* (Brooklyn: Watchtower Bible and Tract Society, 1975), p. 209
11. Isaiah 9:6; Hebrews 7:3; Isaiah 44:24; John 1:3; Revelation 1:7-8, 17-18; 2:8; 22:12-13, 20

12. Matthew 1:20; 26:63-64, Mark 1:1; Luke 1:35; John 1:34, 49-50; John 3:18; John 20:31

13. Wayne Grudem, *Systematic Theology* (Grand Rapids: Zondervan, 1994), p. 530

14. John 1:1,14 ; 1 Timothy 3:14-16; Grudem, pp. 543-563

15. Hebrews 4:15

16. The Watchtower believes being born again involves obtaining a heavenly hope. However, the Bible describes it in terms of replacing the dead spirits we inherited from Adam with new spiritual life. Ezekiel 36:26-27; 2 Corinthians 5:17; Ephesians 2:4-5; Colossians 2:13; because Jesus did not inherit a dead spirit from Adam, he did not need to be born again.

17. *Reasoning from the Scriptures*, p. 255

18. *The Watchtower*, "How Jesus Magnifies God's Righteousness," 8/15/10, p. 8

19. *Reasoning from the Scriptures*, pp. 218, 408

20. *Reasoning from the Scriptures*, p. 255

21. *Should You Believe in the Trinity?* (Brooklyn: Watchtower Bible and Tract Society, 1989, 2006 printing), p. 15

22. *The Watchtower*, "Appreciating the Salvation of Our God," 8/1/73, p. 465

23. *Reasoning from the Scriptures*, p. 306

24. *The Watchtower*, "'Born Again—Man's Part and God's Part," 2/1/82, p. 25

25. *The Watchtower*, "You People Must Be Born Again," 10/1/58, p. 605

26. *Reasoning from the Scriptures*, pp. 217-218

27. Grudem, pp. 237-238

28. Grudem, pp. 636-649

29. *Reasoning from the Scriptures*, pp. 380-381

Chapter 12: The Jesus Isn't Michael Approach

1. *Reasoning from the Scriptures* (Brooklyn: Watchtower Bible and Tract Society, 1985, 2009 printing), p. 218

2. *Reasoning from the Scriptures*, p. 218

3. *Reasoning from the Scriptures*, p. 218

4. *Reasoning from the Scriptures*, p. 218

5. See David Reed, *Jehovah's Witnesses Answered Verse by Verse* (Grand Rapids: Baker Book House, 1986), p. 47

6. For a further discussion of this issue, see Ron Rhodes, *Reasoning from the Scriptures with the Jehovah's Witnesses*, Copyright © 1993/2009 by Harvest House Publishers, Eugene, Oregon 97408, www.harvesthousepublishers.com, pp. 176-178

7. *Reasoning from the Scriptures*, p. 218

8. *Reasoning from the Scriptures*, p. 218

9. *What Does the Bible* Really *Teach?* (Brooklyn: Watchtower Bible and Tract Society, 2005, 2013 printing), p. 50

10. *The Watchtower*, "Appreciating the Salvation of Our God," 8/1/73, p. 465

Chapter 13: The Jesus is the God-Man Approach

1. *Reasoning from the Scriptures* (Brooklyn: Watchtower Bible and Tract Society, 1985, 2009 printing), pp. 214-215

2. See Philip DelRe, *Answering Jehovah's Witnesses With Questions* (Belvidere, IL: Voice Publishing, 2007), p. 27

3. *Reasoning from the Scriptures*, p. 213

4. *Reasoning from the Scriptures*, p. 414

5. *Reasoning from the Scriptures*, pp. 412-413

6. *Reasoning from the Scriptures*, p. 413

7. Taken from *Reasoning from the Scriptures with the Jehovah's Witnesses* by Ron Rhodes, Copyright © 1993/2009 by Harvest House Publishers, Eugene, Oregon 97408, www.harvesthousepublishers.com, p. 228

8. This definition can be found in Greek lexicons. See also Rhodes, pp. 133-135, 177

Chapter 14: The Holy Spirit is God Approach

1. *Insight on the Scriptures*, Volume 2 (Brooklyn: Watch Tower Bible and Tract Society & International Bible Students Association, 1988), p. 1020

2. *Insight on the Scriptures*, Volume 2, p. 1019

3. *Awake!* "What Is the Bible's View? Satan the Devil—Personification or a Person?" 12/8/73, p. 27

4. *Reasoning from the Scriptures* (Brooklyn: Watchtower Bible and Tract Society, 1985, 2009 printing), p. 380

5. *You Can Live Forever in Paradise on Earth* (Brooklyn: Watchtower Bible and Tract Society, 1982), p. 41

6. See David Reed, *Jehovah's Witnesses Answered Verse by Verse* (Grand Rapids: Baker Book House, 1986), pp. 85-86

7. *Reasoning from the Scriptures*, p. 407

8. For an expanded discussion of this issue with suggested questions to ask Witnesses, see Ron Rhodes, *Reasoning from the Scriptures with the Jehovah's Witnesses*, Copyright © 1993/2009 by Harvest House Publishers, Eugene, Oregon 97408, www.harvesthousepublishers.com, pp. 203-204

9. *Insight on the Scriptures*, Volume 2, p. 1019

10. *Insight on the Scriptures*, Volume 2, p. 1020

11. Homer Duncan, *Heart-To-Heart Talks with Jehovah's Witnesses* (Lubbock: Missionary Crusader, 1972), p. 99

12. Duncan, p. 99

13. *Insight on the Scriptures*, Volume 2, p. 1019

14. Duncan, p. 97

15. Duncan, p. 98

16. *Reasoning from the Scriptures*, p. 407

17. *Insight on the Scriptures*, Volume 2, p. 1019

18. Robert M. Bowman, Jr. *Why You Should Believe in the Trinity*, (Grand Rapids: Baker Book House, 1989), pp. 27-33. For quotations from these and many other church fathers, see www.bible.ca/H-trinity.htm

Chapter 15: Watchtower Signature Issues

1. *Reasoning from the Scriptures* (Brooklyn: Watchtower Bible and Tract Society, 1985, 2009 printing), pp. 196-197

2. *The Watchtower*, "What Birth of the Nation Has Meant for Mankind," 7/1/82, pp. 24-25

3. Matthew 6:9; John 17:1, 5, 11, 21, 24-25; 18:11; Acts 1:4, 7; 2:33; 4:24; Wayne Grudem, *Systematic Theology* (Grand Rapids: Zondervan, 1994), pp. 157-160

4. *What Can the Bible Teach Us?* (Brooklyn: Watchtower Bible and Tract Society, 2015), p. 131

5. *Reasoning from the Scriptures*, pp. 269-270
6. *Reasoning from the Scriptures*, pp. 176-182
7. *Reasoning from the Scriptures*, pp. 68-69
8. *The Watchtower*, "You Received Free, Give Free", 8/1/03, p. 20
9. *Jehovah's Witnesses—Proclaimers of God's Kingdom* (Brooklyn: Watchtower Bible and Tract Society, 1993), p. 343
10. Acts 4:34-37
11. *Reasoning from the Scriptures*, pp. 89-93
12. Galatians 5:11; 6:12, 14; Matthew 10:38; 16:24; 1 Corinthians 1:17-18; Ephesians 2:16; Philippians 2:8; 3:18; Colossians 1:20; 2:14-15; Hebrews 12:2
13. *Reasoning from the Scriptures*, pp. 375-380
14. *Reasoning from the Scriptures*, pp. 168-175
15. Grudem, pp. 472-486
16. Grudem, pp. 1142-1143, 1148-1153
17. Revelation 20:10; Grudem, p. 419
18. *What Can the Bible Teach Us?*, pp. 138-141
19. *What Can the Bible Teach Us?*, pp. 33-34, 91

Chapter 16: The Divine Name Approach

1. *What Does the Bible* Really *Teach?* (Brooklyn: Watchtower Bible and Tract Society, 2005, 2013 printing), p. 195
2. *The Divine Name That Will Endure Forever* (Brooklyn: Watchtower Bible and Tract Society, 1984, 2006 printing), p. 3
3. *What Does the Bible* Really *Teach?*, p. 196
4. Matthew 4:4,7,10; 5:33; 21:42; 22:37,44; 23:39; Mark 12:11,29,30,36; Luke 4:8,12,18,19; 13:35; 20:42; John 6:45; 12:38
5. Mark 5:19; 13:20; Luke 20:37
6. *The Kingdom Interlinear Translation of the Greek Scriptures* (Brooklyn: Watchtower Bible and Tract Society: 1969), p. 11
7. *The Kingdom Interlinear Translation of the Greek Scriptures*, p. 11
8. *The Kingdom Interlinear Translation of the Greek Scriptures*, p. 17
9. *Reasoning from the Scriptures* (Brooklyn: Watchtower Bible and Tract Society, 1985, 2009 printing), p. 64
10. *The Watchtower*, "The Challenge of Knowing God by Name," 7/1/10, p. 5

Chapter 17: The Christian Freedom Approach

1. *Reasoning from the Scriptures* (Brooklyn: Watchtower Bible and Tract Society, 1985, 2009 printing), p. 272
2. *Reasoning from the Scriptures*, p. 69
3. *What Does the Bible* Really *Teach?* (Brooklyn: Watchtower Bible and Tract Society, 2005, 2013 printing), p. 157
4. *Reasoning from the Scriptures*, pp. 69-70
5. *Reasoning from the Scriptures*, pp. 176-182
6. *Good News to Make You Happy* (Brooklyn: Watchtower Bible and Tract Society, 1976), pp. 128-129
7. *Reasoning from the Scriptures*, p. 180
8. *Reasoning from the Scriptures*, p. 182
9. *The Watchtower*, "If God Is For Us, Who Will Be Against Us?" 6/1/01, p. 16
10. *The Watchtower*, "Why Do the Witnesses Keep Calling?" 8/15/94, p. 10
11. *Awake!*, "God Let Us Find Him", 3/22/96, p. 11
12. *The Watchtower*, "Serving With the Watchman", 1/1/00, p. 9
13. See David Reed, *Jehovah's Witnesses Answered Verse by Verse* (Grand Rapids: Baker Book House, 1986), pp. 82-83
14. *Reasoning from the Scriptures*, p. 92
15. *Reasoning from the Scriptures*, p. 92

Chapter 18: The Justice for the Wicked Approach

1. *Reasoning from the Scriptures* (Brooklyn: Watchtower Bible and Tract Society, 1985, 2009 printing), p. 174
2. *Reasoning from the Scriptures*, p. 175
3. *The Watchtower*, "God is Vengeful—Is It True?" 10/1/11, p. 6
4. *The Watchtower*, "Demons—How Can We Resist Them?" 3/15/07, p. 27
5. *Reasoning from the Scriptures*, pp. 174-175
6. *The Greatest Man Who Ever Lived* (Brooklyn: Watchtower Bible and Tract Society, 1991), Chapter 88

Chapter 19: The Life and Death Issues Approach

1. *Reasoning from the Scriptures* (Brooklyn: Watchtower Bible and Tract Society, 1985, 2009 printing), pp. 72-76
2. https://wol.jw.org/en/wol/d/r1/lp-e/2004448
3. *Reasoning from the Scriptures*, p. 73
4. *Knowledge That Leads to Everlasting Life* (Brooklyn: Watchtower Bible and Tract Society, 1995, 2006 printing), p. 129
5. *Jehovah's Witnesses—Proclaimers of God's Kingdom* (Brooklyn: Watchtower Bible and Tract Society, 1993), p. 183

Chapter 20: The False Prophecies Approach

1. *The Watchtower*, "Praise Jah! You Who Attend the Memorial," 3/15/51, p. 166

Chapter 21: Where Will You Go from Here?

1. Leonard and Marjorie Chretien, *Witnesses of Jehovah* (Eugene: Harvest House, 1988), p. 15
2. Don Cameron, *Captives of a Concept* (Morrisville, NC: Lulu, Inc., 2011), p. 120

SUBJECT INDEX

1914, 209, 285, 290-291.
See also False prophecies
144,000, 7, 49, 55-56, 59, 68-69,
103-105, 111, 116-117, 129-130,
133-137.
See also Anointed class; Little flock

Anointed class, 7, 55-56, 68-69,
129-130, 133-137.
See also 144,000; Little flock
Armageddon, 24, 63, 69, 209,
281-282, 286-287, 290
Author's testimony, 1-8, 11-15, 21-23,
33-34, 81-82

Bible
reliability, 216-218
translation issues, 44-45, 117-119,
162-171, 174-179, 187-188,
195, 205, 211-218, 220-221,
230, 242-246, 254, 258-261
Birthdays and holidays, 206-207, 225,
232-236
Blood transfusions, 208, 265-268,
272-279
Born again, 34-35, 37, 55-60,
129-138, 142, 144.
See also New birth

Camping, Harold. *See* False
prophecies, Harold Camping
Christendom, 25-27, 90, 141, 148,
204, 211-212, 226, 239, 241-246,
285, 291, 295, 303
Christian love, showing to Jehovah's
Witnesses, 27-28, 36-41, 282,
301-302, 305

Church. *See* Inviting Jehovah's
Witnesses to church
Collections, 207, 225, 239-240, 303
Context, importance to Bible
understanding, 5, 11-22, 43, 48-49,
100-101, 111-116, 125-126,
137-138, 160, 175, 220-221,
228, 254-256.
See also Passive v. active
involvement
Cross, 207-208, 225, 241-246, 303
Paul's view, 244-246
torture stake (Watchtower view),
207-208, 242-246

Devotional approach, 73-87
Doctrinal and approach chapters
explained, 8-9
Door-to-door preaching, 12-13, 16,
26, 33, 37-39, 63, 90, 101-102,
238, 281-282, 291, 295-296, 298

Encountering Jehovah's Witnesses
choices, 1-10
opportunities, 295-305
active Witnesses, 296-297
at a Kingdom Hall, 303-304
ex-Witnesses, 299-300
inactive Witnesses, 297-298
internet outreach, 301-303
people studying with Witnesses,
298-299
Witness children, 297
Witnesses doing street
witnessing, 300-301
Encouragement to witness to
Jehovah's Witnesses, 9-10,
295-296, 305

SCRIPTURE INDEX

Made in the USA
Middletown, DE
15 May 2021